THE CHOICE
WE FACE

THE CHOICE WE FACE

How Segregation,
Race, and Power Have
Shaped America's Most
Controversial Education
Reform Movement

JON N. HALE

Boston
BEACON PRESS

BEACON PRESS
Boston, Massachusetts
www.beacon.org

Beacon Press books
are published under the auspices of
the Unitarian Universalist Association of Congregations.

24 23 22 21   8 7 6 5 4 3 2 1

This book is printed on acid-free paper that meets the uncoated paper
ANSI/NISO specifications for permanence as revised in 1992.

Text design and composition by Kim Arney

Library of Congress Cataloging-in-Publication Data
Name: Hale, Jon N., author.
Title: The choice we face : how segregation, race, and power have shaped
America's most controversial education reform movement / Jon N. Hale.
Description: Boston : Beacon Press, [2021] | Includes
bibliographical references and index.
Identifiers: LCCN 2021005011 (print) | LCCN 2021005012 (ebook) |
ISBN 9780807087480 (hardcover) | ISBN 9780807087503 (ebook)
Subjects: LCSH: School choice—United States—History. |
Discrimination in education—United States—History.
Classification: LCC LB1027.9 .H33 2021 (print) | LCC LB1027.9 (ebook) |
DDC 378.1/61—dc23
LC record available at https://lccn.loc.gov/2021005011
LC ebook record available at https://lccn.loc.gov/2021005012

To Claire, Edith, and Nina, with all my love,
and for whom all choices are made.

CONTENTS

INTRODUCTION   The Choice We Face. 1

CHAPTER ONE   The "Divine Right" and Our Freedom
of Choice in Education 17

CHAPTER TWO   Milton Friedman and the Problems
with Choice in Chicago 38

CHAPTER THREE   Racism by Yet Another Name: Busing,
White Resistance, and the Foundations
for a National School Choice Model 62

CHAPTER FOUR   Federal Support of the School
Choice Movement 90

CHAPTER FIVE   The School Choice Menu 116

CHAPTER SIX   Race and a Civil Rights Claim
to School Choice 139

CHAPTER SEVEN   The Sinking Ship of Public Education
and the Failure of Choice 164

CHAPTER EIGHT   Resisting School Choice Through
Counternarrative and Coalitions 189

Acknowledgments 215
Notes 217
Index 267

INTRODUCTION

The Choice
We Face

ONE DAY IN APRIL 2015, I attended a town hall about the future of
Burke High School, a historically Black public high school in Charleston, South Carolina. At the time, I was a faculty member at the College
of Charleston, teaching classes on the history of education and the civil
rights movement. The meeting piqued my interest. It was organized
by local White parents who demanded reform to improve Burke High.
Though the school was modern and within walking distance for most
students, most Whites refused to send their children to the school, citing subpar test scores, poor teaching, and a weak curriculum—perceptions that were not always supported by research. The nominal purpose
of the meeting was to improve a Black high school. But what was really
at stake—as what is at stake at most meetings of this kind that occur
every week in communities across America—was the heart and soul of
public education.

The room was crowded by Charleston standards. Over two hundred people were in attendance. The fact that nearly half the crowd
was Black made it one of the rare integrated meetings in the city. It was
classically local and grassroots. Notice for it was publicized by word of
mouth and through Facebook, the preferred social media of parents in
Charleston, if they used any at all.

Burke High School was founded as the Charleston Industrial Institute in 1894. It is the only high school that remains a traditional, non-charter public high school on the peninsula of Charleston. It is also 97 percent African American. Racially, the school stands in stark contrast to the popular historic homes that surround it, which are mostly occupied by Whites. The gentrified neighborhoods of Charleston are now over 70 percent White, a dramatic shift since the 1980s, when the city was two-thirds Black. The city, historically, was predominantly Black. Before the Civil War, the numbers of enslaved African Americans outnumbered Whites by at least two to one, at times five to one.[1] Charleston is now the whitest it has ever been in history. Though Black parents and community members have long labored to improve Burke, the concerns of White parents who called the meeting seemed to garner more attention. These underlying truths and the dramatic gentrification of this historically Black city added to a palpable tension in the room.

Moving in droves since the early 2000s to this newly "discovered" tourist destination, Whites wanted better options for their kids. Burke High School's reputation, like that of many segregated Black schools, left much to be desired. The school was consistently tagged as "at risk" or "failing." Unfounded rumors of violence and inept teaching circulated among White Charlestonians. Alternatives to Burke were appealing yet limited. The magnet schools serving middle and high school students in the area were great but were very difficult to get into. The local paper, the *Post and Courier*, likened entry into the premier Charleston schools to admission at Harvard. The private Porter-Gaud School is indicative. Porter-Gaud is routinely lauded as one of the best in the state and enjoys status as a nationally ranked private school. It is also one of the most expensive, with tuition for the lower school set at $22,000 per year.[2]

Avoiding Burke and largely excluded from the alternatives, parents demanded more choice. Like other gentrified areas across the country, Charleston embraced charter schools as a way to provide more choice with wide support among both African Americans and Whites. In fact, a Black alumnus weeks before the meeting submitted a proposal to convert Burke into a charter school. The proposal, driven by a growing desire among Whites to use the public schools if they were "chartered," was almost guaranteed success. The last public high school standing in

Charleston was about to become a charter school, and the meeting set the stage for how the debate would unfold.

Public education and the politics surrounding it were personal for me. My wife and I are White. We were then without children. But if and when we did have children, we had decided to commit to using the public schools in the area. We would have skin in the game, as problematically White as it was.

I was also captivated intellectually, which only fueled my interest in the future of Burke High School. The school was for me steeped in symbolism and significance. With my students I studied the history of education in South Carolina and the struggle to achieve a quality education, one of the hallmark struggles of the Black freedom movement. In 1740, it became illegal to teach African Americans in South Carolina. After the Civil War, a paltry education was reluctantly offered, provided it was segregated. During the civil rights movement, Whites vehemently resisted integration, putting forth insidious mechanisms to preserve their privileges and investment in a segregated system, most notably through "freedom of choice" plans that eventually included charter schools.

The deeper meaning of events was obvious to me. At the center of debate was school choice. As school choice advocates and some scholars have noted, "choice" or the principles behind it have existed since the earliest years of our republic. Philosopher John Stuart Mill warned of state intervention in education. Other theorists, including Thomas Paine or even Adam Smith, have backed the use of vouchers or public support for private education. It has been noted that states such as Vermont, New Hampshire, and Maine (which has covered some of the cost of private school tuitions since the 1870s) supported vouchers over 150 years before the *Brown* decision. And across the country parents practiced choice to some degree when they enrolled their children in a private school, which was often religious in nature, most notably Catholic. Choices driven by a "market" existed over a century before the founding of a common public school system in the United States.[3]

But school choice as understood and practiced today is an education policy that took on new significance in the politics of massive resistance after the *Brown v. Board of Education* decision in 1954. Calls for vouchers and minimalist state intervention prior to *Brown* occurred when schools were segregated by race in the United States or, before 1865, when formal education was denied to Black families. Race and racist policy after *Brown* have shaped the emergence of school choice and are inextricably linked to its contemporary manifestation. Segregationists used vouchers along with an ideology of choice that fundamentally shaped what we mean by "choice" today. Vouchers and calls for subsidized private education fell into the hands of influential segregationists after *Brown*. This is not to say that everyone who discussed vouchers in the 1950s was racist. However, to ignore the determining role of race and the politics of massive resistance or to claim that the origins of choice are not racist—as so many have done and continue to do—is to conceal problematic and paradoxical development of school choice over time. Such myopic definitions ignore the very premise of public education in the United States, which was indelibly shaped by racist policy.

As practiced today, school choice allows parents to select alternatives to their local public school to improve all schools through competition. Since the *Brown* decision, school choice includes a myriad of choices alternative to traditional public schools, including but not limited to charter schools, publicly funded but privately managed schools; magnet schools, public schools with specialized curricula to attract White students; school vouchers, publicly funded "coupons" used to cover the cost of private schools; private schools, education funded by private tuition that often provides religious instruction; and homeschooling, the education of children in their own homes.

School choice often encompasses where we choose to live too, since this is often determined by a desire to enroll in the best possible schools. It is baked into White flight. The choice includes the decision to move to more desirable locations, many times suburbs but increasingly pockets of urban areas once deemed unsuitable by Whites after desegregation. Since school choice hinges on claiming the right to attend a school that you select, making a good choice involves decisions about purchasing homes in proximity to excellent schools.[4] One's choice and the history that shapes this choice are irrevocably linked. Yet an emphasis on the right to choose schools while citing test scores or real estate–based assessment of "great schools" essentially masks the racist origins of school choice since the 1950s while perpetuating the racism behind it.

School choice is more than mere policy. It is more than vouchers and charter schools. School choice is an ideology and a way of thinking about public schools. It is an idea that fermented during desegregation in the 1950s and is grounded in the politics of massive resistance. School choice—in particular "freedom of choice" plans—gained popularity as a way to avoid racially desegregated schools. School choice provided new ways to talk about public education as the system was being desegregated. It put forth new ways of thinking about one's "right" to an education. Its promoters rivaled civil rights advocates who claimed and demanded a right to a quality education unfettered by racial discrimination. Instead, after courts mandated that students attend desegregated schools, parents demanded their individual right to choose their children's school. The way school choice emerged as a popular idea and policy in the aftermath of desegregation distinguishes it from any previous "choice" and demarcates the policy as one of the most controversial in the history of US education.

Today, using choice does not make one racist. But it is grounded in a racist history and racist policy. The ideology of choice today includes a right to choose or a demand for that right. It is often used to escape failing "government schools"—a coded term with direct links to racist origins. But choice is also used in paradoxical ways that challenge its racist past. Some cities that have been roiled in desegregation struggles, such as Boston, employ "controlled choice"—a comprehensive approach to student assignment that intentionally promotes racial and economic integration through use of a rank-order system in which all families choose.[5] Civil rights advocates as well as racist politicians and "school choice" advocates claim that school choice is, in fact, a civil right. It is, in short, complicated. What is meant by "choice" depends on one's racial, social, and economic position in the United States, not to mention one's connection to and awareness of this history.

But race and racism are critical components in understanding the choices before us. The very school choice plans discussed at this meeting in

Charleston were clearly and unequivocally linked to these historic attempts to preserve segregation. At first, I was lost as to how so many people supported school choice at the meeting that evening, not to mention the ferocity with which Whites cut down Burke High School. They cited a litany of reasons why they would not send their kids to the state-of-the-art school with modern facilities and amenities that defined quality public education. Burke in many ways stood as a monument that disproved the "if you build it, they will come" theory. The county invested in new buildings and a state-of-the-art auditorium to replace the older historic buildings. They installed the latest technology and upgraded the entire campus by 2005. The county invested heavily in Burke to attract Whites and spent much more per student at the school than they did on the largely White suburban schools. The county had built a shiny new school, but no Whites came.

I was also lost—and would have been mildly entertained if it had not been so real—as a multitude of "progressive" Whites denied that race was a factor, dancing and tiptoeing around the reality that Burke was virtually an all-Black school. Test scores, teachers, courses, and discipline—though contested when one parsed the data—comprised the litany of reasons Whites refused to send their children to Burke. Race, racism, and racial microaggressions—illustrated by the White parent who convened the meeting and regularly *shushed* the audience when people started to speak out of turn—was the elephant in this crowded room.

In the follow-up conversations on social media and board meetings at the district office, it seemed that the charter school proposal was likely to pass. Supporters cut across race and class lines and included many Black parents and alumni who believed that a charter could improve the school. Conversations about charters were also shaped by the general feeling that civility had to be honored. The people of Charleston who fervently debated the future of Burke beseeched us to keep "politics" out of the meeting that night and all other discussion about improving Burke. Any improvement was supposed to be solely for the children.

At the moment it was also clear that if the charter proposal did not pass—and it ultimately did not pass, this time at least—Whites would only seriously consider going to Burke if it adopted some sort of charter, magnet, or private option they endorsed. Choice appeared to be one of the more viable ways to build consensus in this racially divided city.

I was stunned. Whites' disavowal of race and the way they skirted discussion of race was embarrassing. It crystallized how color-blind ideology operated in modern times, further perpetuating inequity. It demonstrated with poignant clarity that many White liberals either ignored race altogether or failed to comprehend its nuanced manifestations.

I was also perplexed by the nearly universal desire that politics should be left out of the conversation. Education is inherently political. It deals with the provision of a public good that imparts the knowledge necessary to compete in the job market as skilled workers and to participate in our democracy as informed voters. The quality of public education correlates with the strength of our nation. To assert that education should remain above and beyond politics, as so many had argued in Charleston, was ignorant and ahistorical. American education has been politicized from the very beginning. Thomas Jefferson articulated this in the nation's first call for public education in 1781, Frederick Douglass demonstrated this in his first autobiography in 1845, and the NAACP enshrined the political nature of education as they argued the *Brown v. Board of Education* case in 1954. Even the quintessential Dixiecrat of South Carolina, Strom Thurmond, understood the political implications of education.

The practically unquestioned acceptance of school choice was confounding, as were the choices it spawned, such as charter schools, magnet schools, and private schools. As a student of the civil rights movement, I saw choice as the worst possible solution to improving Burke. There was a painful history of school choice in South Carolina, but parents, advocates, and White homeowners in Charleston seemed to be wholly unaware of this.

Debates that gripped Charleston in the ensuing months were unnerving, to say the least. The situation inevitably became what all could agree was indeed political. Scores of parents, teachers, scholars, organizers, and clergy entered the fray, each putting forth their opinions on the matter. Anger and distrust permeated school board meetings. Whites passionately policed Facebook pages devoted to the issue, attempting to enforce politeness. This was Charleston, after all, where civility and paternalism reign supreme.

In the midst of this heated debate, a horrific event transpired. On the evening of June 17, 2015, twenty-one-year-old Dylann Roof—a high school dropout from outside Columbia, South Carolina—entered the Emanuel AME Church in downtown Charleston. He opened fire on those gathered for Bible study, killing nine people. When his manifesto declaring White supremacy and a desire to start a race war was released, Charlestonians stood strong. Such racism did not and would not define their "holy city." As the city and nation mourned—including President Barack Obama, who traveled to the city and sang "Amazing Grace"—the intense local fights over school choice subsided.

Yet deep-seated racism and educational inequality were still everywhere, and it was everything. Dylann Roof symbolized racial ignorance and a failure of the state's education system. Educators reeled over how anyone could enroll in a public education system and still spout racist ideology and history as Roof had done.

The proximity of the education problem to the Charleston shooting is also telling. Buist Academy, a highly selective magnet school, stands directly across the street from the AME church. The school tells a different story of injustice than that which unfolded across the way. This school symbolizes a more insidious injustice that plagues the entire public school system. Buist is one of the best elementary and middle schools in the district. It offers Spanish and French beginning in kindergarten, its teachers practice a child-centered pedagogy with low student-teacher ratios, and the school prepares students for the college track at an early age. District officials established Buist to provide a better "choice" in public education, theoretically spurring innovation and better schools across the district.

Yet Buist and the theory of choice that supports it has only perpetuated racial and class divisions. To ensure race-neutral admission policies in schools like Buist, local lawyers cited reverse discrimination and threatened to sue the district to great effect, ensuring that race would *not* be used in admission criteria. The vast majority of Black students who are not granted admission to exemplary choice schools are relegated to some of the least desirable schools in the district, like Burke and other predominantly Black schools. The system of racial segregation repeats itself. Once the news cameras left and the flowers left by mourners outside the AME church began to wilt, the fight over schools ensued once more.

The tensions on display in Charleston are emblematic of public education today. It is contentious and tumultuous. The debate is political. The schools we choose impact how we raise our children and where we live. How we interface with this system is one of the most difficult choices we face today.

The Choice We Face traces the history of an idea. It follows the social and political forces that gave rise to a ubiquitous "school choice" reform movement. Since its origin in the 1950s, school choice has become entrenched in our national outlook on school reform. It is nearly unquestioned in areas that have fully converted to "choice districts," and there are many such districts across the country. All but six states have enacted charter school legislation, bringing into being the defining characteristic of school choice today. Between 2000 and 2015, the proportion of public schools that operated as charter schools rose to 7 percent. The number of charters more than tripled to nearly seven thousand in the same period. EdChoice, a private advocacy organization founded as the Friedman Foundation for Educational Choice in 1996, cited twenty-nine states that have enacted legislation including education savings accounts (ESAs), school vouchers, tax-credit scholarships, and individual tax credits and deductions that support private schools under the umbrella of "school choice." In 2016, over 40 percent of parents with children in school indicated that public school choice was available to them. If choice or popular manifestations of it like charter schools are not in one's own district—and the majority of districts do not have a charter school and most parents claim they get their first choice of public schools—it is a topic of national significance and in the talking points of both political parties.[6] School choice as an *idea* is everywhere, even when it does not exist in local policy. The American public has been sold the idea that school choice is the panacea for a broken system.

Yet this great reform movement is paradoxical. While "school choice" has captivated a significant part of the country, it remains sorely misunderstood. One study claimed that 41 percent of Americans do not understand the term or inaccurately define it in terms of its current application. A Gallup Poll in 2014 found that between 40 and 60 percent of Americans were unclear about the very nature of charters on a series of points ranging from religion to tuition and overall quality of charter schools.[7]

We hear so much about school choice on the news, at school board meetings, and with our friends that most people, especially White Americans, see it as their inalienable right. Since the Reagan era, both Republicans and Democrats have seemed to agree that choice is not only a proven way to reform schools but something they must provide their constituents. Despite the best of intentions, most choice advocates—including those on the left—disconnect the issue with its troubling past. Most Americans fail to see how school choice is grounded in a complex history of race, exclusion, and unequal competition for scarce resources.

The Choice We Face unravels this paradox through time. It uncovers the clear line from the birth of school choice in the 1950s as a weapon against integration to the endemic problems we see in our schools today. It traces its development to a wide-scale divestment from public education in the wake of the civil rights movement, catalyzed by a self-fulfilling narrative of failure. The 1983 publication of *A Nation at Risk*, a federal report that argued that our failing school system put the country in peril, affirmed the gloomy assessment of US schools.[8] News stories, published reports, and national discourse harangued us with alarming narratives about the failure of public education. Today, we are told, children continue to fall behind their international peers in China, Japan, Korea, Finland, Estonia, and a host of other countries we at one time surpassed.[9] Schools are not preparing our children with the technological skills to compete in the twenty-first century. Children are exposed to violence, poor teaching, and a host of other problems. School choice in the current context becomes an easy sell if not a lifeline for those stuck in a failing system.

To be sure, critics on all sides point to falling test scores, incompetent teaching, scarce resources and a myriad of other valid concerns. Yet this was not always the case. Since the Second World War, the American public's view of public education has plummeted. In the 1940s, Gallup and public opinion polls found that 85 percent of Americans agreed "that young people today are getting a better education in school than their parents got." One study found that 87 percent of parents were satisfied with the schools their children attended. When asked for criticisms of the schools they attended, 40 percent said they could not identify anything wrong with the schools. Educators fared well too, as 60 percent of teachers earned top distinctions in a public survey. Yet by the 1970s and early 1980s, after desegregation and the acerbic debate it spurred, Americans held far less favorable opinions. Polls and surveys revealed that only 35 percent thought contemporary schools were better than those of the past. By the 1980s, Americans gave the public school system a marginally passing C- grade.[10]

School choice is understandably a celebrated solution to a perceived crisis. Millions have taken advantage of it. By 2018, over 10 percent of parents, which translates into over five million students, had opted out of traditional neighborhood public schools and elected to attend either public schools of choice (often privately managed) or a traditional private or religious school.[11] Tens of millions more seek to leave traditional public schools. Since school budget formulas are largely determined by the number of students enrolled, over $33 billion each year has followed students who have left traditional public education—a sizable endowment that would otherwise go to traditional neighborhood public schools.[12] Radically shortchanged, these schools are then asked to perform educational miracles on a shoestring budget.

School choice today is not without racial undertones. Race, in fact, makes school choice one of the most controversial—and misleading— reform policies to date. The percentage of White families with children attending neighborhood public schools has fallen to 50 percent. The percentage of African Americans is 16 percent, and Latinx and Asian students comprise 30 percent of the public school population. In regard to choice schools, Whites comprise 35 percent of the charter school population while 27 percent are black and 30 percent are Latinx students. Private school enrollment, which is 70 percent White, is also telling.[13] Whites have left our public system in large numbers for private and charter schools. In their wake they have left behind a crumbling infrastructure for those who do not benefit from the same privileges.

Much to the chagrin of many White liberals, school choice enjoys sizable support from Black, Indigenous, and People of Color (BIPOC) families. Parents who have been historically slighted by public education clamor for reform. BIPOC students make up the majority of the charter school population. Numerous studies have indicated strong support for charter schools among Black respondents—nearly 50 percent—and Latinx communities support choice with similar enthusiasm. Such studies also show that support for choice among people of color has risen over 10 percent in the past ten years. School choice is popular and getting more popular, cutting across racial divides.[14]

Part of the reason for the success of school choice advocates is that high-profile politicians, education reformers, and civil rights luminaries have touted it as a pressing civil rights issue. The broad bipartisan support of choice, one of the few issues that unites a politically divided nation, complicates the issue of choice as well. On the campaign trail in 2016, Donald Trump vowed to "fight to make sure every single African American child in this country is fully included in the American dream." For Trump, this struggle entailed "the new civil rights issue of our time: school choice." In 2020 and in the midst of nationwide protest and rebellion, Trump once again affirmed the notion, stating "frankly, school choice is the civil rights statement of the year, of the decade and probably beyond." The secretary of education, Betsy DeVos, a controversial advocate of religious school vouchers, supported choice by similarly invoking civil rights ideology. Without acknowledging a history of de jure segregation, DeVos claimed that historically black colleges and universities provided proof that "choice" benefited African Americans.[15]

Black civil rights advocates liken school choice to civil rights as well. The National Civil Rights Museum awarded Geoffrey Canada, a former teacher and charter school founder in New York, the National Freedom Award in 2013. "Dr. King taught me something," Canada noted in his acceptance speech, "that if you know something is wrong, you need to stand up, no matter what the price." His solution, the Harlem

Children's Zone, is one of the most revered charter school programs in the country. Even the children of Dr. King support choice. In 2016, Martin Luther King III led one of the largest school choice rallies in the nation. "This is about freedom," King told the crowd gathered in Florida, "the freedom to choose for your family and your child."[16]

Still, as much as racial justice underpins the school choice movement, opponents cite ongoing segregation and racial disparities in public school funding, academic achievement, discipline, and other areas that remain unaddressed by school choice. Since 2013 the Southern Poverty Law Center has filed suits against school choice laws in Mississippi and Alabama, arguing that charter school funding, education tax credits, school vouchers, and other mechanisms of choice violate state constitutions because they divert resources from traditional public schools. The NAACP issued a moratorium on charter schools in 2016 and 2017, urging instead the strengthening of "free, high-quality . . . and equitably-funded public education for all children." The NAACP declared: "We are dedicated to eliminating the severe racial inequities that continue to plague the education system."[17]

Efforts to profit from school choice cloud the issue as well. Under school choice, for-profit charter schools operate with legal protection. Corporations that fund charter schools stand to profit through subsidiary companies that provide educational services. Individuals who run charters are paid substantial salaries that are supported by public dollars, and, at times, salaries are drawn from money gained through the fraudulent exploitation of tax laws or funding formulas designed to fund schools for all children.[18] The very language of business—"consumers," "competition," and "product"—creates an educational "marketplace" that can be driven by profit alone. The fact that people or corporations can financially benefit from providing an education contradicts the inherent notion that education reform is "all about the children."

Largely funded through the same property taxes and state funds as traditional public schools, schools of choice siphon off scarce resources, talented teachers, and other forms of capital. Poor communities and students of color make up the majority of the public school system and are often relegated to schools that are forced into extreme parsimony through budget cuts and staffed with fewer experienced teachers. They are disproportionately punished in a school-to-prison system that the contemporary Black Lives Matter movement seeks to abolish. Though complicit in the perpetuation of choice that benefits their own best interests, White families are casualties as well. Increasingly corralled in homogenous schools, White children often grow up ignorant of their privilege and the complexities of a diversifying society often divided by issues of race.[19] The very nature of public education, in short, is under threat, and those who continue to rely on neighborhood public schools outside affluent areas—BIPOC and students living in poverty—are getting the short end of the stick.

Choice, not further investment in traditional public schools, is the Department of Education's solution to a failing education system.[20] The appointment of Betsy DeVos symbolized the triumph of choice, the ignorance that shrouds it, and the resultant threat to public education. As a person with no teaching experience and a record of donating millions from her family's fortune to the privatization of public education, she recently occupied a position that enabled her to further dismantle the public school system.

As offended as some Americans were by DeVos's unabashed support for school choice and privatization, the widespread acceptance of choice should have come as no surprise. The policies of President Barack Obama and his first secretary of education, Arne Duncan, funded reform initiatives that used the same paradigm of choice. Democratic presidential candidate Hillary Clinton in 2016 advocated for the same policies. She urged the teachers' unions in New York: "Continue to stand behind the charter school/public school movement, because I believe that parents do deserve greater choice within the public school system to meet the unique needs of their children."[21] DeVos may have rubbed Clinton supporters the wrong way, but she continued a bipartisan legacy.

Shallow understandings of school choice policy, negligent comprehension of its history, and failure to grasp its consequences constitute a gross misunderstanding of educational policy today. Wealthy conservatives, liberal reformers, and grassroots community organizers—and those who stand in judgment—all make competing claims to "school choice." Advocates of choice are not simply what historian Adam Laats called "the other school reformers"—conservative advocates who integrally shaped the trajectory of American public education.[22] People of all political stripes have jumped aboard. The school choice terrain is complicated, entrenched, and often confusing. Today, over half a century after the inception of school choice, many people treat it as an unalienable right granted by the Constitution and, in the more complicated cases, as a civil right that can be used to guarantee access to full citizenship. They feel the freedom to choose their school is protected alongside other freedoms inherent to the founding of the United States. Choice may have been conceived as an objective and universal right, but the truth is that it has enabled a quasi-public system to function for the benefit of some students as it undermines support for and weakens a traditional public system with economic, ideological, and political disinvestment.

The Choice We Face unpacks the genealogy of school choice and sheds light on this misunderstood and often misconstrued history, tracing the direct link between its troubled past and its controversial manifestation today. Originating from an esoteric theory of the economist Milton Friedman, school choice was applied by "liberal" parents and policymakers from New York, Chicago, and Boston at the same time as it was used by segregationists in Charleston and Birmingham. When the Democratic Party, under both Bill Clinton and Barack Obama, scrapped some of the ideology but maintained the essence of school choice, they molded choice into a popular and bipartisan program.

School choice today, in its most salient forms, is defined through both its purported ideals and documented shortcomings. Parents face a bevy of choices—magnet schools, charter schools, private schools, voucher programs, online schools, homeschooling, and combinations of these. Repackaged with promises of liberation, most are misunderstood, though they all connect to past efforts to maintain a racist school system or in some cases to abolish it. Grounded in a troubled history and repackaged with promises of liberation, it's a choice we all must face.

CHAPTER ONE

The "Divine Right" and Our Freedom of Choice in Education

THE VENERATED CONGRESSMAN and civil rights activist John Lewis was fourteen years old in 1954 when the Supreme Court ruled in *Brown v. Board of Education* that school segregation was unconstitutional. The ruling held tremendous potential for the young Lewis, who was acutely aware of the indignities of a Jim Crow education. Attending school in Pike County, Alabama, Lewis rode daily past White schoolhouses that were, he later remembered, "very sleek, very modern, with nice playground equipment outside, nothing like our cluster of small cinder-block buildings, with the dirt field on which we played at recess and the privies out back." To get to school, he and his peers shared a bus, a "rattling, rusty jalopy, an old hand-me-down." It was prone to stalling. Lewis recalled several occasions when he emptied out of the bus with his classmates to shoulder the lumbering vehicle back onto the muddy road to complete the trip to school.[1] The accumulated slights of segregation, from school buses to schoolhouses, were daunting to young people like Lewis trying to make it in America. Yet the *Brown* decision and the struggle to achieve it offered hope.

Education for Lewis—like millions of others—was a civil right. The acquisition of literacy was the means to full citizenship, greater opportunity, a path toward upward mobility promised in the rhetoric surrounding education in the United States. It held a deeper meaning of freedom and resistance. Those enslaved and oppressed by America's stringent racial caste system attached a liberating significance to literacy and passed it down each generation. "I had a wonderful teacher in elementary school who told me, 'Read, my child, read,' and I tried to read everything," Lewis recalled. "I was obsessed with learning all I could about the world beyond the one I knew, and that's why the school library became like a second home to me." For Lewis's teachers and elders, "education represented an almost mythical key to the kingdom of America's riches, the kingdom so long denied to our race."[2]

The Black newspapers found in Lewis's second home printed victorious declarations about the decision. Harlem's *Amsterdam News* proclaimed, "The Supreme Court decision is the greatest victory of the Negro people since the Emancipation Proclamation." The popular *Chicago Defender* postulated that the decision meant "the beginning of the end of the dual society in American life." The *Pittsburgh Courier* editorialized, "The conscience of America has spoken through its constitutional voice . . . idealism and social morality can and do prevail in the United States, regardless of race, creed or color."[3]

On the other side of the American racial divide that cut across Pike County and the rest of the nation, however, Whites vilified the decision. They cursed it. They broadcast their disdain for the decision through the pages of the southern press. As one editorial in Jackson, Mississippi, stated, "May 17, 1954, may be recorded by future historians as a black day of tragedy for the South."[4] The Jackson *Clarion-Ledger* editorialized, "The ruling will go down in history as the most unwise, unnecessary, unfair and ineffective decision that the Supreme Court has ever made."[5] The very prospect of desegregation prompted the Speaker of the House in Mississippi, Walter Sillers, to state in 1953 that "if a non-segregated system of school were established the white race would be mongrelized." He asserted, "I would gladly give up my property and my life if necessary to preserve the integrity of segregation."[6] The New Orleans *Times-Picayune* expressed skepticism at best: "The disappointment and frustration of the majority of southerners at the revolutionary overturn of practice and usage cannot immediately result in the improvement of race relations."[7]

After the *Brown* decision, there was no issue likelier to stir turmoil in the United States than education. People of color demanded a better education, which included additional litigation in support of Black children's right to enroll in White schools across the nation. Students joined civil rights activists and used other nonviolent means such as walkouts, peaceful demonstrations, and boycotts to reform the schools. Activists demanded a curriculum more inclusive of Black history, stronger representation on student councils, and fairer treatment in schools. Whites, by and large, resisted vehemently, employing every legal and extralegal means at their disposal.

During John Lewis's accomplished career as a student, civil rights movement leader, and statesman in the US House of Representatives, equal and quality education would become defined as a civil right by many African Americans and movement allies. But White segregationists defined school choice as an inherent right. The right and struggle to "choose" schools stems from this deep-seated, racialized tension. John Lewis and those Black children who came after him would never know the equality promised by the *Brown* decision. The educational landscape forever changed to accommodate the "right" for White families to choose the school they wanted to attend.

School choice in its contemporary form developed in fierce opposition to desegregation. Instead of complying with the *Brown* edict, Whites initially opted for what US senator Harry F. Byrd Sr. of Virginia dubbed "massive resistance"—a system of local and state laws designed to thwart desegregation. In the 1956 "Southern Manifesto," ninety-eight southern US senators and representatives vowed to resist desegregation: "We decry the Supreme Court's encroachment on the rights reserved to the States [and] commend the motive of those States which have declared the intention to resist forced integration by any lawful means." The southern delegation pledged to "use all lawful means to bring about a reversal of [the *Brown*] decision which is contrary to the Constitution and to prevent the use of force in its implementation."[8]

Southern lawmakers changed their state constitutions and passed new laws that funded tuition waivers for White families who wanted to enroll their children in private, all-White schools. They allowed locally elected school officials to close public schools if ordered to integrate. The legislative agenda of massive resistance comprised the most serious constitutional overhaul of the South's educational infrastructure since Reconstruction. To those predisposed to use violence to preserve the social order of Dixie, the Southern Manifesto implied that their representatives supported them. Recalcitrant racists felt protected if not justified in what they viewed as a noble defense of the southern way of life. It emboldened many to think—not inaccurately—that White policymakers would look the other way if their less sophisticated constituents opted for violence to register their discontent. Whites could lynch African Americans in broad daylight with impunity. The murder of fourteen-year-old Emmett Till proved this to the world just one year after the *Brown* decision.

These acts of violence would eventually become part of the nation's collective memory of desegregation in the 1950s and 1960s. The first cases of integration in the South, where a small number of African Americans entered all-White schools, were met with scorn and terrorism. On September 4, 1957, Black student Dorothy Counts walked alone to Harding High School in Charlotte, North Carolina, to integrate the school. White students surrounded Counts to mock her. They spit on her, verbally assaulted her, and tormented her.[9]

That same day in Little Rock, Arkansas, Governor Orval Faubus ordered the Arkansas National Guard to "maintain the peace and good order of the community" by physically blocking nine Black students from entering Little Rock Central High School. What followed was a display of massive resistance that would become iconic thanks to national news coverage. In one infamous picture captured that day, a White student, Hazel Bryan, exhibits vitriolic fury against a Black student, Elizabeth Eckford, who walked alone to school that day. Protected by city police, a White mob and the state National Guard turned the Black students away. Three weeks later, President Eisenhower issued an executive order that sent soldiers from the US Army's 101st Airborne Division to ensure that integration would take place. Though federal troops would escort Black students into the school, a horrific ordeal followed. White students physically assaulted, verbally berated, and socially ostracized the designated nine every day for the remainder of the school year, leaving emotional (and sometimes physical) scars on both the students and those who witnessed it.

Melba Pattillo Beals, one of the nine students to desegregate Little Rock Central High School, would later write about the experience. Her powerful narrative, *Warriors Don't Cry*, opens: "In 1957, while most teenage girls were listening to Buddy Holly's 'Peggy Sue,' watching Elvis gyrate, and collecting crinoline slips, I was escaping the hanging rope of a lynch mob, dodging lighted sticks of dynamite, and washing away burning acid sprayed into my eyes."[10]

The reality of the situation stood in marked contrast to the hopes and dreams of John Lewis, who felt that the highest court in the land had promised him a chance of attending a better school in the fall of 1954. Yet Lewis and his peers got nothing but the same discrimination and segregation they'd had the year before. "As I began my sophomore year in the fall of 1954 by climbing onto the same beat-up school bus and making the same twenty-mile trip to the same segregated high school I'd attend the year before," Lewis later recalled, "*Brown v. Board of Education* notwithstanding, nothing in my life had changed."[11]

By any measure, White southerners successfully maintained their sacred doctrine and practice of segregation, much to the disappointment of Lewis and the millions of others who read promise and opportunity in the *Brown* decision. Though school choice would eventually dominate the discussion of educational policy and reform, children like John Lewis had little to no choice after *Brown*. After the decision—and massive resistance—Whites closed some public schools and opened many private ones. If Whites allowed Black students to enter White schools, it was often a living hell for them. Within the decade there were indeed some desegregated public schools, but, with predominantly Black student populations and greatly declining public support, virtual segregation continued. New legislation at the state level was passed to ensure that White supremacy would remain protected—that it was up to Whites whether or not to desegregate.

Southern legislatures had already been occupied with evading desegregation well before the *Brown* decision. White southerners were cognizant in the early 1950s of the possibility that courts would order desegregation. By 1953, the NAACP had engaged in litigation that directly challenged school segregation in South Carolina, Virginia, Kansas, Washington, DC, and Delaware. Often led by grassroots organizations who mobilized local support, the challenges caused segregationist legislators to rethink their strategy.

In an effort to appease local Black communities if not federal courts after the *Brown* decision, state legislatures adopted "equalization plans" in an effort to live up to the "separate but equal" doctrine upheld in the Supreme Court's 1896 *Plessy v. Ferguson* decision. The *Plessy* verdict upheld a New Orleans train segregation ordinance and was subsequently used to sanction all Jim Crow laws, including those pertaining to formal education. If Black schools were equal to White schools, many White legislators reasoned, then African American families would opt to voluntarily maintain segregation. Governor James "Jimmy" Byrnes of South Carolina captured the rationale behind equalization in 1954, stating, "I believe the vast majority of Negroes . . . would prefer to send their children to the splendid schools now being constructed for them."[12] Though reluctant to part with already scarce funding, southern legislatures in South Carolina, Mississippi, and Georgia consented to investing more in Black education. South Carolina passed a 3 percent sales tax, the first such tax in the state, and a $75 million bond issue in 1951. Two years later, Mississippi legislators considered spending $34 million annually with over $140 million to begin the equalization process. That same year Georgia proposed a sales tax and bonds to secure over $86 million to equalize Black education. Legislators earmarked these funds to invest in teacher salaries, brand new facilities, buses, textbooks and other supplies.[13]

Though new and unprecedented forms of investment in Black education were promised, genuine support for equalization never materialized. Greater investments were made, to be sure. New buildings for Black students were constructed. Black teachers made a little more money. Facilities were upgraded. But southern states only halfheartedly supported equalization efforts. It was more of a distraction meant to delay desegregation indefinitely.[14]

Southern legislators also opted to amend their state constitutions and to pass new laws that protected segregated school systems despite *Brown*. Once the *Brown* decision was reached, they worked overtime and met in extraordinary sessions beyond their required terms to identify legally defensible solutions. They established special commissions and held focused hearings to craft the means to circumvent integation.[15]

South Carolina voters in 1952 overwhelmingly passed a referendum to eliminate the constitutional requirement to provide free public schools. Legislators in the same state also repealed compulsory education laws and passed other legislation designed to strengthen the authority of local school boards to determine pupil placement laws.[16] Legislators in Georgia proposed an amendment to the state constitution to provide publicly funded grants to cover the tuition of private education and eventually passed legislation funding such scholarships. Mississippi ratified a constitutional amendment to make the provision of public education a legislative option as opposed to a constitutional requirement. Louisiana passed legislation that repealed the compulsory education laws in districts subjected to any federal decisions mandating desegregation, which effectively meant all districts by the late 1960s.[17] In John Lewis's home state of Alabama, legislators passed a bill in 1955 that delegated to local school boards the authority to place students in schools according to their discretion alone.[18] Other new codes permitted states and local districts to preserve the right to abolish public education if they so desired when faced with federal integration orders. The result of all these changes was a convoluted web of laws, policies, and constitutional amendments that made it exceedingly difficult to desegregate.

The option to indefinitely close the public schools constituted the most extreme form of legal resistance. In notable instances, southern governors and school boards shuttered their public schools to avoid desegregation orders. For southern policymakers contemplating the decision, it would be the first time since the creation of a public education system during Reconstruction that schools would actually close. Governor Faubus in 1958 closed all public high schools in Little Rock for one year after the desegregation of Central High, ending the widely publicized showdown. District officials in Virginia closed schools instead of succumbing to integration, with intended dramatic effect. With desegregation cases still pending in the federal courts, Virginia governor J. Lindsay Almond closed schools for the 1958–59 school year in Charlottesville, Norfolk, and Warren County. The most nefarious instance of school closure occurred in Prince Edward County, Virginia. In this case, the local school board, in consultation with the state legislature, closed the public school system for five years from 1959 to 1964—the longest school closure in history—to avoid desegregation orders.[19] Such resistance ended when federal courts, in cases such as *Griffin v. County School Board of Prince Edward County* (1964), reopened schools and insisted on at least token desegregation. Yet southern legislators showed their hand in their embrace of extreme methods that circumvented integration.

While passing new legislation, southern officials simultaneously condoned, encouraged, and participated in unofficial methods of intimidation. Segregationists founded the first Citizens' Councils in Mississippi in 1953, organizing chapters in seventeen counties, many with high Black populations or where African Americans were challenging segregation. Drawing members from the middle and upper classes of southern society, the Citizens' Councils became the South's revered "moderate" incarnation of segregationist organization, committed to resisting desegregation through social and economic means rather than violent ones. Within two years of the *Brown* decision, Citizens' Councils enrolled between 250,000 and 300,000 dues-paying members in Mississippi, Alabama, Georgia, Louisiana, and South Carolina.[20]

The strategies embraced by the Citizen's Councils, though nonviolent, were deeply harmful. Many Black parents who tried to enroll their children in all-White schools were fired from their jobs. They were denied credit at banks and grocery stores. Their names were printed in local newspapers. Crosses were burned in their yards. They received incessant telephone calls late at night "encouraging" them not to apply for their children to enroll in a White school. News of the harassment of Black students spread like wildfire in the Black community, which slowed efforts to integrate.[21]

White segregationists also founded private schools to avoid integration while preserving access to education for their children. Segregationists carefully created an alternative system of private schools to educate those Whites whose parents had taken them out of public schools after federal orders to integrate. South Carolinians had explored privatizing their school system a full decade before the *Brown* decision. When a handful of Black students sought admission to the College of Charleston in 1944, the school privatized to preserve its all-White student body. It was a move fully endorsed by the conservative press. Thomas Waring, editor of Charleston's influential *News and Courier*, stated that orders for integration were "without justice." He urged readers to leave public schools and establish their own private schools to save themselves from the massive "burden" of funding Black education.[22] Three years before the *Brown* decision, Governor Jimmy Byrnes articulated how privatization would be an unfortunate but necessary outcome: "If the Court changes what is now the law of the land, we will, if it is possible, live within the law, preserve the public school system, and at the same time maintain segregation. If that is not possible, reluctantly we will abandon the public school system. . . . The White people of South Carolina could pay for the education of their children [but] Negro citizens would suffer."[23] Public views by leaders such as Byrnes led to a spike in private school enrollment.

The architects of segregation after *Brown* leveraged funding to establish all-White private schools with public money. South Carolina legislators passed laws denying funds to schools that had been "forced" to integrate by federal decree. Virginia legislators approved a state constitutional amendment to publicly fund tuition grants for White families attending private schools. Voters in Georgia ratified a state constitutional amendment that allowed the state legislature to provide "grants of state, county or municipal funds . . . for educational purposes, in discharge of all obligations of the state to provide an adequate education for its citizens." Mississippi legislators passed similar legislation to use tax dollars to defray the cost of attending private schools established to avoid desegregation.[24] Such publicly funded tuition grants would eventually become known as "vouchers"—an effective means of abdicating the public and constitutional responsibility to fund an equitable public school system.

Through public funding, tax cuts for those who enrolled their children in private schools, and other modes of state support, segregationists across the South established a network of nonsectarian "segregation academies," private schools established immediately prior to and well after the *Brown* decision to avoid desegregation. These private schools enjoyed the support of Citizens' Councils, adding ideological depth and significance to the schools' presence across the embattled South. Legislators in South Carolina passed the Tuition Grants Bill in 1963, which allocated $250,000 to cover the tuition costs carried by families to enroll in schools founded solely to provide refuge from desegregated public schools. By 1967, the state operated forty-four private academies. Mississippi underwent a similar pattern of privatization and growth. By 1968, there were forty-three state-supported private academies and hundreds of other private schools outside the jurisdiction of the state.[25] When the Supreme Court finally enforced full-scale desegregation of every grade level by 1969, Mississippi doubled the number of private schools it funded, to at least one hundred, about 40 percent of the private schools in the state. Across the South, between three hundred and four hundred state-supported private schools were part of an informal private school system of over fifteen hundred private schools that served approximately three hundred thousand children. The Southern Regional Council, an organization committed to "interracial peace," estimated that five hundred thousand students enrolled in segregation academies after the US Supreme Court's *Green v. County School Board* (1968) and *Alexander v. Holmes County Board of Education* (1969) cases that effectively vacated guidelines to desegregate with "all deliberate speed" and ordered desegregation in all grades immediately. The private school population doubled in less than two years.[26]

Despite the growth of private schools, they were not pervasive throughout the South, and they were not an option for White families without the money for tuition. Ten years after the *Brown* decision, during the fall of 1964, fewer than ten private schools were open in Virginia, for instance. Many were organized on short notice and were located in private residences or church buildings, and tuitions were high.

In Prince Edward County, Virginia, less affluent White families had to take out second mortgages on their farms, homes, and other properties to afford private school for their children.[27]

Though never the panacea envisioned by segregationists, these academies redefined the role of private education. These schools did not so much function as religious institutions, as their predecessors had since the founding of public education in the United States. As public education deteriorated in the wake of the school wars over access, private education became a southern ideal. Observing White flight and deterioration of public education during the 1960s, John Sessions, a member of the board of education in Washington, DC, noted prophetically in 1966: "The schools have deteriorated so badly that regardless of their race, people who can afford the cost are taking their kids out of public school." The chair of the board commented, "[It is] disturbing to think that our school system could become not just all-Negro, but that it could be made up almost totally of poor children."[28]

White architects of continuing school segregation did not go unchallenged. Disappointed in his government for maintaining oppression, John Lewis committed himself to the burgeoning civil rights movement after high school. He emerged as an influential activist with the Student Nonviolent Coordinating Committee, working with Dr. Martin Luther King Jr. and gaining notoriety for publicly criticizing President John F. Kennedy. Lewis and the rising army of student activists, along with the NAACP, forged ahead. Using the courts (NAACP), grassroots organization (SNCC), and protest (King and others), they took it upon themselves to painstakingly desegregate state by state, district by district, school by school.

Massive resistance to school desegregation ultimately failed because it could not be sustained under the judgment of a nation increasingly supporting John Lewis and those who joined him on the front lines of the civil rights movement. Within this tension between maintaining segregation and dismantling it, school choice emerged as a new form of resistance to desegregation and an effective policy that would withstand the test of time.

For White segregationists, the NAACP's push for integration assaulted their individual right to choose where their children went to school, forcing them to attend schools with children they wanted to avoid. It was not only states' rights that fell victim to federal jurisdiction after the *Brown* decision; Whites' individual rights and liberties pertaining to the freedom of association—or the right to voluntarily join or leave groups, in this case school—were at stake. White southerners had historically detested what they saw as federal meddling in the affairs of the states, linked to the region's defense of slavery during the early republic. This perceived threat to their individual right to associate—to choose where their children attended school and with whom—was tantamount to tyranny. After *Brown*, southern segregationists articulated a stringent defense of this new right to choose schools, and they mobilized to protect it.

Segregationists viewed the freedom to choose as grounded in the constitutionality of the freedom of association and the rights of the individual, the same rights Whites increasingly felt were under attack by federal desegregation orders. In South Carolina, Governor George Bell Timmerman, who led efforts to repeal compulsory education laws, noted, "The parental right to determine what is best for the child is fundamental. It is a divine right. It is a basic law of nature that no man, no group of men, can successfully destroy."[29] He stated without equivocation: "We must preserve for the parents of the children of this state the right to send their children to separate [segregated] schools."[30] In Virginia, a prominent group of businessmen earned a state charter for an organization they developed in the wake of the *Brown* decision. They called themselves the Defenders of State Sovereignty and Individual Liberties and were clearly concerned about desegregation, though the group's founding statement avoided mentioning segregation and race, emphasizing instead the state's "right to regulate within its borders . . . its own domestic arrangements . . . whether education, recreational, economic, social or otherwise."[31]

Alabama policymakers employed a similar tone, further building on the ideology of choice. Forney Johnson, a segregationist lawyer and early advocate for "freedom of choice" plans, spoke of the rights of

Whites: "If Negroes are to have the right of free choice in attending separate or mixed schools if they wish, then even the Supreme Court cannot deny to white people that same free choice of sending their children to separate or mixed schools." He went on to assert, "Freedom of choice [or] the liberty of parents to direct the basic conditions under which their children shall be educated shall not be denied."[32]

Beginning in 1955, Alabama passed freedom of choice provisions to its constitution after intensive study by a state commission devoted to preserving segregation. Through freedom of choice plans, Alabama legislators defended their right to determine the process of educating the state's young citizens, including protecting the right of families to choose where their children attended school. They removed all constitutional obligation to maintain public schools, which continued the trajectory established by several southern states. But they did not necessarily abolish the public school system. Their actions were interpreted as giving White people choice in uncertain times, providing them with the choice to send their children to segregated schools if they wanted. To facilitate this process, Black students and students of color were free to apply to enroll in White schools. But White school boards at the district level retained control of how and where students would be placed. Their plans included pupil placement laws based on a variety of measurements, including intelligence and aptitude tests, which ultimately discriminated against Black students because pupils in underfunded, segregated schools were not provided the resources needed to perform well on the exams. They also authorized local, all-White school boards to determine pupil placement based on the "safety" of students who had been removed from their background and associates (i.e., racially homogenous peers) under federal desegregation orders. If desegregation was viewed as dangerous, then Black students would not be assigned to White schools. Freedom of choice plans also provided local districts with the choice to transfer public funds to private schools. As one administrator quoted in the *Southern School News* noted, the new legislation provided the "freedom to give away public school buildings, give away public school equipment, give away public school sites and give away public school tax money to non-public schools."[33]

Freedom of choice was ultimately a political compromise among Whites divided on the issue of how to preserve segregation. In a campaign to spread the gospel of freedom of choice provisions in Virginia in 1958, Governor J. Lindsay Almond struck an important compromise between advocates of massive resistance—those who wanted to close public schools indefinitely—and moderates who wanted to maintain a system of public education. A rhetoric of rights and choice united extreme and moderate segregationists. The idea gained momentum when Leon Dure, a retired southern newspaper editor, began publishing his ideas in the southern press around the "freedom of choice of association." For Dure, the *Brown* decision assailed Americans' right to associate, a fundamental liberty protected by the First Amendment. His proposal was to accept the *Brown* decision but protect the right of individuals, irrespective of race, to "assemble and associate without restraint by law." In obeying the decision, states could provide "freedom of choice in education" without restraint or federal oversight. Governor Almond addressed a special session of the legislature, iterating Dure's major ideas, arguing that "the right to associate carries with it the right not to associate."[34] White Virginians began to discuss the preservation of their rights in the impending onslaught of federal intervention. The freedom of choice plan passed by the Virginia legislature consisted of new pupil placement laws, much like those passed in Alabama, as well as public funding for tuition grants for White families seeking their children's admission to private academies.

The ideology behind freedom of choice rested on race-neutral rhetoric. Southerners were able to craft legislation that addressed race without explicitly naming it. The platform of the Virginia States' Rights Party of 1956 is indicative. "It should be left to state and local governments," it noted, "to decide how much and exactly what kind of education they are willing to support. There is no popular demand for federal control or direction of education. As a matter of fact, this invasion of states' rights is a pure political grab for power."[35] In South Carolina, the Gressette Committee—the legislative group assigned to find the legal path to circumvent desegregation—noted, "We can dare to hope to offer to all our citizens the broadest possible freedom of choice of the kind of schools to which they wish to send their children." The Gressette Committee went on to report in 1963 that "South Carolina at all costs must prevent the development of its grammar and high schools into the lawless 'blackboard jungles' that integration has made."[36] As H. Harrison Jenkins, the editor of the South Carolina–based *Columbia Record*, noted, "The singular important factor to remember in an acceptable freedom-of-choice program is that the child or parent has the liberty to make a choice and that the degradation of compulsory attendance at a particular school, solely because of race, is absolutely removed."[37]

Regardless of one's race, parents had a choice under the new spate of legislation passed across the South. As Fritz Hollings of South Carolina noted on the Senate floor in 1970, "This is a freedom of choice . . . that wasn't drafted by southern bigots or by southern illiterates or by southerners wanting to turn the clock back, or by southerners with prejudice or by southern red necks."[38] Freedom of choice allowed all families—regardless of race and without racial discrimination—to determine where to go to school. Hollings asserted, "The thrust of the 14th Amendment is that rights not be denied the individual. If the individual is given the right he chooses, then the spirit and letter of the Fourteenth Amendment is complied with."[39]

The rhetoric of choice permitted token integration while maintaining the essence of segregated schooling. While the majority of White Americans were not thrilled about the prospect of sending their sons and daughters to school with Black and Brown students, they were also not enthused about White southerners burning crosses, verbally accosting children, and physically assaulting students. Massive resistance broadcast to a national audience the racist sentiment behind the caustic rebellion of Dixie. Massive resistance was also bad for business. Black economic actions, from the Montgomery bus boycott to the boycott of five-and-dime stores across the nation, withheld capital from White "moderate segregationists" concerned with the bottom line. Meanwhile, southern legislatures wanted to prolong the postwar economic boom and federal investment in the South. Freedom of choice became a solution that segregationists could live with.

It was federal funding coupled with a defense of the right to choose, not a moral compass, that ultimately forced the South to enroll a handful of Black students in formerly all-White schools. Through Title VI of the Civil Rights Act of 1964, President Lyndon B. Johnson threatened to cut off federal funding to institutions or persons who practiced segregation, including schools. The following year, Johnson signed into law the Elementary and Secondary Education Act, a sweeping bill that appropriated over $1 billion to public schools. The most significant part of the bill was the Title I program, in which federal dollars were directed to schools that enrolled student populations of whom 40 percent or more lived in poverty. It was Johnson's noble attempt to win his "war on poverty" and build his Great Society. Federal funding partly filled the coffers of financially strapped school districts, including southern districts that had begun desegregating.[40]

The new legislation encouraged compliance with desegregation efforts since the act outlawed discrimination based on race while simultaneously leveraging fiscal consequences to uphold the law. The stakes were high: many southern districts were poised to receive a sizable infusion of federal money. When Johnson signed the Civil Rights Act into law, eleven states of the former Confederacy received over $370 million in federal aid. After the passage of the Elementary and Secondary Education Act in 1965, southern states were projected to receive an additional $503 million. In Mississippi, federal funds were projected to account for nearly one-fifth of the education budget, making it the state most dependent on federal funds.[41]

Whites began looking for opportunities to have it both ways: to separate students by race but also preserve the constant inflow of federal dollars. They did not have to look too far, as they had already crafted the language and ideology of "choice." The rhetorical strategy drew on a positive conception of choice that was quintessentially American, the right to choose one's own destiny, and free market ideology. Framing matters this way, White legislators insisted on the right of individuals to choose where they enrolled their children.

Under mounting pressure to retain funding, hundreds of districts submitted evidence of desegregation. Three-fourths of the South's nearly three thousand school districts agreed to comply with federal stipulations before the summer break in 1965, and over 90 percent had submitted plans for compliance by the time school began that fall. The state school superintendent in Florida put it succinctly when he declared to the press, "We have no choice."[42] Yet, contrary to the perception of those who felt they were giving in to desegregation mandates, defenders of segregation developed a score of "freedom of choice" plans across the South and invested in them wholeheartedly. After the Civil Rights Act, these plans presented viable means to maintain both segregation and federal funding. Whites used them to project an image of compliance with the federal mandate while at the same time maintaining control of public education for their benefit. The federal government permitted southern school districts to meet minimal standards by submitting plans stating that anyone regardless of race was free to apply to any school in their district. The burden of desegregation was thus shifted to individual Black families and framed as their choice.

Freedom of choice plans initially met the immediate requirements established by the Office of Health, Education, and Welfare. Massive resistance, with armed guards protecting the schoolhouse door, was replaced by "choice" rhetoric and token desegregation, to the relief of the Office of Health, Education, and Welfare.

What federal officials, liberal and conservative alike, did not see when validating freedom of choice plans, or what they chose to ignore, was the persistent harassment that Black children and their families endured after applying to enter White schools. Black families were "free to choose," but the reality was a living hell for doing so. Freedom of choice plans looked good on paper, but they represented a watered-down compromise—compliance—far from the ideals of both sides. Such plans offered a very different sort of desegregation as that envisioned by the NAACP and activists who wanted immediate and full integration. But the law contained loopholes and opportunities to repudiate the spirit of integration once again.

A decade of struggle between integrationist and segregationist reformers transformed the educational landscape of the US South. By 1964, at the height of the civil rights movement and the time of the Civil Rights

Act passage, new choices were on the horizon for African American students. Small groups of Black students entered formerly all-White schools across the South through a bevy of freedom of choice policies. The US District Court for the Southern District of Mississippi ruled in *Evers v. Jackson Municipal Separate School District* (1964) that Mississippi schools had to allow Black students to enter White schools. Ten years of resisting desegregation came to an end as White schools opened their doors to a handful of Black students in Mississippi—the last state in the nation to do so. The Supreme Court also issued a clear message that same year in *Griffin v. School Board of Prince Edward County*, noting that "the time for more 'deliberate speed' has run out, and the phrase can no longer justify denying these Prince Edward County children their Constitutional rights."[43] (In Prince Edward County, Virginia, recall, public schools had been shut down since 1959.) At the end of the 1960s, the Supreme Court issued a final rebuff in its *Alexander v. Holmes County* (1969) decision: "Continued operation of racially segregated schools under the standard of 'all deliberate speed' is no longer constitutionally permissible."[44] The writing was on the wall that African American students were protected if they enrolled in all-White schools.

As much as choice was grounded in White resistance, it also advanced the civil rights movement's integration goal. The NAACP, the lead organization behind litigating desegregation, and supportive civil rights activists outlined the choices Black students faced, holding grassroots meetings in churches and homes across the South. Students could enroll in all-White schools, helping dismantle legal barriers and fulfilling their ancestors' dreams, or they could remain in the segregated institutions they had always attended and were expected to attend. Choosing a well-funded White school with state-of-the-art facilities, brand-new books, impeccable science labs, safe transportation, and highly paid teachers, among other amenities, appears to be the obvious choice, yet it was extraordinarily fraught. This decision placed a tremendous burden on young people.

But White officials comfortably spoke of freedom of choice. They could point to the handful of Black students in White schools—almost unthinkable ten years prior—as evidence of desegregation. As long as schools simply declared they were open to all students and pointed toward good faith efforts, the federal government funded them. The federal government was not mandating significant integration, only the appearance of it, and the appearance of federal compliance was something most segregationists could live with. With this "desegregation," White southern legislators distanced themselves from the open racism of massive resistance.

While freedom of choice policies at first passed the muster of federal compliance, they did not ultimately withstand the scrutiny of the Supreme Court. Freedom of choice plans did not achieve genuine integration. This was evident in South Carolina, one of the first states to champion freedom of choice. There, 92 of the 108 school districts were operating under such plans by 1969. Across the South, just over 1 percent of Black students were enrolled in schools that were at least 50 percent White, and just over 2 percent of Black students were in desegregated White schools overall.[45]

Token desegregation and ongoing recalcitrance were suspect, especially to the former NAACP attorney Thurgood Marshall, who President Johnson appointed as a Supreme Court justice in 1967. Marshall's appointment in and of itself was a milestone. As the court's first Black justice, Marshall would continue to make history, ruling in favor of decisions to strike down the so-called "freedom of choice" policies in both *Green v. County School Board* (1968) and *Alexander v. Holmes County Board of Education* (1969). In no uncertain terms, the majority of Supreme Court justices forbade any further delay in desegregating schools. From the perspective of southern segregationists, it appeared that all was lost when the *Green* and *Alexander* rulings ordered immediate and full desegregation.

Yet the clarion call of choice continued to resound widely across the South. In 1970, Mississippi governor John Bell Williams called a large meeting that signified the beginning of a new era of education reform. The site was the Jackson Coliseum, the largest venue in the capital city, a location that was strategic in announcing a new form of resistance. The coliseum sits on the other side of the hill from the fairgrounds, where in 1961 local police had converted cattle, swine, and horse yards into temporary holding cells for activists when they ran out of jail space. The meeting nine years later was no less ominous, but the appearance of the 1970 meeting was much more palatable to a "progressive" South.

Although Governor Williams officially called the meeting along with former Jackson mayor Allen Thompson, Whites came to the Jackson Coliseum to support the launch of a national initiative founded by Thompson, the Freedom of Choice in the United States (FOCUS). An acolyte of massive resistance, Thompson had the support and trust of segregationists. During his tenure as mayor between 1960 and 1964, he had militarized the state to confront "outside agitators"—civil rights activists who had moved to Mississippi to help crack segregation. He had built to his own specifications what *Newsweek* dubbed "Thompson's Tank" for law and order during the freedom struggle. A multimillion-dollar armored vehicle, the tank was "a 13,000-pound armored battlewagon" replete with shotguns, tear-gas guns, and a machine gun.[46] While mayor, Thompson had overseen the incarceration of activists at the Jackson fairgrounds.

Covered in the regional press, the 1961 FOCUS meeting drew a crowd of more than four thousand people. By Thompson's side stood US senator John Stennis: Dixiecrat, staunch defender of segregation, signer of the Southern Manifesto in 1956, and soon to be a Republican defector in support of Barry Goldwater.[47] Given the backgrounds of these White supremacists, it was clear that "choice" would be used to maintain segregation. This time, however, they did not publicly demand segregation. They did not call in Thompson's Tank to intimidate African Americans seeking to enter White schools. They did not dispatch the police to arrest Black youth. Instead, they reissued the call to defend the rights of White parents to choose where to send their children to school. It was time for resistance by another name on a much grander scale.

John Lewis asserted that "education represented an almost mythical key to the kingdom of America's riches, the kingdom so long denied to our race."[48] Southern legislators like Stennis were throwing away the key. Real school choice would continue to be denied.

An even larger platform for school choice would emerge. Schools were segregated in all major northern cities, and these schools were subject to desegregation orders after the *Green* and *Alexander* decisions. Many northerners would embrace the same strategies of resistance, but for school choice to be palatable to the wider American public, it would need the support of pundits and policymakers far removed from the South and its avowed white supremacists. Award-winning economist Milton Friedman would prove just the one to turn regional massive resistance into national policy.

CHAPTER TWO

Milton Friedman and the Problems with Choice in Chicago

A RISING ECONOMIST at the University of Chicago at the time of the *Brown* decision in 1954, Milton Friedman was the ideal spokesman for school choice. Friedman was the first to present school choice as an application of free-market economic theory to education. His argument, which criticized a liberal state he saw as overreaching, nurtured distrust of the federal government, the same distrust harbored by segregationists. Friedman's argument for school choice sparked nothing short of a revolution. Chicago also provided the stage from which to amplify the promises of school choice to parents outside the South. When civil rights activists made the demands for integration in cities like Chicago, they shocked northern sensibilities. Northerners shunned the images of violent mobs attacking innocent Black children simply trying to go to school. The nation largely treated segregation and the violence it engendered as a regional aberration confined to the South. Northerners were above this. Or so they thought.

Chicago was a petri dish for school choice in the North. Like other northern cities, Chicago faced the challenges of integration and drew on the same "freedom of choice" plans negotiated in the South. Friedman, arguably colorblind in a detrimental way, proclaimed that all parents were free to choose and that this choice would remedy a system broken by government control of the schools. But Chicago was especially fraught with structural problems, not to mention the contradiction of being a northern "liberal" city governed by the same racist policy that defined the South. The city where Friedman developed and published his ideas demonstrated racism at its roots, akin to the structural racism underpinning his proposal.

The racially segregated housing market throughout the Windy City showed no semblance of equality, and residence determined school attendance, enrollment, and thus the racial composition of schools. Under local neighborhood school policies that had been in place since the nineteenth century, district officials zoned students to attend the school closest to them. School zones therefore reflected the composition of neighborhoods. Since neighborhoods were racially segregated, it followed that schools were racially segregated. But schools and the neighborhoods they served were not "naturally" segregated or segregated by choice. Racist housing policies such as mortgage redlining, White vigilante neighborhood associations, and elaborate plans to resist desegregating neighborhoods—many of them supported by the University of Chicago—infected the "marketplace" in which so-called choices were made.

Despite the obviously uneven playing field evident in his own neighborhood, Friedman could effectively sell the school choice idea to the American public because in many respects he epitomized the American Dream. He was born in 1912 to Jewish immigrants from Hungary who barely spoke English upon arriving in New York. Growing up in poverty, Friedman had worked diligently to pursue an education. He read voraciously. He studied between jobs, graduated from high school before the age of sixteen, and enrolled at Rutgers University after winning a scholarship.[1] In short, Friedman seemed to demonstrate how one could pull oneself up by the bootstraps to overcome economic hardship.

Graduating from college in 1932 in the depths of the Great Depression, Friedman studied firsthand the economic problems that aggrieved the nation and beleaguered the economy. First understanding the Depression as caused by (and thus to be corrected by) government regulation, he later devoted his career to the libertarian notion that the government should not be actively involved in the economy. Prior to his ascent to renown as an economist and fame as a public intellectual in the 1950s, Friedman was marginalized and at times chastised for challenging the reigning orthodoxy of his field. The prevailing view at the time was based on the ideas of John Maynard Keynes, a British economist who postulated that the Great Depression was caused by economic instability triggered by failing markets and banks, the solution to which was a greater level of government intervention. According to Keynesian thought, the government should set fiscal policy, including tax rates, and increase government spending and borrowing to spur aggregate, large-scale economic activity.

Friedman began making a name for himself by challenging this view. In 1963, Friedman argued in his coauthored volume *A Monetary History of the United States, 1867–1960* that the Depression was caused by the Federal Reserve Bank's misguided monetary policy—not by Wall Street panic or consumers who hastened to withdraw money from banks. Monetary policy that focused on central bank activity—rather than fiscal policy that addressed spending and taxation—held more importance for Friedman, who advocated for changing interest rates and changing the money supply through a central bank as opposed to the network of smaller commercial banks.[2]

Friedman would not only ruffle feathers through his analysis of monetary policy. His largest contributions to the national political debate extolled the virtues of a free and competitive market in relation to a wide array of fields, including education. As Friedman continued to critique Keynesian economic thought within the ivory tower of academia and began to garner a growing influence and following, he began to articulate theories of the free market and the idea that human freedom was inextricably linked to it. For Friedman, the government should play only a limited role, thereby "freeing" individuals and the market to operate of its own accord. Friedman's work established the basis for a revolution in regard to the role of government in the economy but also in schools.

Friedman was challenging the core assumption of federal fiscal policy of his time. The Keynesian economic doctrine extended President Franklin D. Roosevelt's New Deal economic policies of the Great

Depression into the 1950s and 1960s. It was often criticized among anti-interventionists or advocates for a smaller government as a tax-and-spend liberal frenzy of congressional Democrats under President Lyndon B. Johnson, himself a mentee of FDR. By the 1960s, LBJ's Great Society programs and legislation like the Elementary and Secondary Education Act of 1965 were grounded in the same principles of Keynesian economics. It followed that the government should also guide, or intervene in, a host of other aspects of American society, including education.[3] To Friedman and others, federal education policy was the most recent example of an entrenched interventionist government.

Friedman was in a position to advocate for school choice outside the American South, effectively distancing it from a region associated with virulent racism. In academia, Friedman struck many of his teachers, colleagues, and disciples as sharp, witty, and even brilliant. A quirky, charismatic speaker with a reputation for impeccable debating skills, he spread his doctrine through speaking tours, published research, and, most notably, in meetings with high-profile politicians in the Republican Party—those who sought to woo White southern voters to the GOP. He was, in short, a force to be reckoned with.

To question the basis of federal intervention as Friedman did guaranteed political isolation. Even though he was an insider at an elite institution, Friedman put forth outsider views that resonated with those who had advocated for school choice in the South. Friedman first and foremost bucked the system with gusto, and his willingness to do so was seen as an admirable trait in an era remembered for its rebelliousness. "My maverick status did not keep me from receiving more requests than I could accommodate," Friedman later recalled.[4]

Exemplifying the American Dream, Friedman also espoused one of its most widespread myths. For Friedman, hard work and steadfast effort with a little luck could catapult one to the top. *Two Lucky People*, the autobiography he wrote with his wife, Rose, highlights the latter. "In all," they wrote, "it was pure luck that . . . enabled us to have an extraordinarily rich and varied life." For Milton in particular, it was "luck" that he'd had an inspiring math teacher in high school in New Jersey who offered a course in Euclidean geometry. It was luck that he had teachers at Rutgers University who enabled him to go to Chicago.

It was mere chance that Friedman met the faculty he did at the University of Chicago.[5] For Friedman, it was all happenstance luck, an uncontrollable factor in economics. Of course, he acknowledged, it was not all providence. His American-inspired ingenuity, work ethic, and keen intellect rounded out the American Dream that he exemplified. These traits precipitated his rise as an influential, Nobel-winning economist.

Though a growing number see the American Dream as unattainable, the idea remains popular. Popular psychologist Angela Duckworth used the word "grit" in 2007 to encompass the idea that with the right combination of passion, perseverance, and tenacity, most people, if not all, can overcome great challenges to achieve life goals.[6] Though this belief is criticized, it remains widely accepted in education circles, and many Americans are comfortable embracing it. They are in turn likely to endorse the ideas of someone like Friedman, son of immigrants, born in Brooklyn, who worked numerous jobs to help pay for his education.

Yet there are privileges and an unequal playing field that explain the rise of someone like Friedman. Nothing in this archetypal narrative mentions the privilege of his race. It disavows race and racialized policy altogether. It ignores the reality of segregated schooling enforced by housing segregation and policy decisions that enabled new forms of segregation in spite of a growing movement against it. It discounts northern housing covenants that relegated BIPOC families to "ghettos" that stripped away the same protections and promises offered to Friedman. He may have been a poor child of immigrants, but Friedman was White. Intellect, merit, and hard work played a role in his life, to be sure. But so did his Whiteness, which was protected and privileged through law, policy, and custom. This was neither the American Dream nor "grit" but a racialized system of advantages that was as American as apple pie.

There were structural limitations to Milton Friedman's ideas about school choice too. As an economist, Friedman grounded his policies in a bottom-line objectivity that assumed individuals were rational actors who for the most part acted in their own best interest. Yet in the 1950s, in the city of Chicago, there was much irrationality on full display. The housing market in particular and neighborhood segregation were governed by policies that intentionally separated White and Black families.

White neighborhood associations chased Black families out of homes in the neighborhood in and around where Friedman lived. His employer, the University of Chicago, meddled in local housing policies to clear out urban "slums" occupied by Black families. White homeowners and elected officials created policies that displaced Black families—all to effect and maintain segregation. Just as in the South, Whites undertook massive resistance to avoid sending their children to desegregated schools. And the Chicago neighborhoods created by racialized policies were intricately linked to Friedman's "educational marketplace"— the place where ostensible free choices were made about where to go to school.

Friedman may have seen that nothing was fair or equal. He may on some level have known something about racism and how it played out on the streets, outside his office window. Regardless, these did not factor into his analysis or the school choice theory that reshaped American education.

Friedman was awarded the Nobel Prize in economics in 1976. He earned the award for his "brilliance and independence" in challenging the predominant view of Keynesian economics, arguing that "money matters."[7] By the time he was awarded the Nobel, internationally esteemed economists credited Friedman with shifting the macroeconomic policy of major nations including the United States, spurring revision and reexamination of previously accepted truths that undergirded monetary policy. "It is very rare for an economist to wield such influence," the Royal Swedish Academy of Sciences noted in 1976, "not only on the direction of scientific research but also on actual policies."[8] His influence continued to grow. In 1980, he published *Free to Choose*, also cowritten with his wife, and it rose to the top of the best-seller list and inspired a popular PBS series of the same name.[9]

Some of Friedman's most influential ideas are about education policy, and his platform as a renowned public intellectual amplified his influence. Friedman put forth what would be dubbed "school choice" in an essay first published in 1955 as part of the edited volume *Economics and the Public Interest* and later included in his highly influential *Freedom and Capitalism*. In "The Role of Government in Public Education" Friedman first challenged a deeply entrenched acceptance of an interventionist state, which he claimed entailed a "concentration of attention and dispute on the areas where new intervention is proposed and to an acceptance of whatever intervention has so far occurred as natural and unchangeable."[10] Government influence in education policy, like government intervention in a plethora of other fields, constituted an intrusion that had grown to the point where it seemed immutable by the mid-1950s. Though he never specifically mentioned it, the *Brown v. Board of Education* decision represented one of the most profound interventions in the field of education since Reconstruction. By publishing his essay in 1955, one year after the *Brown* decision and the dawn of desegregation, Friedman was wading into one of the most contentious debates of the century.

As evidenced by vocational education, discussions of academic tracking, and the presence of business owners in local school governance, schooling in America had long been susceptible to the idea that education should be run as a business, or at least that the aims of education should align with those of the job market. Friedman built on this, envisioning the entire field of education as a free market. Schools would function as places of business in the larger market. Teachers and administrators would act as service providers. Students and their families would be viewed as consumers. Schools that met consumer demand and provided good services as measured by test scores would remain open. It followed that education would be viewed as a business, but Friedman's logic transformed the entire context of how education should be provided and the government's role in it.

Friedman used rational choice and free market theory to argue that the nation's education system would become more responsive to the needs of parents if they were free to choose where their children attended school. Redistributing school funding directly to the individual, or consumer, rather than to local school districts or state agencies would provide a better education, or product. As in a free market, the best schools would stay in business as they gained the tuition dollars of customers who used vouchers. The worst schools, like bad businesses, would close due to their inability to attract customers.

Parents, acting as consumers in their own best interest, would inspire competition among schools, which would theoretically improve the entire market. Parents, as rational consumers, would select the best educational services the market offered. Friedman argued that "competitive private enterprise is likely to be far more efficient in meeting consumer demands than either nationalized enterprises or enterprises run to serve other purposes."[11] But he seemed to offer no insights into how race and racism played a determining role in where parents would send their children to school and with whom. At first glance, Friedman's thoughts appear to transcend race, but his essay includes a long footnote that is often overlooked in the history of school choice. Just before he published his essay, Friedman was made aware of plans to use public money to privatize education in the South, and he used this footnote to distance himself from southern opposition to integration. He opposed this southern resistance, but not on moral grounds. He thought that southern plans were "a striking case of the possible defect" of his idea of "public financing but private operation of education."[12]

Upon further reflection, evident in a later revised version of the essay, Friedman saw the South as the ultimate test of the government's commitment to individuals' right to select their children's school. While Friedman made sure to say that he detested segregation and racial prejudice, he noted, "It is not an appropriate function of the state to try to force individuals to act in accordance with my—or anyone else's—views."[13] This included racial prejudice, so long as the attitudes did not physically harm others. If the government had no business intruding upon free speech, Friedman reasoned, then the government also had no right to intervene with the individual's freedom of choice. Based on his articulation of the proper role of government in education, Friedman concluded that the government had no right in a free market, capitalistic society to force segregation or, conversely, "nonsegregation." People had a right to be racist in views and action, he maintained, as much as people had a right to be nonracist or antiracist.[14]

For Friedman, private schools resolved the dilemma presented by the "evils" of being forced by the government to choose between segregated and nonsegregated schooling. Under his proposed system of school choice, "there can develop exclusively white schools, exclusively colored schools, and mixed schools. Parents can choose which to send their children to."[15] This "third alternative" was precisely what

Virginia's freedom of choice plans advocated. Virginia legislators adopted a freedom of choice policy and, by the time Friedman published *Capitalism and Freedom* in 1962, Prince Edward County had closed its public schools, denying all children a public education. Tuition grants and vouchers supported by the state in practice only went to White families. It was a policy that Friedman endorsed in principle. He even predicted success: "We should see a flowering of the schools available in Virginia," he noted, "with an increase in their diversity, a substantial if not spectacular rise in the quality of the leading schools, and a later rise in the quality of the rest."[16] The disastrous results of closing public schools for five years proved otherwise.

In a belief that is widely shared among school choice advocates, Friedman claimed that race did not and would not matter in an ideal application of choice. He predicted marked improvement through school choice plans for "the ablest and most ambitious Negro youth."[17] If one is able, ambitious, committed, and dedicated—like he himself had been— one could succeed. These ideas resonated with southern "freedom of choice" advocates because he placed the onus to desegregate on those who supported integration. It was up to them, not the government, to persuade individuals to support desegregation. Friedman argued, in the long footnote in his 1955 essay, "The appropriate activity for those who oppose segregation and racial prejudice is to try to persuade others of their views; if and as they succeed, the mixed schools will grow at the expense of the nonmixed, and a gradual transition will take place."[18] In his revised essay seven years later, he urged his readers to "try by behavior and speech to foster the growth of attitudes and opinions that would lead mixed schools to become the rule and segregated schools the rare exception."[19]

Friedman was a principled libertarian, which complicated any "conservative" label. Friedman applied the same principles in his opposition to fair housing legislation, arguing that the government had no right to intervene in the management of negative or nonviolent harm, as he conceived it. He argued that business owners have a right to apply racially discriminatory hiring practices if desired by a majority of customers or employees, just as they have to the right to *not* discriminate based on race.[20] He also extended his opposition to intervention in the budding discourse around "right-to-work" or anti-union legisla-tion.[21] For Friedman, government intervention to ban unions was tan-tamount to the same overreach he so adamantly opposed in the field of education. As historian Nancy MacLean has demonstrated, Friedman was part of a larger network led by other economists, such as James Buchanan at the University of Virginia, who established the intellec-tual foundations for a network of wealthy elites to restructure state and federal policy to protect *their* rights (and their privileged position) from being diminished by the majority of Americans, who were not in the upper echelons but potentially wielded the power to regulate the elite.[22]

Clearly, Friedman stood in direct conflict with the civil rights move-ment. Beyond providing intellectual rationale for the "freedom of choice" plans that emerged across the South, Friedman, in principle, opposed the milestone legislation of the movement: the Civil Rights Act of 1964. Speaking to the Young Conservative Club at Harvard just three months before the passage of the act, Friedman criticized the bill on principle, upholding his assertion that freedom must be applied equally by asking: "If we pass a law saying that race shall not be a factor in employment, then what grounds do we have for opposing a law that race shall be a factor?" He again reinforced "the general principle that the state [should] not interfere in these [civil rights] matters."[23] To put it simply, according to Friedman, the government should not be used to protect the rights of the routinely and historically disenfranchised.

Friedman's opposition to federal spending and advocacy for free markets would soon be leveraged by the New Right, a movement to oppose federally mandated desegregation and interventionist economic regulation. Part of this rising tide of conservative policymakers, Arizona outsider Barry Goldwater hired Friedman to serve as economic advisor during his 1964 presidential campaign, and Friedman's economic theory turned even more conservative while he continued to ardently oppose government intervention. Friedman later noted that he "was impressed with Goldwater's firm adherence to basic principles, his courage in tak-ing unpopular positions, his willingness to sacrifice what seemed like political expediency to stand up for what he thought was right, and, not least, his quick wit."[24] Friedman helped shape Goldwater's economic platform and provided numerous engagements in New York as he taught as a visiting professor at Columbia. In the *New York Times*, he outlined Goldwater's basic philosophy, which dovetailed neatly with his own. Goldwater believed in the "freedom of the individual to pursue his own interests so long as he does not interfere with the freedom of others to do likewise; opportunity for the ordinary man to use his resources as effectively as possible to advance the well being of himself and his family."[25] The ideology did not win the converts he sought in the New York intellectual community—a lot he chastised as homogenous and provincial. To Friedman, the liberals of New York accepted "a standard set of views complete with cliché answers to every objection, of smug self-satisfaction at belonging to an in-group."[26]

Though Goldwater was defeated by Lyndon Johnson in the landslide election of 1964, a major change further upset America's troubled political waters. Friedman and Goldwater's philosophy captured the heart of Dixie, and their proposals shaped the reorganization of the Republican Party's economic platform. Through his connections during the Goldwater campaign, Friedman met Ronald Reagan, not yet governor of California, who would also be key in the conservative economic realignment of the Republican Party. Their movement similarly embraced race-neutral rhetoric and a defense of individual rights. This attracted southern segregationists with whom Friedman personally disagreed but whose right to school choice he supported.

But race could not be dismissed in a footnote. It was an absolute factor that shaped individual decision-making. Many Americans were not permitted to enroll their children in the school of their choice. The nation watched as White segregationists harassed, threatened, and terrorized Black students who enrolled in White schools. And White school "consumers" often conformed to a racist logic, making this a truth of their economic "rationality."

While Friedman's ideas would flourish, the "educational marketplace" remained harmfully unfair. In the years after the *Brown* decision, public schools, especially in the South, grew stagnant, and those who relied on them suffered. Hopes were dashed. Opportunity was denied. As historian Ansley Erickson noted of the period after World War II and before the onset of desegregation in the mid-1960s, "Schooling interacted with a broad range of municipal policy areas, from city planning practice, housing development and urban renewal plans to local and state economic efforts."[27] In Chicago, where Friedman lived and wrote, this dynamic led to White flight to the suburbs, with the weight of concomitant problems, such as failing schools, squarely on the backs of Black people.[28] Contrary to Friedman's assertions, school choice perpetuated inequality.

The University of Chicago was Friedman's incubator. While serving on the faculty, Friedman published his most important work, served as economic advisor to a burgeoning conservative movement, and accepted the Nobel Prize in economics. The school's location, the city of Chicago, was a potential laboratory to study how his ideas could reform education. Friedman asserted in 1962: "There is also no doubt at all that if the Virginia [school choice] system were introduced in Chicago the result would be an appreciable decrease in segregation, and a great widening in the opportunities."[29] As with Virginia, this outlook proved tragically false.

The foundation of the grand experiment in choice was inherently flawed from the start. Friedman never factored into his analysis the endemic racism and segregationist history of Chicago, and the violence racism fomented there during the 1950s and 1960s. His position in the ivory tower colored—or, rather, whitewashed—his way of seeing it.

Chicago was a deeply segregated city. It still is today. The city's segregation barriers grew in direct relation to the arrival of over half a million African Americans between 1910 and 1970, when six and a half million Blacks left the South as part of the Great Migration. The Black population in Chicago rose to over one million by the end of the massive migration to the North. In 1920, Black residents constituted only 4 percent of the city's population, but by 1956, two years after the *Brown* decision, African Americans and other communities of color made up 19 percent of the city's population, and, by the height of the civil rights movement, African Americans made up 30 percent.[30] The Urban League in Chicago, the historic African American association for empowerment founded in 1910, extrapolated in 1958 that 80 percent of the Black population in the Chicago area would be concentrated in the city by 1965 while only one-half of the White population would reside within city limits.[31]

Once African Americans arrived to the promised land of Chicago, they encountered the same codified racial segregation that existed in the South. Whites implemented racially discriminatory housing policies and practices to confront what they largely saw as a Black "invasion." Real estate boards and agents across the city coordinated a code of racially restrictive covenants, which dictated where to sell and to whom. These covenants became embedded in property deeds, home loans, and business ethics. After the Supreme Court found racial ordinances to be unconstitutional in *Buchanan v. Warley* (1917), racially restrictive covenants rested on private agreements, unspoken understandings, and contracts among real estate brokers, homeowner associations, and business owners.[32] The exclusionary process was also determined by federal programs including the Home Owner's Loan Corporation, the Federal Housing Administration, and the Veterans Administration that refused or grossly limited access to home loans and other financing to families of color. Those steered to areas that were demarcated on maps by literal red lines—"redlining"—found it exceedingly difficult to gain financial assistance at all or loans to buy homes anywhere.[33] Denying the capital needed to buy homes and build wealth, lending policies were frighteningly efficient tools to corral people of color into racialized ghettos. In Chicago, covenants ultimately relegated Black tenants and property owners to the South Side, where they had traditionally lived in mixed neighborhoods. As in other northern cities employing the same practices, African Americans were boxed in, shut out, and denied access to other affordable neighborhoods in the city.

Whites militantly enforced the strict racial boundaries they drew. Violence was not uncommon. Historian Arnold Hirsh asserted that the late 1940s was "an era analogous to that of 1917–21, when one racially motivated mobbing or arson occurred every twenty days."[34] Instances of violence across the city defined the lived experiences of people of color. Harvey Clark, a veteran of the Second World War, and his wife and two children were relegated to a one-room tenement unit on the segregated South Side. By 1951, they'd found a place in Cicero, the virtually all-White working-class neighborhood on the city's West Side. As the moving truck pulled up to their new, larger apartment, a small White mob greeted them with jeers and taunts. The Clark family ultimately left that day, once the police ordered them to do so. When, later that summer, the Clarks managed to go back and move their belongings into their new abode, the White Circle League, a segregationist vigilante association, inspired another mob to invade the apartment. Ransacking The Clarks' home, the mob threw their furniture out the window, piled it next to other family belongings, and then torched it. This was only the start. The mob then firebombed the entire building and threw bricks at arriving firefighters. They owned the streets. The violence subsided only when the governor called in the National Guard to quell the riot, which lasted for four days. Over one hundred Whites were arrested, yet none were indicted.[35]

A Black recording artist who had earned the respect of White America at large fared no better. As Mahalia Jackson searched for a home in a White section of the South Side, Whites protested, organized meetings, and rallied their neighbors to resist. Once she moved in, Whites fired shots into her home. They harassed her and her family with late night phone calls. They threatened their lives. Police were stationed outside her home.[36]

This violent reality belies the claim that residential segregation was "natural" and that those who lived in segregated neighborhoods voluntarily chose to do so. Self-segregation is nothing more than a myth, and Chicago provided the tangible evidence. The area surrounding Milton Friedman's neighborhood and the University of Chicago was the site of fierce and highly visible lawsuits over housing segregation. In 1938, Carl Hansberry, the father of playwright Lorraine Hansberry who was eight years old at the time, purchased a home in Woodlawn, an all-White neighborhood just southwest of the university. Whites harassed the Hansberry family and threw bricks through the windows at night. Mrs. Hansberry kept watch throughout the night, pacing through their new home or sitting in a rocking chair with a loaded gun in hand. Anna Lee, a White woman, filed suit on behalf of the Hyde Park–Woodlawn Improvement Society, charging that the Hansberry family had violated a restrictive agreement that prohibited home sales to African Americans.

Whites seeking to drive the family out won in the local and state courts. Though the Supreme Court eventually overturned the case in *Hansberry v. Lee* (1940), the family was forced to leave the neighborhood. The ordeal inspired young Hansberry, who would pen the acclaimed *A Raisin in the Sun*.[37]

As courts struck down racial covenants after *Hansberry* and established legal precedent, Black families moved where and when they could to escape the overcrowded and overpriced conditions of racialized ghettos. In response, Whites moved out. The suburban population of Chicago exploded after the collapse of overt racial covenants and during the years of the civil rights movement, growing by more than 400,000 or 15 percent. More than 270,000 Whites left in the early part of the 1950s alone, a massive White flight out of the city. Outside the city limits, people of color—denied the loans and capital to build and buy homes—composed only 5 percent of the suburban population, a percentage that remained steady throughout the 1950s. As Whites moved out of the city, African Americans moved into previously all-White urban neighborhoods. These parts of the city were "in transition" to becoming all-Black, triggering serious alarm among Whites who stayed.[38]

Some Whites cashed in on the housing crises that they had carefully engineered. When Black families began to move into White neighborhoods, Whites opted to sell their homes under unfavorable circumstances rather than live next to Black homeowners. White speculators swooped in to capitalize, purchasing the homes of Whites, who often panicked and sold for far less than their houses were worth. Speculators could offer cash up front, which Whites needed for down payments on their new homes. Speculators then sold to African Americans, who were eager to move and willing to pay more for the same home. They charged, on average, 73 percent more than they purchased a home for. They relinquished the title only once the mortgage was paid in full—a prospect that remained a distant dream.[39]

To further enhance their profit, White speculators scaled back on maintenance and general upkeep. Their negligence led to increased deterioration of homes and neighborhoods, urban decay and blight. And White Chicagoans were terrified. It appeared that the entire city was crumbling before them.

Violence and flight were the most visible forms of White resistance to desegregation, but Whites also mobilized an elaborate defense of what they marked as their space, drawing on myriad local economic and political decisions. In a coordinated effort under the rubric of "urban renewal" to stave off "blight" and the Black "invasion," affluent Whites, civic leaders, and business owners formed partnerships with corporations that had financial stakes in the city. They tapped public funds available from local, state, and federal agencies after powerful coalitions pushed through legislation such as the Illinois Blighted Areas Redevelopment Act of 1947. Later supported by federal policies such as the American Housing Act of 1949, legislation around urban development authorized "slum clearance" and the construction of new public housing. "Slums" and "ghettos," in the common parlance used to denote all-Black or all-Brown segregated areas, were to be cleared, literally. Led by the Chicago Land Clearance Commission, White Chicagoans called on officials in bodies such as the Chicago Land Clearance Commission to "check the blight" and physically remove Black neighborhoods in disrepair while "renewing" the cleared areas. For the victims of this policy, the process was tantamount to "Negro Clearance."[40]

There was nothing equal about urban renewal. The Urban League in the 1950s launched an investigation into Chicago's renewal problems and preservation efforts. Its conclusion in 1958 was unsurprising: "Urban renewal, as conducted up to now, in Chicago, is working great and undue hardships on the Negro population, and, on balance, is working more and more harm on the city as a whole." The Urban League also observed a pattern of racial segregation in the city that surpassed that of any other urban area in the nation and claimed that Chicago was the most segregated major city in the United States. Between 1948 and 1956, approximately eighty-six thousand Chicagoans were displaced by urban renewal projects, 67 percent of whom were African American. Roughly 11 percent of Chicago's Black population was forced to relocate.[41]

Chicago developed a solution to urban "decay" attributed to Black families moving outside Black neighborhoods. City leaders initiated public-private ventures between city, state, federal, and corporate interests. It established a national protocol that influenced urban renewal in the 1950s and 1960s throughout the nation. As Chicago renegotiated racial boundaries under the guise of de facto or "natural" segregation, a pattern was emerging in the North that not only maintained residential segregation but also kept school integration at bay.

Milton Friedman took up residence in the South Side's Hyde Park neighborhood to teach at the University of Chicago at a time when Whites thought that urban blight was a threat to the school's very existence. University officials and neighborhood residents anxiously anticipated a Black invasion. More and more Black families were moving into the area. Thousands would soon follow. Whites wanted to avoid what they saw as a point of no return—a line that, once crossed, would make their "interracial" neighborhood an all-Black ghetto. Chancellor Lawrence A. Kimpton claimed in 1959 that the university's effort in urban renewal was "no less than for the university's survival."[42] Enrollment was already dropping due to a perceived urban crisis, propagated by racialized fears of the "blackboard jungles" of urban education.[43]

The University of Chicago, and the Hyde Park and Kenwood neighborhoods that surrounded it, were desirable areas for Black families who felt the stress of overcrowding. In Black neighborhoods, housing was deteriorating and families were increasingly packed into jammed tenements and overfull apartment buildings. Essentially forced into legally and politically constructed ghettos, African Americans were isolated and primed to move to other parts of the city. The Hyde Park and Kenwood neighborhoods were a logical destination and were increasingly more valuable as the Black population continued to boom. In 1950, only 6 percent of the Hyde Park–Kenwood neighborhood was African American. By 1956, one year after Friedman published his essay on school choice, about 37 percent of neighborhood residents were Black and other people of color.[44] Whites were panicking, to be sure. They were attuned to what the Chicago Urban League cited in 1958: that once 25 percent of a neighborhood was occupied by families of color, the community quickly became virtually all-Black.[45]

In the 1950s, Whites saw what they angrily interpreted as an approaching storm. The transition their neighborhoods were experiencing was unstable, the growth unsustainable. Over 60 percent of families in Hyde Park–Kenwood had been in their current homes for less than three years. Over 33 percent had been in their present home for less than a year. Streets were congested. Parking spaces were limited. Some buildings were unsightly and unkempt. Crime increased. "On its northwest border was a segregated Negro area," the *Chicago Tribune* noted of the university neighborhood, "bursting at its seams."[46] As one neighborhood organizer noted, "The tremendous population densities in the ghetto that almost surrounds Hyde Park–Kenwood will continue to build up and roll right over us. The very existence of the ghetto makes for unrest, tension, and flight throughout the whole South Side."[47]

Following a pattern established across the city, university officials by 1960 had teamed up with local and state governments to "save" the university area and maintain a "stable, interracial community."[48] White, affluent, well-educated Hyde Park residents joined other Chicagoans who sought to delay what they saw as "inevitable decay" or the "'natural history' of all cities for the center to change from a highly desirable living area to a blighted and decayed slum as the city expanded."[49] Behind a banner of integration and progress, the institution participated in clearing slums on the South Side, especially Hyde Park. It was a practice that was part of what sociologist Margaret Weir and historians Thomas Segrue and Matt Delmont call "defensive localism," Whites defending their right to own property and maintain boundaries around that property by racially segregating their neighborhood. Hyde Park was cited as the third-largest urban renewal project in the country after projects in New York and Philadelphia, cities also threatened "by encroaching slum and crime problems."[50] In 1958, the University of Chicago demolished four blocks in the southwest portion of the city, an area bordering Washington Park, the neighborhood that had transitioned after the *Hansberry* case.[51]

Hyde Park neighborhood associations sought to control the extent of integration. This amounted to limited desegregation that carefully projected images of diversity while preserving the essence of the White neighborhood. They even recruited African American residents to work with them in cultivating a "stable" interracial neighborhood that adhered to a middle-class White aesthetic and sensibility.[52] It was in their own best interests to permit token desegregation with people of color who engaged in the politics of respectability. The neighborhoods did not necessarily have to be all-White for university officials and local homeowners. However, it still had to be majority White, and families of color were expected to conform to White norms.

The university maintained racial covenants in the housing it continued to operate. Though working under a superficial call for interracial communities, building managers catered to Whites, refusing to rent or lease to students of color, even those enrolled at the university.[53] As historian Arnold Hirsh noted, "The university was hardly engaging in a noble experiment on the viability of interracial communities."[54]

The University of Chicago was a powerful ally of fearful white residents in the urban renewal project on the South Side. Its law school supported urban renewal efforts by threatening litigation against "slum landlords" in violation of city ordinances.[55] The board of trustees contributed over 20 percent of the budget of the local neighborhood commission that directed urban renewal in the area, the South East Chicago Commission. Board members, who included banker David Rockefeller, grandson of the university's founder, contributed money and helped leverage private and corporate donations toward renewal.[56] The university worked with local neighborhood organizations as well. Since the 1940s, White homeowners there had been organizing neighborhood associations to combat impending blight. Stories of violence and fears of Black bodies that drew on racial stereotypes heightened the sense of urgency.

The University of Chicago and the Hyde Park–Kenwood neighborhood successfully maintained the "interracial" neighborhood they desired. The project was heralded a success. Mayor Richard Daley, reflecting in 1960 on the renewal of the area, stated: "The program of conservation and renewal in Hyde Park–Kenwood is an excellent example of what can be done through the cooperation between government and private enterprise. But the key to democratic progress . . . has always been citizen interest."[57] Daley's reflection captured the ardent belief that not only was progress made in saving the neighborhood but also that private enterprise and individuals drove that success. These were the cornerstones of the new ideology that would drive privatization and school choice for the remainder of the century.

Racial covenants and residential segregation policies alone did not create Chicago's segregated schooling. As historian Elizabeth Todd-Breland writes, the school boards and school district administrators perpetuated segregation by "manipulating school assignment policies, meticulously districting attendance areas along racial lines, creating barriers to student transfers, and building new schools to maintain this segregation."[58] Such policy decisions from various housing, government, and school agencies at the local, state, and federal level helped remake what historian Ansley Erickson called the "unequal metropolis."[59] Students in Chicago were subject to state-sponsored, legal segregation, though it was more subtle and hidden than the de jure school segregation in the South.

Starkly segregated public schools defined life in the Windy City as much as racialized ghettos, drawing the scorn of civil rights advocates. The Chicago branch of the NAACP filed reports in 1957 with the city's board of education, sharing its estimates that over 90 percent of elementary schools and over 70 percent of high schools were de facto segregated. Parents and civil rights activists took matters into their own hands. They launched Operation Transfer in 1961 and sought to transfer 160 Black students to all-White schools. The transfers were denied. They filed *Webb v. Board of Education* in 1963 through civil rights lawyers, and the NAACP urged Superintendent Benjamin C. Willis and the Chicago Board of Education to refrain "from maintaining and requiring attendance at racially segregated public schools."[60] The courts ultimately ruled that "school segregation resulting from residential segregation, alone, is not a violation of any right over which this Court can take cognizance."[61] In a long pattern validated by the federal government, school district administrators and city officials claimed they did not intentionally segregate by law. Segregation, they claimed, was caused not by intent—which was unconstitutional—but by circumstances and conditions beyond the control of the schools. Courts did not find this de facto segregation to be in violation of the law.

The *Webb* case was ultimately settled out of court and prompted a formal investigation into the nature and status of segregation in city schools. The 1964 *Report to the Board of Education of the City of Chicago by the Advisory Panel on Integration of the Public Schools* found that 90 percent of Black students attended racially segregated schools. The report also found a pervasive lack of qualified teachers, poor test scores, higher dropout rates than White schools, and generally far fewer resources in Black schools.[62]

To evade court action and to stave off criticisms and further demands for integration, district officials drew up and used a voluntary transfer plan that allowed families of color to apply to transfer to or otherwise enroll in White schools. Much like the "freedom of choice" plans in the South, this placed the onus of desegregation on the backs of Black families. Withholding transportation to White schools while harassing Black transfer students, White parents and officials ensured that plans were largely ineffective, leading only to token desegregation.[63]

To add insult to injury, Superintendent Willis ordered the arrangement of aluminum mobile classrooms for Black and underfunded schools as a way to assuage concerns about overcrowding. Dubbed "Willis Wagons" by civil rights activists and Black parents, the mobile units symbolized the intentions of the city to avoid integration and dismiss demands for quality public education.[64]

The city of Chicago and the White men who dictated its education policy made it painfully clear that both neighborhoods and their schools would remain segregated or marginally desegregated, to their own benefit. Even as the civil rights movement won desegregation victories in the South, northern cities like Chicago stood in Dixie-like defiance.

Supported by a prevailing notion that segregation was somehow "natural" or not produced by law and policy, Chicago was spared the federal intervention that enabled integration of segregationist strongholds in the South during the 1960s. But civil rights activists continued to petition for such intervention. The Coordinating Council of Community Organizations (CCCO), the civil rights coalition working to desegregate Chicago schools, applied mounting pressure to address racist policy. It organized boycotts, demonstrations, and protests calling for Willis's resignation and immediate desegregation. The coalition sought legal redress and took advantage of Title VI of the Civil Rights Act of 1964—the provision stating that institutions, including schools, that practiced segregation would not receive federal funding. In 1965, the CCCO filed a formal complaint of discrimination to the Department of Health, Education, and Welfare (HEW). The federal government found Chicago to be in violation of the law and planned to withhold $32 million of federal funding to force the city to desegregate.[65]

It was the first test case of the segregation clause of the Civil Rights Act in a major northern city. Infuriated by the prospect of federally enforced desegregation—presuming it designed only for the racist South—Mayor Richard Daley flexed his political prowess, personally intervening with President Johnson and threatening to withhold the support of Illinois senators and representatives. Johnson and HEW backed off.[66]

The city later implemented "voluntary" desegregation plans, which included limited busing routes to transport Black students to White schools. These plans, coupled with an expressed commitment to desegregation, were enough to meet minimal compliance under the Civil Rights Act. The city was free to move forward without federal oversight.[67] It would not be until the Carter administration that a federal court decree was issued to desegregate Chicago schools.

The potential for federal oversight in the North shocked the sensibilities of northern politicians who had passed the Civil Rights Act, assuming that de jure segregation was a problem confined to the former Confederacy. But it also fomented resistance to desegregation in the North, confining "forced integration" to the southern states.

As no formal Jim Crow laws existed in Chicago, Superintendent Willis, the Chicago Board of Education, and Mayor Daley maintained that they were not perpetuating racial segregation. Friedman concurred, noting: "Chicago has no law compelling segregation. Its laws require integration."[68] Such claims ignored both the real threats of violence against people of color moving into White neighborhoods and the breadth of systemic policy that undergirded segregation in Chicago. Whites defending the "racial integrity" of their neighborhoods did not use the openly racist language of southern segregationists or Jim Crow laws. But they sustained the same racist practices and unequal results through the use of color-blind rhetoric. They also acted on the premise that residential segregation was beyond their control—and the courts agreed. In a pattern that would define desegregation efforts in the North, courts did not account for past housing codes or private, if not vigilante, efforts to maintain residential segregation. The courts often blurred the lines between de jure and de facto segregation. But barring any explicit legal racism or intentionality, northern segregation remained free from any meaningful federal oversight and went largely unchecked.

From Milton Friedman's perspective, Chicago represented a limited victory for free market education. The education market in Chicago was free to operate without court-ordered or federal desegregation mandates. Yet Friedman's "free market" was not free to all. When the courts in cases such as *Webb v. Board of Education* (1963) would not recognize the entrenched policies behind the residential segregation that perpetuated school segregation, they proved unwilling to create the level playing field required to participate fairly in Friedman's educational marketplace. Whites' intimidation and terrorism went unchecked. Whites firebombed Black homeowners with impunity, using fear to wield influence that outweighed that of civil rights groups opposing segregation. These Whites who acted with violence and vitriol while retaining a position of power further confounded Friedman's theory, exposing the sanctioned violence of "rational" actors and the influence they yielded.

As Friedman emerged as the economist of the New Right, he largely ignored the racism of the supposedly liberal or progressive northern city of Chicago. As Dr. Martin Luther King Jr. stated of a rally in Chicago in 1966: "I've been in many demonstrations all across the South, but I can say that I had never seen—even in Mississippi—mobs as hostile and as hate-filled as in Chicago."[69] Friedman registered a very different reality. He would recall of the tumultuous period, "Despite [my] having [held] views that were not 'politically correct' . . . I do not recall any significant unpleasantness in those years."[70] Friedman remained aloof, distant, and privileged, adamant that all would work out for the best if the government just left things alone. He fiddled as Chicago burned. Friedman's theory gave northerners an alibi for their racism, a phenomenon he noted in his opposition to the Civil Rights Act, observing that northerners supported the act only because they thought segregation was a "regional problem" limited to the South.[71] Whites could claim they wanted their children to live in the suburbs and attend suburban schools because they were superior in quality, not because they were lily-white. School choice and the dismantling of public education could now proceed on a national scale.

CHAPTER THREE

Racism by Yet Another Name

Busing, White Resistance, and the Foundations
for a National School Choice Model

JOSEPH RAKES was a seventeen-year-old White high school student in South Boston in 1976. Long-haired and decked out in denim, Rakes looked like a typical teenager of the era. On the morning of April 5, he linked up with a group of his friends from South Boston and Charlestown High Schools at City Hall Plaza. They gathered to protest mandated busing—a transportation plan in Boston that bused White students and students of color across the city to achieve "racial balance." Their schools had been all White until busing, though that is not how Rakes or others saw it. "When the busing started, it was, 'You can't have half your friends'—that's the way it was put towards us," Rakes recalled thirty years after this tense moment in history. "They took half the guys and girls I grew up with and said, 'You're going to school on the other side of town.' Nobody understood it."[1] At the time Rakes and his crew descended upon the plaza, the city had been torn asunder by racial violence over the busing issue. The demonstration at city hall that morning was the most recent of hundreds of busing protests upending the city. Ted Landsmark, a Black lawyer unaware of the rally, was rushing to a meeting when he ran into the mob in the plaza. Rakes and his friends turned on Landsmark and assaulted him.[2]

Stanley Forman, a photographer for the *Boston Herald American*, was there, camera in hand, to capture the moment. In a now-famous photograph, *The Soiling of Old Glory*, Rakes wields a US flag like a polearm, appearing to be about to spear the lawyer, who is frozen in time, leaping back, contorted, to evade the flag. In fact, the flag missed Landsmark, but other blows landed, breaking his glasses and his nose. Forman would be awarded a Pulitzer Prize that year for his photograph.[3]

Published locally in the *Boston Herald American* but eventually circulated around the globe, the photograph shocked the sensibilities of White northerners vested in the idea that the North was a haven of freedom and equality. The image and the reality it communicated were especially haunting to those who had toiled in the southern movement against Jim Crow. Millicent Brown, one of the first eleven African American students to desegregate schools in Charleston, South Carolina, was one of these. After a harrowing experience as a full-time civil rights movement activist in the South, a battle-scarred Brown had moved north to Boston to pursue studies at Emerson College. As someone who had grown up "indoctrinated with the North-South divide," she later said, "I first went to Boston because . . . I needed to get out of the South. I had decided that these problems were of the South. I said, 'I'm getting the heck out of Dodge. So I'm going to go North where things were different.' And where do I go? Boston. When? Right at the height of the Boston busing controversy." Brown added, "I ran away from southern racism but ran into something else."[4] The something else was a system of racism that transcended the Mason-Dixon Line. The lived reality of the North presented the same problems as Dixie, just under a different name. And, as in the South, it was public education that comprised a battleground. The rhetoric of the southern school choice movement was going nationwide.

The unrest in Boston—like much of the racial tension of the 1960s and earlier—involved buses. This mode of transportation held enormous significance in educational history. School buses were regularly used to transport children across vast tracts of rural America. For those who had formerly walked miles to school, buses could be a godsend. For John Lewis in Alabama the "rattling, rusty jalopy [and] old hand-me-down" bus was a constant reminder of inequality.[5] But for Rev.

Joseph DeLaine in South Carolina, a bus was a symbol of simple justice. In 1947, wishing to ensure the safe transport of the kids in his community to school, Rev. DeLaine led his congregation in rural Clarendon County in petitioning the school board to provide a bus for Black students. When the board denied their request, they sued. As lead counsel, NAACP attorney Thurgood Marshall argued the case in Charleston and leveraged the bus complaint to argue that de jure segregation was unconstitutional. Though the NAACP lost this particular case, it later became one of the five cases that comprised the monumental *Brown v. Board of Education* (1954) decision.[6] Less than one year after *Brown*, Rosa Parks refused to give up her seat in a White section of a city bus in Montgomery, Alabama. In the boycott that followed, which precipitated the meteoric rise of the young Rev. Dr. Martin Luther King Jr., the bus emerged on the national scene as a quintessential symbol of freedom. In 1961, young activists boarded buses for freedom. The Freedom Riders associated with the Congress for Racial Equality and the Student Nonviolent Coordinating Committee (SNCC) intended to desegregate interstate buses and bus terminals from Washington, DC, to New Orleans. Despite being firebombed and physically assaulted and having to resort to flying the last leg of their route via airplane, the Freedom Riders bestowed new symbolic meaning on buses.

By 1976, as Boston erupted in violence over integration, the classic American school bus—the yellow bus with retractable stop sign—had come to stand for desegregation. Many White Americans despised it, seeing it as an unwanted jalopy.

From the *Brown* decision in 1954 through the late 1960s, the American public largely viewed desegregation as a southern issue. According to the prevailing logic of the North, what happened in Boston was an anomaly. The conflict in Boston was not really based in racism like it was in the South. For centuries, the North had beckoned those who toiled and suffered under the chains of slavery and the oppressive laws of Jim Crow. Yet the lived realities of African Americans who escaped or moved to the North were at odds with the region's reputation as a haven. Dr. King's observations in 1966, for instance—that Chicago was no different from Birmingham, Alabama—did not conform to the mythology of northern freedom. His biting remark merely affirmed the realities of millions like Millicent Brown.

Whites in Chicago, New York, Boston, and Detroit responded with violence to the mere notion of integration. Northern Whites pleaded that court-ordered desegregation infringed upon their rights. Rather than integrate schools, they sought different options, all of which weakened the traditional public school system. Whites fled to the suburbs, leaving behind cities depleted of investment and a tax base. Building on a long national history of racial redlining and discriminatory loan practices since the early 1900s, legal and extralegal barriers ensured that suburban enclaves remained White. Whites also claimed to be paying more taxes than Black families and families of color and therefore entitled to better schooling, even if unequal. When busing remedies were proposed to rectify ongoing segregation, Whites across the North actively demonstrated against it. In the most "liberal" of American spaces, like Chicago and Boston, Whites practiced the same modes of resistance as they did in Dixie to avoid integration.

White parents in the North made it clear that they were not opposed to sending their kids to schools with Black or Brown children, per se. Northerners had witnessed a decade of civil rights struggle in the South, where children were harassed, protesters and activists killed, and the US military called in to escort Black students to White schools. Northerners were not like *that*.

Northern Whites instead directed their angst against the *process* of desegregation. To them, the process was unfair, especially busing. Many northern cities had developed plans to transport students across neighborhoods to mitigate the effects of segregation. This was a way of responding to increasing pressure from civil rights coalitions whose members held no illusions—segregation was upheld north of the Mason-Dixon Line as fiercely as it was below it. Infuriated Whites across the North raised such a clamor against busing that it effectively shaped the platforms of presidential candidates and the Civil Rights Act of 1964. Though busing by court order or by school districts voluntarily actually affected a miniscule portion of the northern school population, the issue captured the attention of the nation.

The impact of White northern reaction to desegregation was widespread and ultimately devastating to public education. Parents and policymakers in New York, Chicago, Detroit, and Boston inspired widespread divestment from education. Many northern Whites perpetuated the belief that public education was broken beyond repair. It was now a broken system not worth investing in. Former Harvard president James Conant's influential book *Slums and Suburbs* portrayed a dismal scene of urban education while using the rhetoric of "slums" that framed Black neighborhoods as inherently inferior places. Best-selling author, education reformer, and homeschooling advocate John Holt even referred to students in urban public schools as "slum children." Americans widely saw public schools in "blighted" cities as a "blackboard jungle," believing that such schools—and consequently their children—were in peril. Jonathan Kozol, a teacher in the Boston public schools who published the award-winning *Death at an Early Age*, provided a view from the trenches in the 1960s. For Kozol, public education was not only failing; it was slowly killing kids, existentially and physically. He claimed that students in American schools were part of "a losing battle to survive." The same message was reinforced by popular historian Nat Hentoff in *These Children Are Dying.*[7]

Calls increased for America to heed the warning signs and scrap the public school system altogether. This toxic mindset made choice palatable to the majority of Americans nationwide, not just as a way to avoid the prospect of widescale desegregation in the South.

Much like the civil rights movement in the South, an impressive coterie of activists was coordinating strategies to desegregate northern cities. In New York City, coalitions such as the Intergroup Committee on New York's Public Schools, Parents' Workshop for Equality in New York City Schools, and the New York Citywide Committee for Integrated Schools challenged the city to live up to the ideals of integration. Working alongside the NAACP, grassroots coalitions flourished under the leadership of civil rights luminaries such as Ella Baker.

They coordinated with the Southern Christian Leadership Conference and SNCC. Drs. Kenneth and Mamie Clark, whose famed "doll tests" that illustrated the adverse effects of segregation among children and were cited as critical evidence in the *Brown v. Board of Education* (1954) decision, were active in New York as well. Rev. Milton Galamison, a Princeton Theological Seminary graduate and president of the Brooklyn chapter of the NAACP, facilitated the rise of a grassroots cohort committed to exposing and addressing segregation in their city.[8] The experience of northern activists who had fought in the southern civil rights movement proved useful in the North as they successfully pressured school districts to adopt desegregation policies.

The coalition prompted school officials in New York to respond by the 1960s, but the city's solution was limited to "free choice transfer," "open enrollment," or "permissive zoning" plans. Much like the freedom of choice plans in the South, only a select number of families of color were permitted to transfer to schools outside their allotted attendance zones. The plans, limited to select neighborhoods, impacted less than 5 percent of all students of color who were eligible, resulting in token desegregation that left a segregated system intact.[9]

Though limited in scope, the plans were enough to incite violence and protest among Whites. In March 1964—just one month after civil rights activists led over 450,000 students in a New York City boycott of public schools to protest segregation—over 10,000 White parents marched on city hall, directing vitriol against plans to bus students across district lines.[10] White parents, led by mothers, used the same protest methods that civil rights activists had used to capture national attention in the South. They marched, carried signs, and chanted. Placards across the Brooklyn Bridge read, "We will *not* be moved." Another said, "I will not put my children on a bus."[11] In September 1964, the same mothers staged a larger boycott that kept over 275,000 students out of school. "I would rather go to jail," one mother noted, "than see my kids bused out of the neighborhood."[12] In response to the White protests, the board of education called for the transfer of about 13,000 students, only 383 of whom would have to travel by bus.[13] White fears of compulsory busing were out of sync with the actual numbers proposed by the city's very modest desegregation plans.

Many parents drew rhetorical distinctions that distanced themselves from those they saw as virulent racists in the South, in part by making claims as taxpayers. As historian Camille Walsh noted, White segregationists across the nation put forth arguments that they were taxpayers who paid more into the system than Black parents did and that therefore their children were entitled to a better education or to attend the school their parents chose for them. Parents in New York named their coalition "Parents and Taxpayers" to articulate that it was not desegregation that they opposed. It was the affront to their rights as parents and taxpayers that they so bitterly protested.[14] The false claim that their rights as taxpayers had been violated was connected to a larger ideology of libertarianism including fiduciary liberty and individualism that resonated with the more nuanced or "moderate" calls for segregation in the South. Whereas White southerners under the banner of "freedom of choice" claimed that the federal government trampled on their right to choose a school, Parents and Taxpayers in New York claimed that the local and state governments treaded on their rights as taxpayers. New Yorkers could oppose busing (and other ostensible desegregation plans such as freedom of choice) because such plans were not based on their consent as taxed citizens.

Such claims as taxpayers were also an affirmation of *White* rights. As one sign read in a "White boycott" in New York City in September 1964: "Give us back our neighborhood school, our children also have civil rights."[15] Whites reacted vehemently in Queens, where a "pairing plan" aimed to pair—or merge—a predominantly White school in Jackson Heights (P.S. 149) with a school in a predominantly Black district (P.S. 92). White parents contended that the plans "denied their children the right to attend their neighborhood school because they are white," charging racial discrimination against Whites that violated the principles of the *Brown* decision.[16] In this vein, parents angrily and publicly opposed *busing*, not desegregation, at least on the surface. Elected officials tended to follow suit. Joseph Krasowski, an Illinois state senator, captured the sentiment, noting, "I don't oppose school integration, but the school board shouldn't stress integration more than education . . . you can't foist this upon the people."[17]

The *New York Times* polled New Yorkers in the midst of growing unrest. The results are instructive. A majority of respondents in one poll
from 1964 believed that the civil rights movement had "gone too far,"
and 54 percent thought that the movement and its demands for equality
and integration were going too fast.[18] Over 80 percent said they opposed the school transfer plans. Nearly 50 percent claimed they would
send their children to a private school rather than permit them to be
part of desegregation plans, whether or not that meant busing.[19] Under
the guise of individual rights, New York Whites opposed desegregation
with a fervor that matched that of Whites in the South, embracing the
same strategies to preserve a system that worked to their advantage.

As a collective rejection of desegregation gained traction in New York,
Whites in Chicago used very similar forms of resistance to busing.
Mayor Richard Daley managed to elude federal enforcement of desegregation mandates in Chicago, rendering the Department of Health,
Education, and Welfare impotent in pressuring northern cities to integrate meaningfully. Still, in response to the US Office of Education's
complaint against school segregation in Chicago, the Chicago Public
Schools announced a desegregation plan, albeit limited in relation to
the depth of segregation in the city. Known as the "Redmond Plan" after the city's superintendent James Redmond, it proposed the two-way
busing of 3,500 students that would have created an "integrated" school
population technically desegregating schools but maintaining a student
body in the participating schools that was 70 percent White. To assuage
White concerns, the plan was reduced to one-way busing, transport-
ing just over 500 Black students from Black elementary schools on the
south and west sides of the city to White schools in the area. On the
first day, a mere 249 students showed up to get on their buses. The
modest measure sparked dramatic racial transition and White flight. In
less than five years, elementary schools affected by busing transitioned
from being 80 percent White to over 80 percent Black.[20]

White parents vehemently denounced even these minimal desegregation efforts. Thousands protested, many of them mothers of children

who were "threatened" by the busing plan. Much like their counterparts in New York, parents argued that since the *Brown v. Board of Education* decision had ostensibly struck down all racial discrimination—that White or Black students could not be singled out by race—Redmond's desegregation plan violated the law because it required transportation and pupil placement policies based specifically on race.[21] They also took to the streets. Approximately fifteen hundred Whites rode city buses downtown to the board of education building to protest in person, creating a media spectacle that garnered citywide attention. Whites drew a firm line and attacked any plans for desegregation, no matter how moderate. When Cardinal John Cody (who was White) publicly supported the plan and framed racial integration as a moral issue, Whites burned him in effigy in front of his Chicago home.[22] Across the North, tens of thousands of parents demonstrated that busing was not in their interests.

In their attacks on busing, northern desegregation opponents acted in defense of the "White neighborhood."[23] As protesting mothers in Chicago claimed, the plans to bus and rezone their children constituted an "attack on the concept of the neighborhood school" that took their children "out of their home neighborhoods and into alien ones."[24] Connecting the desegregation issue to choice, one concerned parent petitioned the board in Chicago, noting: "Some of these people worked hard for many years to choose their neighbors and environment. Now you want the Negroes to have the right to choose their neighbors but not the whites who pay most of the tax dollars."[25]

School officials similarly downplayed or denied any charges of intentional segregation. New York school superintendent William Jansen repudiated claims that he and other administrators intentionally engaged in school segregation. As Jenson noted less than two months after the *Brown* decision: "We did not provide Harlem with segregation. We have natural segregation here—it's accidental."[26] Additionally, northern school officials took lengths to avoid terms like "segregation," opting instead for terms like "separation" and "racial imbalance." Such rhetorical devices were deliberate attempts to distance the northern situation from southern problems. But it was not only an issue of public relations. Claims that segregation existed, but not by any legal means, sanctioned Whites to maintain the system that had been carefully constructed to their own benefit. As historian Matthew Delmont wrote, "These word choices emphasized that northern-style school segregation was innocent, natural, and lawful."[27] If segregation in the North was natural, there was nothing that could be done about it. Northern politicians agreed.

Attempts to desegregate northern schools affected the drafting of key civil rights and education legislation, including the Civil Rights Act of 1964 and later the Equal Education Opportunity Act of 1974. The volatility of the busing issue spurred northern congressional representatives to narrowly define any approach to desegregation in their home states. With the support of both liberal and moderate civil rights supporters, federal lawmakers made sure that only de jure segregation was addressed in the historic legislation, not the more hidden forms of segregation that existed in their home districts. Title IV of the Civil Rights Act of 1964 defines school desegregation as "the assignment of students to public schools and within such schools without regard to their race, color, religion, or national origin" but immediately adds that "'desegregation' shall not mean the assignment of students to public schools in order to overcome racial imbalance."[28] While barring de jure segregation in the South, the law made remedies to segregation such as busing in the North very difficult to implement. It communicated an implicit yet clear disavowal of transferring or busing students to achieve integration. The language of the act selectively used the phrase "racial imbalance" as opposed to segregation, cultivating the ground to allow de facto distinction. Such discourse and legislation shrewdly protected the North—which could argue it had unintentional or "natural" segregation—from federal desegregation mandates and busing orders, much to the chagrin of southern segregationists.[29]

The busing issue shaped influential federal elections in the North. In New York, an incumbent US senator, Republican Kenneth Keating, spoke out amid the busing protests during the fall of 1964. Acknowledging the angst of Parents and Taxpayers, Keating publicly asserted that busing constituted a "costly and burdensome drain on the school system and a hardship upon the children involved." Just days later, his

Democratic opponent, Robert Kennedy, declared his opposition to busing as well. For him, education was best left to local decision makers, not the Senate.[30] With Kennedy entering the fray, the popularity and influence of antibusing rhetoric was made clear, illustrating the extent to which even the arguably most "liberal" city in the United States opposed busing. The busing debate had become a conflagration by 1964, and conservative presidential candidate Barry Goldwater fanned the flames. To a crowd of over eighteen thousand at Madison Square Garden, Goldwater decried the practice, noting that "forcibly busing your children from your chosen neighborhood school to some other one just to meet an arbitrary quota." He said that he wanted to preserve "neighborhood" schools as opposed to seeing them "sacrificed by a futile exercise in sociology which will accomplish nothing—but lose much."[31] For this, Goldwater received a standing ovation.

The issue went far beyond the New York senatorial race and the failed Goldwater campaign in 1964. When running for president in 1968, Richard Nixon would embrace a conservative agenda on a national platform, one that appealed to his southern constituents. Nixon drew on a distinction between de jure and de facto segregation that emerged in national discourse. As was expected by the mid-1960s, Nixon personally disavowed overt segregation. But his tepid support of desegregation ended there. Nixon did not believe in extending the reach of the federal government beyond current legislation to achieve "racial balance" in the schools. This included withholding federal funds and busing to achieve balance. Harking back to the restrictive language of the Civil Rights Act, he reminded the nation that 'desegregation' shall not mean the assignment of students to public school in order to overcome racial imbalance."[32] The stage was set for a national showdown over busing—and northern desegregation.

Legal and political posturing in the North framed segregation as an issue confined to Dixie. This meant that federal desegregation orders would apply only in instances of de jure segregation, which could only be found in the South. Southerners were quick to point out the inherent hypocrisy behind this. The contradiction even prompted Mississippi governor John Bell Williams to propose a $1 million campaign to file desegregation suits in the North. It was part of a larger strategy among southern senators to focus desegregation plans north of the Mason-Dixon Line, exposing the hypocrisy of their fellow senators who denounced segregation in the South but tolerated it in the North. As historian Joseph Crespino highlights, it was just one strategy of ardent segregationists who wanted to force desegregation outside the South to inspire national White backlash.[33] While the façade of "natural" segregation, or segregation without blame, defined the North, the concept did not go uncontested.

As unpopular as busing was, it was a remedy the courts were willing to uphold. In *Swann v. Mecklenburg* (1971), the Supreme Court approved of busing in a case from North Carolina in which school officials who governed a district of over eighty-three thousand students were ordered to eliminate all racially identifiable schools. The justices reasoned that county-wide desegregation was an appropriate remedy to remediate past wrongdoing.[34] Their ruling was based on the precedent of *Green v. County School Board of Kent County* (1968), which held that school boards had the authority and "the affirmative duty to take whatever steps might be necessary to convert to a unitary system in which racial discrimination would be eliminated root and branch."[35] Building upon the urgency of *Green*, the *Swann* decision was the high-water mark for desegregation. In addition to approving busing as a remedy to racial imbalance, the decision also ruled that a quota system was a starting point for desegregation plans.[36]

The decision merely exacerbated tensions around busing and desegregation, and Boston came to define the peak of antibusing demonstrations. Like other northern cities, racial tensions already existed in Boston. The city had experienced a growth rate of Black residents of 300 percent between 1940 and 1970, to comprise nearly 20 percent of the city or over one hundred thousand people. At the same time, suburban growth pulled over five hundred thousand Whites outside the city limits. Residential segregation, enforced through covenants as in Chicago, confined a growing Black population to overcrowded and overpriced parts of the city plagued by the highest unemployment rates. The schools, as was to be expected, lost support. By 1972, over 75 percent of public school students in Boston lived at or near the poverty line.[37]

Since the early 1950s, African Americans in Boston had been organizing for higher-quality education through the NAACP. Civil rights activists boycotted schools and established temporary Freedom Schools during the winter of 1963 and the summer of 1964. They organized Operation Exodus, which bused Black students to participating White suburbs, with over two thousand Black students involved in the herculean effort.[38] Under pressure from civil rights activists and a Black legislative caucus, in 1965 the Massachusetts legislature passed the Racial Imbalance Act, which defined schools in which over half the student population was non-White as "racially imbalanced." But these efforts yielded little relief from systemic racism, hardly achieving anything beyond token desegregation by 1968.[39]

With their backs against a wall, African Americans argued in a federal case that the City of Boston violated the equal protection clause of the Fourteenth Amendment. Judge Arthur Garrity found in *Morgan v. Hennigan* (1974) that the Boston School Committee "took many actions in their official capacities with the purpose and intent to segregate the Boston public schools." Drawing upon the *Swann* decision, Garrity ordered the city to adopt an aggressive desegregation strategy in 1974. The subsequently infamous plan, created by the state board of education and ultimately enforced by Garrity, called for reassigning forty-seven thousand students—nearly one-half of all students in the district—and busing as many as seventeen thousand.[40]

The desegregation plan attracted fierce opposition from Louise Day Hicks—Boston city council member and antibusing stalwart—and the Boston School Committee. The committee sought to protect the White "ethnic" neighborhoods that emerged as the center of resistance to busing—primarily South Boston and Charlestown. These two neighborhoods identified as White, working-class, and Irish Catholic.[41] When Hicks—the central figure in White resistance—left the Boston School Committee to take a seat on the city council, she and likeminded parents formed an association called Restore Our Alienated Rights (ROAR).[42] As historian Elizabeth Gillespie McRae writes, Hicks was one of numerous White American women using a form of maternal politics to claim moral authority in defending individual rights from perceived federal encroachment.[43]

The two-way busing plan included segregated Black schools in proximity to South Boston and Charlestown, primarily Roxbury High School.[44] Whites lambasted Judge Garrity and politicians who spoke in favor of busing. Senator Ted Kennedy, one of these politicians, was jeered and publicly vilified at a gathering at City Hall Plaza on September 9, 1974, with one incensed bystander shouting: "Why don't you let them shoot you like they shot your brothers?"[45] Anticipating violence, less than 10 percent of students attended school in South Boston that day. Angry mobs stole headlines, however, when the first Black students arrived at South Boston High School. Signs like "No N*****s in South Boston" and "Bus 'Em Back to Africa" greeted the yellow buses. White rioters threw rocks, cans, wood, and bottles. Fights between Black and White students broke out. A special force of city police trained for anti-war protests was used to quell antibusing riots and marches. Eventually federal marshals were employed to keep the peace.[46] For the next three years, sporadic violence and mass demonstrations against busing rocked the city. The young Joseph Rakes, wielding a flag as a weapon, encapsulated this violent history.

Much like segregationists in the South, antibusing protestors explored privatization as a means to avoid desegregation. Antibusing protestors and mothers of children in Boston public schools established four private schools in White neighborhoods directly impacted by "forced" busing, three of which were opened within one year of Garrity's decision in 1975. Like the first private academies that opened after desegregation orders in the South, the Boston private schools were hastily organized. The buildings that housed the schools needed new walls, lighting, and bathrooms. One school was founded in the basement of a medical building. The Massachusetts Commission Against Discrimination, a governmental agency, scrutinized the schools for charging tuition at higher rates to residents of other neighborhoods, which curtailed students of color from enrolling.[47] Thomas Atkins, president of the Boston branch of the NAACP, observed: "I consider them to be the same segregationist academies as the ones which sprung up in Mississippi, Alabama, and Georgia when desegregation began there."[48]

The private schools were a point of pride for White resisters, and they enjoyed modest support. South Boston Heights Academy enrolled nearly 450 students by 1976. Hosting open houses and proudly pinning student work on the wall, the grassroots unaccredited schools evaded court busing orders and vague threats by the state courts and the state board of education that their students would be considered truant. Additionally, numerous proposals called for public financial aid to assist in the establishment of the schools, an initiative the mayor of Boston, Kevin H. White, supported.[49] Though not receiving the same level of funding as they had in the South, the Boston academies did have implicit support from Judge Garrity and the state legislators, who opted not to invoke school attendance laws and did not charge the private school students as truant.[50]

In June 1976, the Supreme Court refused to hear the case that appealed the busing mandate, which allowed Judge Garrity's order to stand. By default, Garrity was left in a position to oversee Boston public schools. After eleven years and 415 orders issued, Garrity issued his last order and began to relinquish his control over city schools to the Boston School Committee in the fall of 1985.[51] But the tenure of busing in Boston—and cities across the North—left a devastated system in its wake.

As historian Matthew Delmont notes, both sides of the busing divide were painted as extremists. The media portrayed White antibusing protestors—often employing the same nonviolent protest and direct action tactics of the civil rights movement—as radical. But, at the same time, they also labeled pro-busing candidates, predominantly Black civil rights activists, as extremists too. The public by and large reduced the issue to a false binary, trivializing the work of the civil rights movement and failing to comprehend the nuances of the demands for quality education. Media coverage of the crisis largely lacked the moral clarity that footage from the southern civil rights battles had possessed, and it fell short of exposing institutional racism.[52]

Additionally, desegregation through busing became cemented in American consciousness as inherently violent. Despite the sensational television and media coverage of the time, seventy-nine of the eighty schools that were involved in the Boston busing plan remained free from violence. But the enraged mob at South Boston High School would define the issue for decades to come, and newsreels depicting the scene played on TV sets across the nation in other cities experimenting with busing, including Louisville, Nashville, Dallas, Cleveland, Los Angeles, and Indianapolis.[53]

Northern Whites took measures to explain that it was not the fact that their children would be going to school with Black students; it was that they were being forced to attend what they identified as inferior schools. After events in New York and Boston, a growing core of White liberals criticized the "social experiment" of desegregation, which in their estimation endangered their own children and neighborhoods.

How busing was covered by the media and how it was received among northern Whites limited the extent to which people could see the deeper issues behind it and the potential solutions it offered. Media coverage by and large dismissed the fact that Black parents and civil rights activists were not all that excited about busing. Black parents did not view busing as sufficient to address the larger social, political, and economic problems that continued to plague their communities.[54] Placing Black children next to White children did not have some type of mystical power that would improve education. Nor did civil rights activists or families of color make that claim. Desegregation by any means—busing or otherwise—did little to address the magnitude of White supremacy that underpinned the entire school system. Desegregation policies did not include the promotion and hiring of Black teachers, the election of Black representatives to school boards, or African American curricula. Moreover, there was demeaning logic behind the arguments that framed the *Brown* decision. The decision to desegregate schools and the policies implemented to achieve this largely rested on the racist reasoning that Black education and Black families were inherently inferior. Black schools, students, and teachers were then deemed lesser than their White counterparts. Such logic not only propagated an endemic racism still extant today; it also ignored generations of high-quality education delivered in the most difficult conditions under Jim Crow.[55]

African American voices offered compelling alternatives to busing.[56] Many civil rights coalitions and education advocates coalesced around what Elizabeth Todd-Breland calls the politics of Black achievement, or the pursuit of self-determined means for a better quality education that did not necessarily emphasize or even include desegregation.[57] The movement toward desegregation in the North revealed to many parents and activists most affected by broken public schools that White supremacy had corrupted the entire system. This reality, keenly understood by generations of those who had experienced it firsthand, fostered alternatives to integration into White society, including community control of the schools. This vision held that Black teachers and administrators, families, representatives, and advocates should lead schools. Black demands for community control and the decentralization of schools began in the 1960s. As historian Russell Rickford noted, the "community control movement garnered much of its mass support from a universal impulse: the will to survive."[58]

The community control movement, both ideological and programmatic, took hold in the early 1960s in Mississippi and in such cities as Boston, Chicago, and New York. Black activists established Freedom Schools in order to boycott public school systems that refused to meaningfully desegregate. The Freedom Schools presented a new opportunity. SNCC organizer Charlie Cobb, who proposed the schools in Mississippi in 1963, argued that a movement controlled by people of color required something new: "building our own institutions to replace the old, unjust decadent ones which make up the existing power structure."[59] Movement activists also established Liberation Schools across the country to meet community needs. Liberation Schools, which the Black Panther Party developed after the Freedom Schools, provided curricula and teachers committed specifically to African American students—something sorely lacking in "desegregated" schools.[60] Grounded in a deeper history traced to slavery, education that capitalized on self-determination and empowerment always presented a compelling alternative to working with schools governed by White policymakers.

The busing saga and the process of desegregation captured national headlines, emerging as the mainstream solutions to racially separate or "imbalanced" schools. The narrative eclipsed other solutions and visions for quality education that sprang from the civil rights movement, like the Freedom Schools and Liberation Schools that were working alternatives parallel to the segregated academies of the South. These were driven by a different ideology that moved beyond desegregation. Just months after President Johnson signed the Civil Rights Act of 1964, SNCC organizer Bob Moses asked, "Why can't we set up our own schools? Because when you come right down to it, why integrate their schools? What is it that you will learn in their schools? What [students] really need to learn is how to be organized to work on the society to change it."[61] Fellow organizer Stokely Carmichael, who popularized the phrase "Black Power" in the summer of 1966, wrote:

> Integration is a subterfuge for the maintenance of white supremacy. It allows the nation to focus on a handful of Southern children who get into white schools, at great price, and to ignore the 94% who are left behind in unimproved all-black schools. Such situations will not change until Black people have power—to control their own school boards, in this case. Then Negroes become equal in a way that means something, and integration ceases to be a one-way street.[62]

Demands for community control of schools took hold in northern cities that typically prided themselves on being more liberal than the South. Black activists in New York who identified with the Black Power arm of the larger civil rights movement made demands for "local control" that reverberated across the nation by the late 1960s. In the neighborhood of Ocean Hill–Brownsville, Black activists began to assert demands for greater control of schools. In 1966, concerned citizens organized a "People's Board of Education," which elected local activist Milton Galamison as president. The group, gaining strength through collaboration with the New York–based teachers' union, United Federation of Teachers (UFT), organized the "Independent School Board No. 17." Under African American leadership, the group critiqued the very nature of the segregated system. Its members moved beyond calls for desegregation and other forms of incremental change. The civil rights coalition demanded equity and justice through transformative, redistributive reform defined by and for people of color.[63]

In Chicago, Black parents and civil rights activists teamed with the University of Chicago, public school administrators, and a Black advocacy group, the Woodlawn Organization, to establish the Woodlawn Experimental Schools Project in 1968. The organization sought to increase community control of the curriculum, teacher and principal staffing, and extracurricular programming. Rather than waiting for schools to desegregate, Black parents wanted to improve the quality of education immediately in their neighborhood.[64]

Similarly, concerned Black parents and education advocates took matters into their own hands in Detroit. In 1967, the Reverend Albert Cleage, influenced by the autonomy and self-determination promoted by Black Power ideology, founded the Black Christian National Movement. Rev. Cleage and others broke from mainstream calls for integration and demanded community control of Black schools instead. Working in conjunction with the Inner City Parents Council and Citizens for Community Control of Schools, activists issued a declaration in 1968.[65] They said that they were "ready to move to direct action, if necessary, such as pickets, boycotts, sit-ins, liberation of schools and actual takeover of the schoolhouse until the community obtains real decision-making power."[66]

These northern education activists all practiced the politics of Black achievement by demanding greater control of their own schools, and they gained tangible policy shifts. In Michigan, for instance, the state legislature passed a bill that transferred some power to the community and expanded the number of school districts to increase direct representation. They decentralized some of the education decision-making, creating regional boards and a central statewide board that drew members from each of the regional districts.[67] The move reflected what occurred in New York, where ongoing pressure forced state legislators to create nearly thirty community school districts to increase parental and community participation.[68]

Whites who opposed busing and integration found their own interests served by community control initiatives, which promoted the segregation and "school choice" that they wanted. Liberal Whites recoiled at relinquishing some power, exposing the limits of their commitment to civil rights. The case in the Ocean Hill–Brownsville neighborhood of New York City illustrates the fragility of White liberals then as now. In the process of establishing neighborhood schools, Black community control advocates rightly viewed many White teachers as paternalistic and condescending to students and parents of color.[69] It was clear, after all, that Whites refused to integrate in the true sense of the word or share meaningful decision-making. Activists noted that Black teachers were underpaid and rarely promoted to key administrative positions. Whites continued to treat Black students and teachers with disrespect in the schools that desegregated. White teachers who taught Black students largely misunderstood Black culture if not outwardly disrespecting it. As historian Jerald Podair noted, "Ocean Hill–Brownsville citizens saw community control as a chance to change the rules of an unfair market, and end decades of economic and political marginalization."[70]

The state legislature permitted experimentation with community control in Ocean Hill–Brownsville. Supported by a galvanized local Black community fed up with racist, inferior education and limited desegregation plans, and supported with a sizable Ford Foundation grant, Black parents and community members established their own board, the Brownsville–Ocean Hill Independent Local School Board. It circumvented the traditional power structure of the citywide board of education as well as the power of the teachers' union, the local United Federation of Teachers. Black parents and community members acquired power to appoint principals to fill vacancies in their local district. Their first appointment, Herman Ferguson, was a Black Power advocate active in the Revolutionary Action Movement, a militant organization founded in 1963 and inspired by Malcolm X and Robert F. Williams. White professionals in the UFT branded Ferguson and the revolutionary cause as too radical. The union sued on the grounds that Ferguson's appointment violated a law that required a written examination. The union lost the case on the grounds that the position was experimental, and Black appointees remained.[71] But the battle lines were drawn, pitting White progressives against Black community control advocates, and Black activists were clearly willing and able to effectively challenge the union at a time when teacher unionization was on the rise. On the other side, White teachers and the UFT wanted to retain control of any decentralization initiatives. As one White member of the majority-White UFT put it, Black advocates on the local board were progressing too "definitively" for the union.[72] In Detroit, Black advocates demanded Black teachers and administrators for Black schools. The Detroit Federation of Teachers offered a tepid color-blind response: "Color is beside the point if the person is doing the job."[73] As historian Jeanne Theoharis later noted, "With public support of racial segregation viewed as the distasteful purview of Southern racists, 'color-blind' discourses provided a socially acceptable rhetoric to harness many Northern whites' contentment with the status quo (and opposition to housing, school, and job desegregation)."[74]

The community control "experiment" in New York illustrates the triviality of White liberalism in the face of Black power demands on the ground. This reaction presaged White liberal support of school choice today. When the UFT and its president Al Shanker spoke out against Black advocates who demanded control of their own schools in the 1960s, it exposed White liberals who were not ready to concede power or control. White teachers would travel south to teach in Freedom Schools in Mississippi, but when it came time to relinquish control to Black leaders in their own neighborhoods, White liberals drew a line. Predominantly White teacher unions like the UFT insisted on a hiring system in which credentials were valued and rewarded—an "objective" and "fair" process. The UFT relied on notions of equality, merit, and state-sanctioned standardized examinations to "qualify" all appointments in the community control experiment.[75] The union also maintained a commitment to color-blindness—no teacher would be hired or fired based on race.[76] The UFT went on strike against the Black advocates for over a month across the city. By refusing to teach they hoped to retain control of teacher selection. It was one of the most divisive strikes in history, yet White teachers preserved their power, and the UFT retained control over the hiring, firing, and placement of teachers. White teachers would not be moved to concede or even share control over Black education.

The political alliances that supported Black community control in many ways made for strange bedfellows. In New York, conservative Republicans, left-leaning Black legislators, and civil rights activists aligned to provide support for community control and decentralization policies, including vouchers, or governmental stipends or tax breaks to compensate for the cost of private school tuition. The movement also attracted the political support of New York government and civic leaders, not to mention the era's captains of industry, including the presidents of RCA and *Time*, the chairman of IBM, and a former president of Harvard University.[77] As Todd-Breland notes in her analysis of community control, the development of such coalitions established the foundations for relationships between grassroots organizers and the business community that would define school choice in later decades.[78]

White parents looking to enroll their children in schools in northern cities faced a new, uncertain landscape intimidating for those vested in segregated schools. Antibusing riots and increasing demands for Black community control disrupted business as usual. The milieu surrounding school desegregation and civil rights activism unmasked a truth that racism knew no regional boundaries and never had. This, combined with the race riots igniting across northern cities, made the task of building a quality urban school system highly challenging, if not impossible.

The 1965 insurrection in the Watts neighborhood of Los Angeles, which was predominantly Black, demonstrated to many Whites that investing in cities had become unwise. Violence erupted in August that year after an instance of police brutality, hardly a first. President Johnson sent sixteen thousand National Guard troops to Los Angeles in the next six days of rebellion and unrest. Thirty-four people were killed, most by police and National Guardsmen, over one thousand were injured, and nearly four thousand were arrested. The uprising devastated the neighborhood's Black business community, causing nearly $50 million in property damage.[79] The rebellion made national news and caught the country off guard. A bewildered if not clueless Johnson had signed the Voting Rights Act only five days before the violence, aimed at eliminating racial discrimination in voting. "How could this have happened," Johnson is said to have lamented, "after all I've done?"[80]

Two years later in Detroit, African Americans pushed back against police who, in a case typical of police harassment, had raided an afterhours bar. President Johnson again sent in the US Army—nearly five thousand army paratroopers, and, in the riots that followed over the next days, forty-three people were killed, over one thousand were injured, and nearly four thousand were arrested. Similar to Watts, estimates of property damage soared to over $50 million, equal to about $390 million today.[81] The Detroit riots in 1967 stemmed from the same sort of long-standing racist policies behind the rebellion in Los Angeles. The unrest also followed decades of civil rights organizing in the city. Organizers had cultivated a heightened political consciousness and mobilized the Black community to demand change, vote, and hold city officials accountable. In fact, during the same summer of 1967 in the Motor City, Black activists there stepped up demands for community control of schools.[82]

Rebellion also took place in New York, Chicago, Newark, Cleveland, and other northern cities, especially after Martin Luther King Jr.'s assassination in April 1968, when over one hundred cities across the nation experienced racial violence.[83] The nation was literally on fire, and Whites were terrified.

These events contributed to a new perception that public schools were violent spaces. In Detroit, members of Citizens for Community Control of Schools, a local organization aimed at increasing Black citizens' power to oversee education, responded to a deleterious education system and asserted that they were prepared to take "direct action, if necessary, such as pickets, boycotts, sit-ins, liberation of schools and actual takeover of the schoolhouse."[84] When Black students carried the principles of the civil rights and Black Power movements into the schools and physical confrontations ensued at times between students, White parents and school administrators became uneasy, calling on law enforcement to keep the peace in schools. In Boston, the press reported on school overcrowding and discipline problems. South Boston High School defined for many readers the environment of urban public schools, which increasingly beseeched law enforcement to provide discipline and surveillance. "The halls are relatively quiet," Muriel Cohen of the *Boston Globe* reported in 1976 on South Boston High. "The State Police are stationed at the stairways and strategic points in the narrow, pastel colored hallways."[85]

Police in schools were not an uncommon sight at the time. National discourse by the early 1970s posited that "juvenile delinquency" was a problem of significant magnitude, particularly in desegregated schools. The notion was grounded more in fear of desegregation than actual evidence. More and more cities required a police presence in public schools to restore "law and order."[86] Police, armed guards, metal detectors, and other manifestations of disciplinary power grew to become permanent fixtures in our public schools, and schools in turn became pathways to prison for "disruptive" Black students.[87]

White Americans were deeply troubled by desegregation and shaken by the riots of the 1960s. Best-selling nonfiction books about the nation's public schools, with titles like *Death at an Early Age* and *Our Children Are Dying*, captured the sentiment as thousands of Whites fled the city for suburban enclaves. Between 1950 and 1970, Chicago lost 29 percent of its White population, Newark lost 54 percent, and St. Louis lost 48 percent.[88] Beyond city limits, Whites were distanced from the tensions of the civil rights movement and the increasing calls for Black empowerment. As White people left cities behind, they depleted the property tax base that was (and remains) integral to school funding and left the public school system to crumble. Whites still in the cities subject to desegregation orders were, for the most part, wealthy and enrolled their children in private schools, or they were poor, left with little choice but to attend desegregated public schools. When Whites fled, they left behind a "majority-minority" system that was difficult to integrate meaningfully.

White flight was a widespread form of resistance. The movement to the suburbs was not easily framed like the photo of the young Joseph Rakes wielding the US flag as a weapon. But its numbers suggest that northern Whites wanted nothing to do with desegregation. Even before the apex of the busing controversy in Detroit during the early 1970s, massive flight drained the schools of White students. By 1966 in the Detroit public schools, African American students composed over 55 percent of all students, up from 17 percent in 1946.[89] By 1984, nearly a decade after the busing controversy, Whites made up less than 10 percent of the city school district.[90] In Boston, over two hundred thousand Whites left for suburban enclaves between 1950 and 1970.[91] Approximately 60 percent of students enrolled in Boston public schools were White in 1973. By 1980, Whites accounted for only 35 percent and by

the close of the decade, only 26 percent.[92] Hyde Park High School, one
of the centers of busing during court desegregation in Chicago, began
as a White school. After one year of court-mandated busing, the school
was 60 percent White and by 1986, the school was 82 percent Black.
"This school is really not integrated," Doris Brown, a Black senior at
the school in 1986, recalled. "Lots of whites had moved out and the rest
who live around here go to private schools."[93]

Doris Brown's observations could just as easily have been made in
nearly any other major northern city that was implementing desegregation plans. By 1980, Whites accounted for less than 20 percent of
the public school enrollment in Chicago. Those Whites who remained
in the city opted for private education.[94] One White parent in Boston
encapsulated the new function of private schools in the North: "There
were no circumstances under which [our daughter] was going to Boston public schools." For many parents in the aftermath of busing and
desegregation orders, enrolling in public schools "was just not a risk
[they] were comfortable taking."[95] Privatization and White flight decimated investment in Boston public schools as well, and a largely poor
population was left behind. By the 1980s, over 90 percent of students in
Boston were students who qualified for free and reduced-price lunches.
By 1988, nearly 40 percent of public high school students were dropping out before graduating. Over one-third of city schools qualified for
special state assistance due to failing test scores.[96] The lines had been
drawn yet again, this time between urban and suburban areas.

A weighty dilemma was forced upon the nation. If meaningful solutions to segregation were to be tried, suburbs would have to be part
of the plan. Detroit provided a test case. In 1971, after years of deteriorating conditions in city schools, Judge Stephen J. Roth sided with
the NAACP and issued the most extensive desegregation order to date.
Roth introduced a massive two-way busing plan that called for transferring 780,000 students across the city of Detroit, in addition to 53 of
the 86 school districts in the three-county metropolitan area.[97] Busing,
Judge Roth determined, would cross into suburbia.

But the scope of the decision was never realized. The local and national temperament against busing prompted a fierce legal appeal. In *Milliken v. Bradley* (1974), the Supreme Court—with four new Nixon appointees as part of the majority—blocked the ambitious busing plan in a 5–4 decision.[98] The justices ruled that suburban schools were not subject to busing or other desegregation mandates though they were largely segregated by race and class. As residential segregation between urban and suburban areas was seen to have resulted from social custom—not de jure segregation or racial discrimination proscribed by law—the court remitted any role suburbia could play in desegregation efforts. The decision reflected the popular though flawed distinction between de jure and de facto segregation. The former was attributable to laws requiring separate facilities. The latter was attributed to custom or individual prejudice, which the court reasoned was both less harmful and beyond the scope of the law. It was a distinction made in the Supreme Court's *Keyes v. School District No. 1, Denver* decision in 1973, when the court ruled that *intentionality* of segregation was paramount in determining whether or not court-ordered desegregation was permissible.[99] The outlying suburban districts in *Milliken v. Bradley* were not found to be segregating by intent. Justice Potter Stewart wrote in a concurring opinion in *Milliken v. Bradley* that segregation in Detroit was "caused by unknown and perhaps unknowable factors such as in-migration, birth rates, economic changes, or cumulative acts of private racial fears."[100] The law merely forbade explicit racial segregation. Without the language of Jim Crow, the onus of proving de jure segregation fell squarely on the backs of people of color and civil rights activists—but it was nearly impossible to prove.

With *Milliken*, the court essentially absolved White suburbanites of any commitment—legal or moral—to the betterment of the urban schools and neighborhoods many had left behind. Further exonerating Whites, the court went on to note that it would not impose "punishments" for maintaining segregated schools: the responsibility of the court was "not to devise a system of pains and penalties to punish constitutional violations brought to light. Rather, it is to desegregate an *educational* system in which the races have been kept apart without, at the same time, losing sight of the central *educational* function of the schools." For the court, solutions such as busing became "more and more suspect as they require[d] that schoolchildren spend more and more time in buses going to and from school and that more and more educational dollars be diverted to transportation systems."[101]

The *Milliken* decision limited desegregation mandates to American cities and those who resided within city limits, mostly BIPOC families or poor Whites in the 1970s. With the blessing of the Supreme Court, suburban schools continued to receive public funding and were exempt from any desegregation attempts. It amounted to what legal scholar and president of the University of Virginia James Ryan refers to as the "suburban veto"—the ability of suburban communities to limit education reform to protect their own interests and maintain autonomy.[102] If suburbs did not want to participate in desegregation plans or programs identified with "urban" education reform, they would not be compelled to participate. The rights of Whites were protected and upheld.

Thurgood Marshall, appointed to the Supreme Court by Lyndon Johnson in 1965 just over ten years after he argued the *Brown* case, proffered a dissenting opinion that bespoke the perils of the decision. "After 20 years of small, often difficult steps toward [equal justice under law], the Court today takes a giant step backwards." He noted, "The Court's answer is to provide no remedy at all for the violation proved in this case, thereby guaranteeing that Negro children in Detroit will receive the same separate and inherently unequal education in the future as they have been unconstitutionally afforded in the past."[103] He also weighed in on the public pressure of the case, which was immense. "I fear," he wrote in his dissent, "[the decision] is more a reflection of a perceived public mood that we have gone far enough in enforcing the Constitution's guarantee of equal justice."[104]

After attacking Ted Landsmark, Joseph Rakes was convicted of assault with a deadly weapon and received a suspended sentence of two years. In many ways, Rakes's life would be defined by the arresting image— much like Hazel Bryan's was in Little Rock, Arkansas. Thirty years after the assault, Rakes recalled: "The picture—it says what it says, but it doesn't tell the whole story."[105] Without apology, the comment is a self-serving deflection of responsibility. Yet there is an embedded truth to his statement. The photograph accurately captured the violence of White resistance to desegregation and it points to an awareness that an astute Millicent Brown learned firsthand as a student in Boston, reaffirming what Malcolm X declared in 1964, that everything south of Canada is essentially the "South." The same mechanisms of racism functioned in the mythologized "freedom North"—Boston, New York, Chicago, and Detroit—as they had in her hometown of Charleston, South Carolina. Joseph Rakes's assault could have occurred anywhere in the United States.

These truths underpinned the national retreat from not only desegregation but also the entire system of public education. Disdain for desegregation and public education transcended regional boundaries. Whites on both sides of the Mason-Dixon Line thought the civil rights movement had gone too far, that with desegregation *their* rights were infringed upon. The new battle cry to defend the rights of Whites came from those President Richard Nixon referred to as the "silent majority"—law-abiding, patriotic, and quiet citizens. The silent majority constituted a base of support for the New Right and the rebirth of the Republican Party. Their dismal perception of public education facilitated the rise of the school choice movement beyond measure. Much of the country—and its elected representatives—stood ready to embrace school choice policy.

CHAPTER FOUR

Federal Support of the School Choice Movement

ON PALM SUNDAY, APRIL 11, 1965, President Lyndon B. Johnson signed the Elementary and Secondary Education Act at the old one-room schoolhouse he had attended as a child in Johnson City, Texas. At his side sat Miss Katie Deadrich, who had taught Johnson his very first school lessons.[1] It was the most sweeping federal education legislation enacted in history. Up until this moment, both tradition and constitutional law had kept education decision-making at the state and local levels. School boards, district administrators, superintendents, and principals made and enacted education policy. The sites of decision making were local school district offices, board rooms, and town halls. Congress breached the divide in 1958 by passing education legislation aimed at strengthening math and science programs after the Russians beat the United States into space with *Sputnik 1*. But Johnson dramatically expanded federal oversight, investment, and prowess in setting education policy.[2] The federal government could desegregate schools once and for all—or delay it inevitably.

Throughout his presidency, Johnson had done much to advance the cause of desegregation. A year before the Elementary and Secondary Education Act, he had pushed the Civil Rights Act of 1964 through Congress. The Johnson administration, with support from Congress and the courts, enforced desegregation by withholding funds from schools that practiced it. This led to widespread desegregation of public schools in the South; Dixie schools became the most integrated in the country between 1964 and 1970, when the percentage of Black students attending segregated schools (ones that were 90 to 100 percent Black or Latinx, American Indian, or other students of color) dropped to only 24 percent. Three decades after *Brown*, the percentage of Black students attending majority-White schools in the South rose from less than .001 percent to nearly 44 percent by 1988.[3] Johnson, however, had trouble in the North. He struggled to bypass politicians like Mayor Richard Daley of Chicago who refused to acknowledge segregation in their cities.[4] As courts increasingly ordered busing to desegregate schools, they infuriated northerners, shaping national discourse and debate around public education and desegregation. Much as it had in the South, busing and the desegregation process motivated northerners to find alternatives to public school.

The feds were essentially unable to coerce the North to meaningfully desegregate its schools. The 1974 *Milliken* decision extinguished a belief in the merits of desegregation, and the gates were thrown wide for massive divestment from public education. With support at the federal level, from judicial decisions to funding, school choice ideology eventually became a comprehensive policy embedded in the very fabric of American life and effectively nullified the ideals LBJ signed into law in 1965.

Americans were ripe for school choice. Discontent with public schools and resentment of desegregation orders, particularly busing plans, had moved north of the Mason-Dixon Line. Weary of desegregation efforts and ensuing strife, they were ready to welcome alternatives promulgated by Republican presidential candidate Richard Nixon. Rhetoric of antibusing and "taxpayer rights" were part of his successful campaign and the rebranding of the Republican Party during the late 1960s. The party avoided desegregation efforts beyond those addressing de jure segregation.

By capitalizing on the growing discontent with public education and busing, Nixon guided the nation toward school choice. Fostering the narrative of failed public education, he enabled millions of parents to abandon the project of desegregation. The rise of the New Right and the remaking of the GOP was one of the greatest political reformations of the twentieth century.

During his successful 1968 presidential campaign, Nixon promised a slow approach to desegregation, currying favor with southern stalwarts such as Senator Strom Thurmond of South Carolina, the former Dixiecrat behind the new Republican Party when he switched parties in 1964. To entice segregationist southern Democrats to vote Republican, Nixon toed a moderate line, blaming desegregation on the courts.[5] It was a critical shift in national and electoral politics, which marked for Kevin Philips—a political strategist on the Nixon campaign in 1968—a "repudiation visited upon the Democratic Party for its ambitious social programming and inability to handle the urban and Negro revolutions."[6]

To make new inroads in the South by increasing its base, the GOP recruited southern Democrats through racist policy around school desegregation and "law and order"—coded language for upholding acceptable White values and criminalizing Black protestors and activists. Courting Thurmond and other disenchanted Dixiecrats, Nixon attempted to appease a conservative, anti–civil rights base that would support diehard segregationist George Wallace for president. During Nixon's campaign for reelection, Wallace swept the Democratic primary in Florida in 1972 and even captured Michigan, historically a pro-union state but one that was subject to busing. As one *New York Times* poll found among Michigan voters, Wallace's stance against busing was a greater factor among his supporters than the surge of sympathy that had emerged for him after a recent assassination attempt.[7]

Despite Wallace's strength in the South, Nixon drew much of his support from southern and Sunbelt suburbanites who resented "forced busing" and desegregation orders. By reaching the suburbs, Nixon was able to generate a platform that resonated across the nation. "National growth," Kevin Phillips pontificated in *The Emerging Republican Majority* in 1969, "is shifting to suburbia . . . the American future lies in a revitalized countryside, a demographically ascendant Sun Belt and suburbia, and new towns."[8] Though dubbed a "Southern" approach to redefining politics after the civil rights movement, it was a national initiative. White families in Chicago reacted to people of color moving into their neighborhoods with the same vitriol as southern segregationists. So too did White mothers who hurled stones at buses in Boston that transported Black children across town to achieve racial balance. Hatred was not so southern after all.

To win the coveted support of South Carolina's Strom Thurmond, Nixon had to support what moderate southerners had in mind. Thurmond assured audiences across Dixie again and again that Nixon was the man to protect their right to choose their children's school against a federal government hell-bent on enforcing desegregation. At the same time, he had to position himself in the middle of the road. Nixon supported choice while in the next breath affirming the principles behind the *Brown* decision. At best, his rhetoric seemed to be that of a recalcitrant desegregationist, pitting the two extremes against one another: those who wanted immediate integration and those who wanted to maintain segregation.[9]

Unpopular on both sides of the aisle, busing was the clarion call to galvanize the GOP base. An antibusing platform could unite disparate factions across geographical boundaries—it was something that Chicagoans and Dixiecrats in South Carolina could agree on. Nixon astutely anticipated this during his campaign and promised to end busing. Once he was elected, an antibusing stance allowed Nixon to iterate a belief in the principles of the *Brown* decision, that segregation was wrong and any laws enforcing segregation had to be abolished. It also allowed him to have it both ways by drawing a false distinction between de facto and de jure segregation. "*De facto* segregation, which exists in many areas, both North and South," said Nixon in a public statement in 1970, "is undesirable but is not generally held to violate the Constitution." He reminded the nation that "in the case of genuine *de facto* segregation . . . school authorities are not constitutionally required to take any positive steps to correct the imbalance."[10] Coupled with the language codified in the Civil Rights Act against transferring students to address such racial imbalance, Nixon reaffirmed where he stood during a televised address in 1972: "I am opposed to busing for the purpose of achieving racial balance in our schools."[11] In the address he proposed an immediate moratorium on the practice.

Unifying Whites nationwide and others disenchanted with public education and the desegregation process underway, Congress passed laws that undermined both the system and the process. Nixon signed into law the Emergency School Aid Act in 1972 to support voluntary desegregation instead of busing and to slow the desegregation drive. Initially introduced as a package to cushion the blow of desegregation in Dixie by providing more school funding with no strings attached and little to no oversight, Nixon catered to southern districts, encouraging them to voluntarily address de facto segregation through interracial programming and other measures that addressed "racial isolation." In effect, a significant part of the act sought to "encourage the voluntary reduction, elimination, or prevention of minority-group isolation," to support the efforts of those who sought desegregation, but to assuage southern concerns that desegregation would be "forced."[12] The bill stated that federal funding could not be used for busing unless local officials provided a request to do so—falling short of Nixon's moratorium but still a strong prohibitive statement.[13] The Emergency School Aid Act remained the only federally funded program that openly encouraged desegregation.[14]

Nixon also halted progress on the integration front by curtailing the work of the Department of Health, Education, and Welfare as well as the Department of Justice, effectively undoing the progress made by President Johnson. Yet it was his Supreme Court and other judicial nominations that exacted the most lasting impact.[15] Nixon appointed over 230 federal judges and 4 Supreme Court justices, selecting strict constitutional constructionists who favored a narrow reading of the Constitution to scale back the intervention of the liberal, "activist" Warren Court that passed a wave of anti-segregation civil rights decisions from 1953 to 1969. Nixon's first Supreme Court appointment was Warren Burger, considered to be a conservative constructionist and now remembered as "a lightning rod for those who welcomed as well as those who feared the end of an era of judicial activism."[16] Another Supreme Court appointee, Lewis Powell, was an attorney from Richmond, Virginia, and former chairman of the Richmond Board of Education. Moderates praised him for keeping the Richmond schools open during the mid- to late-1950s when segregationist extremists sought to close them down as they had in other parts in Virginia.[17]

Championing narrow interpretations of the Constitution that protected the rights of the individual and enshrined the sanctity of "law and order," Nixon shaped a court that would leave an indelible impact on education policy and the larger intellectual framework for "choice."

Just prior to Nixon's resignation in 1974, the Supreme Court delivered its 5–4 decision in *Milliken*, led by four Nixon appointees, ruling that busing across district lines was a "wholly impermissible remedy" where inter-district segregation did not exist.[18] *Milliken* delivered on Nixon's campaign promise to curtail busing and limit it to cases of de jure segregation. It may not have delivered a complete moratorium on busing, but it effectively removed the air from the buses' tires. In doing so, the court also upheld the distinction of de facto segregation and erected a nearly insurmountable barrier around suburbs, which were now immune to "forced" desegregation orders. The decision, as civil rights scholar Gary Orfield determined, "rendered *Brown* almost meaningless."[19]

As federal desegregation initiatives would not be enforced, school desegregation stalled in the North, and though public schools desegregated in the South, the nation as a whole effectively abandoned the ideals of racial integration. This precipitated a color-blind ideology in education policy that it was wrong to "see" race. Desegregation was great in principle, but "forced busing" was un-American. Additionally, parents who identified with the "silent majority" wanted the means to escape what they saw as a failing public education system. By the time Nixon tendered his resignation in 1974—twenty years after the *Brown* decision—the ideology of school choice was on the rise as a platform for disaffected northerners and southerners alike.

Gerald Ford maintained Nixon's policies. Ford's one-term successor, President Jimmy Carter, made some progressive gains in education, most notably creating the Department of Education in 1979 and garnering the support of the teachers' unions. His successor Ronald Reagan, in many ways completing the Republican revolution of the 1960s, indelibly shaped the field for choice. Reagan advanced the narrative of failed public schools and effectively kept desegregation efforts at bay, both critical to fomenting choice. Reagan would also break new ground by advocating for states' rights in the realm of education policy and privatization from the highest office in the land. By 1980, just one-third of Americans expressed confidence in US public education, down from 59 percent in 1966.[20] Public opinion emboldened more drastic measures. Nixon had sought to play the middle of the road, forestalling any meaningful desegregation efforts or reinvestment in public education. But Reagan was unabashedly reactionary, seeking to roll back any and all federal presence in education and to demand privatization. In 1980, he was the ideal presidential candidate to carry out more fully his conservative predecessors' vision. Reagan was already experienced in national politics, having served as a spokesperson for Barry Goldwater in his 1964 campaign, and he maintained commitment to Milton Friedman's economic vision.

Reagan continued to reject desegregation and the means to achieve it, seeing it, like Nixon, as unnecessary and harmful while expressing personal disdain for racial separation and exclusion. "While racial segregation simply has no place in American public schools," Reagan noted, "neither has forced busing. It has wrought too much damage already." Public school districts should not bus for the purposes of desegregation, Reagan believed, and the federal government should have no role in educational policy making at the local level. "States' rights" ought to be the cornerstone of education policy. On the campaign trail in 1980, Reagan emphasized that if elected he would order federal agencies—in particular the Department of Education that Jimmy Carter had signed into law—"to get off the back of state and local school systems, to leave the setting of policies and the administration of school affairs to local boards of education.[21] In 1980 in Neshoba County, Mississippi, where civil rights activists James Chaney, Michael Schwerner, and Andrew Goodman had been murdered sixteen years before, Reagan outlined the premise of his political agenda. With no mention of Chaney, Schwerner, and Goodman, he declared to a crowd of over fifteen thousand Mississippians at the Neshoba County Fair, "I believe in states' rights." Writes Joseph Crespino, in *In Search of Another Country*, "Reagan pledged that, if he were elected, he would 'restore to states and local governments the power that properly belongs to them.'"[22] States' rights did not correlate to school choice directly, but it threw up a larger defense to protect the individual's right to choose as opposed to "forcing" parents to send their children to "government schools."

Elected president, Reagan was true to his word. His administration did not file any desegregation suits, and, like Nixon, he supported school districts that were sued for de jure segregation. Within his first year in office, Congress rescinded the Emergency School Aid Act, terminating the largest program committed to even a watered-down version of school desegregation. Reagan also slashed desegregation assistance centers, which were authorized by the Civil Rights Act of 1964 to assist desegregation attempts at the local level.[23] He proposed that parents embrace voluntary choice programs such as highly marketable "magnet schools"—though these were selective and few in number—to integrate schools in racially segregated neighborhoods. Such schools were effective but miniscule in scale when compared to widespread mandates to integrate entire districts. Voluntary choice programs like magnets also co-opted choice with an intent to desegregate, expanding choice beyond a simple tool to preserve segregation. The Justice Department actively worked to dismantle large-scale desegregation initiatives, with varying degrees of success, in Nashville, Tennessee, and Norfolk, Virginia. For Reagan's administration, such plans were unfair to the individual and the local school district. Reagan also elevated Justice William Rehnquist—the Supreme Court's leading opponent of desegregation—to chief justice after Warren Burger's retirement in 1986.[24]

Reagan did not stop with cutting or terminating federal funding for desegregation. While calling to restore prayer in schools, Reagan also supported tax credits and breaks for families enrolling in private schools. Republicans in their 1980 party platform reaffirmed their "support for a system of educational assistance based on tax credits" to help cover the costs of private tuition. Reagan also vowed to strengthen the tax-exempt status of private institutions after the courts began to deny such breaks to private schools that discriminated based on race. Reagan sought to restore tax exemption in order to "compensate parents for their financial sacrifices in paying tuition at the elementary, secondary, and post-secondary level." Reagan also proposed throughout his administration federal vouchers for education for the first time since *Brown*.[25]

For Republicans, it was a matter of "fairness" and improving poor families' access to choice and private schools. Claiming that the government had overstepped its bounds by denying tax exemptions, Reagan sought to restore tax exempt status to Bob Jones University, one of dozens of schools explicitly committed to segregation. The Supreme Court ultimately ruled against Bob Jones University and the Reagan administration, but it was clear that the president sided with privatization and stood firmly against any move toward integrating public schools.[26]

One of Reagan's foremost commitments in education was to overturn a crowning legislative accomplishment of his predecessor, Jimmy Carter, who had created a new Department of Education out of the Department of Health, Education, and Welfare. Strongly endorsed by the National Education Association, the largest teacher union in the country, the legislation had passed by four votes and became a divisive, partisan issue. It was an affront to small-government Republicans, especially Reagan, who referred to it as a "bureaucratic boondoggle." Seeking to "not tie them up in red tape," the GOP was committed to abolishing the department and restoring decision-making to local officials.[27]

Reagan appointed Terrell Bell, former teacher and the commissioner of higher education in Utah, as secretary of the Department of Education. Following the party platform, Reagan pressured Bell to abolish the department. Dismantling it was supposed to begin in 1981, when Reagan created the National Commission on Excellence in Education to study the state of education in the country.[28] Bell and the commission, however, triggered an unintended consequence when they released their findings in a report called *A Nation at Risk* in 1983. The report had unfathomable impact. Focusing on a decline in test scores, lax academic standards, and misguided educational aims, no other federal report offered such a decisive, singlehanded blow to the reputation of public education. It fed the bleak outlook on the education system and the low achievement of American students. "The educational foundations of our society are presently being eroded by a rising tide of mediocrity," the report concluded, "that threatens our very future as a Nation and a people." It suggested, "If an unfriendly foreign power had attempted to impose on America the mediocre educational performance that exists today, we might well have viewed it as an act of war."[29]

The report argued that the economy, productivity and, therefore, quality of life were all in peril because of an inadequate, ineffective system of education.[30] Militant in its rhetoric and strident in its tone, the report issued a compelling call to action that galvanized a nation and ironically strengthened the role of the federal government in education. It also framed a state of panic and anxiety in public education that further lowered the perception of schooling in the United States.

As a publication, *A Nation at Risk* was wildly popular. More than five hundred thousand copies were distributed to administrators, teachers, policymakers, school districts, and the press. Over seven hundred articles in forty-five newspapers referenced the report.[31] *A Nation at Risk* only confirmed the fears and suspicions Americans held about public education. The ominous tone crystallized an already popular viewpoint that public education in the United States was a failing endeavor.

Advancing the aims of Reagan and the Republican agenda, the report also established a front from which to attack teachers and teachers' unions. Teachers' unions had been on the rise since the early 1960s, particularly in the urban North. In the aftermath of strikes in New York in 1968, for instance, when the city agreed to meet with union representatives, the city observed that union participation among teachers had grown during the 1960s from 5 to 97 percent. Cities such as Detroit, Newark, and Philadelphia followed suit, and membership in the National Education Association and the American Federation of Teachers grew dramatically. Even as numbers declined in private-sector unions and trade unions, public school teachers were on their way to becoming one of the most unionized sectors in the nation, second only to the postal workers. Unionized teachers constituted a threat to the privatization of education and, as such, stood in the way of the GOP brand of education reform.

Though Reagan's wish of abolishing the Department of Education was not realized, the impact of *A Nation at Risk* inspired a new "accountability" movement—one that held schools and especially teachers to a tougher standard. It is not surprising, then, that teachers were blamed for the mediocrity of public education. With teachers' unions already scorned by an administration supportive of big business, those in the classroom were easy to blame. As the country retreated from desegregation and the ideals of integration—integration that had tangible positive gains for all students—teachers became an even easier target. The report found that the teaching profession failed to attract "academically able" people. Teacher education programs were dismal and inadequate for the task. In short, the report concluded that "the professional working life of teachers is on the whole unacceptable."[32] The report recommended fairer compensation for all teachers, but reformers asserted that "salary, promotion, tenure, and retention decisions should be tied to an effective evaluation system."[33] Policymakers suggested merit-based compensation. As education researcher Dana Goldstein noted, "Stricter revaluation systems, merit pay, the weakening of teacher tenure, and the creation of alternative pathways into the classroom . . . [are] often talked about as a sort of next step in school reform, because integration failed."[34] Teachers were a popular scapegoat, and national animosity toward teachers and their unions only grew over time.

Framed in stark economic terms and with teachers' unions on the defensive, *A Nation at Risk* invited the business community to act, and Reagan's amiable relationship with business forged a new business-education partnership. As a new global economy emerged in the 1980s and the United States sought a lucrative position in it, businesses took a keen interest in education reform. As the Committee for Economic Development, an organization of two hundred educators and corporate leaders, wrote in 1985, the business community's participation in school reform was of paramount importance to the economic success of the nation. Acknowledging the role of educating responsible citizens, they were also aware of "increasing evidence that education has a direct impact on employment, productivity, and growth, and on the nation's ability to compete in the world economy."[35]

Though it was not without its critics, *A Nation at Risk* perpetuated a narrative of failure throughout the 1980s as Americans increasingly supported their governors and representatives in Congress who called for dramatic reform.[36] Not for the sake of desegregation, of course.

In response to the acidity of *A Nation at Risk*, school choice was used as a primary mechanism to improve what was increasingly viewed as a failed public school system. The National Governors Association released a report in 1985 that highlighted school choice as a state-level solution. The Republican governor of Tennessee, Lamar Alexander, was an advocate of choice and connected it to the larger accountability movement. Alexander called for some "good old-fashioned horse-trading. We'll regulate less, if schools and school districts will produce better results."[37] These "results," to be sure, would not include integration or any other civil rights objectives. They did include choice. "It will mean giving parents more choice of the public schools their children attend as one way of assuring higher quality without heavy-handed state control."[38] For Alexander and others interested in choice, the new emphasis on reform under Reagan meant they were in control and desegregation was off the table.

In spite of the report's sweeping recommendations for greater investment in schools, Congress made massive budget cuts—overall funding for the Department of Education was curtailed by 11 percent, and staff was also reduced. They eliminated or converted categorical grants, which regulated how funds could be spent, into more flexible block grants. Taken together with a perennial resistance to higher taxes for education, federal cuts to education exacted a heavy toll on already cash-starved public schools.

Reagan opened the floodgates for corporate and private reform. With teachers demonized, public opinion embraced privatization as people abandoned public education. Subsequent administrations—including both Bushes and Clinton—would build on this discontent and institutionalize the first school choice policies since the 1960s, presenting an opportunity for the South to rise again.

With federal support for privatization, corporate reform, and education policy unencumbered by desegregation, a new cohort of southern governors embraced education reform in ways unseen during the decades-long struggle of the civil rights movement.[39] Typically the stalwarts of segregation, southern governors under Reagan and George H. W. Bush—including Lamar Alexander of Tennessee, Bill Clinton of Arkansas, Richard Riley of South Carolina, William Winter of Mississippi, and, by 1995, George W. Bush of Texas—adopted a new "accountability" movement that called for new, high academic standards and developing new modes of measurement to assess progress. With integration efforts all but abandoned and de facto segregation protected by law, these southern governors were safe from the civil rights "extremists" who demanded racial equity. As the American public and policymakers increasingly connected the nation's schools with the economy, reformers proffered "objective" and often color-blind policies. To shape reform around race—as with affirmative action—was undesirable for most Americans. During the 1980s and 1990s, these southern governors enacted education reform that was race-neutral, ignoring the very issues of segregation and other civil rights–based solutions such as community control. They also grounded the disciplinary measures behind Nixon's "law and order" mandate in education policy. All of this facilitated the ideology and fostered political conditions conducive to widescale school choice.

Southern governors pushed the nation toward choice after the Charlottesville Education Summit in 1989. Convened by President George H. W. Bush and at a site near Thomas Jefferson's home at Monticello, the nation's governors felt the charge to reinvigorate education so that it matched Jefferson's historic vision: schools that were a pillar of strength for the Republic. It was also an appropriate location to advocate a plan that was based on the strength of states and states' rights—a symbolic move away from the seat of federal government in Washington, DC, but still grounded in the South. In the single largest meeting of US state leaders to discuss education reform, the governors at the summit reaffirmed a connection between education and the economy. As Bill Clinton, then governor of Arkansas put it, "This is the first time in the history of this country that we ever thought enough of education and ever understood its significance to our economic future."[40]

After the Charlottesville summit, governors adopted six national goals that focused on early childhood education, student achievement, math and science, dropout rates, functional literacy in a global economy, and safe, drug-free schools.[41] Dubbed "America 2000," the six goals were part of a legislative agenda and a voluntary program embraced by the states, to be achieved by the turn of the millennium.[42] It was an ambitious, optimistic effort. Little education legislation was passed under the first Bush administration, but a national framework for identifying goals and mandating testing to assess academic progress was established.

Building on the momentum generated by *A Nation at Risk* and the Charlottesville summit, Bush also identified school choice at the federal level as a key area of reform to help schools that needed it the most. Linking his initiative to his predecessor Reagan, he noted, "We must hold all concerned accountable. In education, we cannot tolerate mediocrity."[43] In ground that had been mostly fallow for the three decades, Bush planted the seeds for a new era of accountability for educational "excellence," of which school choice was a critical part. In one address, Bush outlined: "We can encourage educational excellence by encouraging parental choice. The concept of choice draws its fundamental strength from the principle at the very heart of the democratic idea. . . . It's time parents were free to choose the schools that their children attend. This approach will create the competitive climate that stimulates excellence in our private and parochial schools as well."[44]

When Bush appointed Lamar Alexander as his secretary of education, he solidified choice as an integral part of education reform discourse. Together they proposed funding both public and private school choice legislation, and they lobbied behind the scenes for federally supported choice legislation. Though their efforts never crystallized in any formal legislation, the Bush administration facilitated the rise of choice at the state level.[45] Choice was no longer framed as a way to preserve Whites-only schools. Choice, as spelled out by George H. W. Bush, was race-neutral. It benefited everyone, regardless of class or race, and it could hold traditional public schools more accountable.

Magnet schools—public schools with specialized curricula focusing on the likes of performing arts, languages, International Baccalaureate, or STEM, and intended to attract White students for the purposes of desegregation—continued under Bush's term in office. Governor Tommy Thompson of Wisconsin signed into law the Milwaukee Parental Choice Program—the progenitor to the state's controversial religious school voucher program that offered publicly funded vouchers to be used for private school tuition.[46] Legislators in Minnesota passed the country's first charter school law into existence in 1991 and established the first charter school—a publicly funded but privately run school—in St. Paul the following year.[47] As states began adopting school choice plans for the first time since the "freedom of choice" of the 1960s, the federal government issued assurances. Governors like Lamar Alexander, who had advocated for choice since the 1980s, were now free to establish a choice agenda in their home states. Reinforcing a race-neutral policy in the best interests of all children, school choice earned national and bipartisan support. By the 1990s, school choice would become a central part of restructuring education.

One of the more salient aspects of the school choice movement is its bipartisan nature, which explains how it has become so entrenched in the school system and ways of thinking about education reform. To this day, in a divided political world, school choice seems to be a rare issue that actually unites people across the aisle. Democratic administrations of Bill Clinton and later Barack Obama did not challenge school choice (and in fact expanded it) as the policy and the ideology behind it continued to attract bipartisan support and gain traction among the wider public. By the 1990s, both major parties could agree that choice was a mechanism to improve education. President Bill Clinton did not stray from his predecessor's platform. Clinton was a proud product of public schools, and he advocated adamantly on behalf of them, yet he did so in a way that maintained the ideological underpinnings of previous Republican initiatives. At the same time, Clinton accelerated the availability of choice options across the country, effectively claiming school choice as a priority for the Democratic Party.

As a governor, Clinton had been an active, energetic participant at the Charlottesville education summit. Then, as president, Clinton expressed an interest in actualizing the goals he had helped establish under the Bush administration. Appointing former governor of South Carolina Richard Riley—who had attended the Charlottesville summit—to serve as the secretary of education garnered bipartisan approval, including that of the outgoing choice advocate Lamar Alexander.[48] Though the parties had shifted, many of the same educational policies and trajectories remained in play under Clinton. Building on the momentum of the preceding administration, Clinton ushered through Congress the Goals 2000: Educate America Act of 1994. He also reauthorized the influential Elementary and Secondary Education Act (ESEA), which codified the national goals in operation under George H. W. Bush and legislated the National Education Goals Panel and the National Education Standards and Improvement Council. It appropriated a relatively modest $2 billion that was to be distributed by way of grants that agencies competed for at the state level. Greater inroads were made in strengthening the states' commitment to testing and accountability, which often meant linking state and local funding to assessment of the schools through a barrage of statewide and national tests.[49]

Clinton was no mere placeholder for choice, however. He helped codify charter schools into federal law and served as a choice advocate, many times connecting options such as magnet schools to desegregation goals as the courts floundered. He also elevated charter schools as a way to meet the needs of communities of color. Clinton demonstrated that choice was the policy of the "left" too and ushered in other significant federal programming. In particular, the reauthorization of ESEA in 1994 established the Federal Charter School Program. The Clinton administration also passed the Charter School Expansion Act of 1998, which provided the first financial and legal support for charters and school choice at the state and federal level.[50] Clinton actively promoted it as well, stipulating in Goals 2000 how funding should be used for "promoting public magnet schools, public 'charter schools,' and other mechanisms for increasing choice among public schools." This included disseminating information to parents about choice and options available.[51] It also established a free-flowing and expanding revenue stream for charter schools and school choice, beginning with a modest yet significant $4.5 million.[52]

School choice—though framed as an avenue of reform in the best interests of all students—gained traction at a time when the national commitment to desegregation had dropped and previously integrated schools were beginning to resegregate. In the South—the region that showed enthusiastic support for choice—the percentage of African American students who attended majority-White public schools reached a high mark of approximately 44 percent in 1988. But within ten years, the number dropped to 32 percent. Across the nation, the percentage of Black students who attended schools that were 50–100 percent Black or Brown rose to nearly 80 percent by 1999.[53] The political will to achieve desegregation had dissipated during Clinton's presidency.

Clinton did not sound too different from his Republican predecessors during his State of the Union Address in 1994. Silent about
resegregation, he confirmed to a national audience that his education
legislation was designed to "empower individual school districts to experiment with ideas like chartering their schools to be run by private
corporations or having more public school choice, to do whatever they
wish to do as long as we measure every school by one high standard."[54]
Allowing for private entities to run schools, he still maintained that
charters should be nonsectarian while also recruiting the support of parochial institutions. On a high-profile education tour toward the end of
his administration, Clinton noted, "There is a role, a positive role, that
faith-based groups can play. My goal is to get more money and more
people involved in the charter school movement, to break down the
walls of resistance among all the educators to it, and to get community
people more aware of it."[55]

Bill Clinton may not be remembered as an "education president,"
but choice was ushered in under his watch. There had been only one
charter school at the beginning of his administration. By the end of
his second term in office, over 1,700 charters existed. Federal financial
support for them had increased every year of his presidency. Clinton
wanted more, too, hoping to reach three thousand charter schools by
the end of his presidency. He may not have achieved that goal, but he
earned a lasting legacy as the "charter school president."

Though Clinton connected choice to civil rights initiatives in limited though influential ways, the courts throughout the 1990s and the
early 2000s kept race out of the question in cases related to education.
In *Board of Education of Oklahoma City Public Schools v. Dowell* (1991),
the Supreme Court ruled that the Oklahoma City school district could
terminate its preexisting desegregation plans after determining it had
achieved a "unitary" or desegregated status in spite of evidence that the
district would experience dramatic resegregation. Similarly, in *Freeman
v. Pitts* (1992) and *Missouri v. Jenkins* (1995), the high court terminated
other integration mandates, officially signaling the end of court-ordered
desegregation attempts.[56]

The case of the school district in Charlotte and Mecklenburg County,
North Carolina, is particularly telling. The district had been under fed-

eral court order to bus students to achieve desegregation since 1971's *Swann v. Charlotte-Mecklenburg*. In 2001, a federal appeals courts ruled that the district was unitary or sufficiently desegregated, and desegregation plans were dropped. The decision came after thirty years of busing and desegregation mandates staving off total racial segregation. Though not racially proportionate and not without its problems, the Charlotte-Mecklenburg school district had become a model of sorts, achieving a high degree of success in desegregating. But after the district dropped desegregation plans, the schools rapidly resegregated. By 2018, the North Carolina Justice Center's Education and Law Project found the district to be the most segregated in the state, three decades of efforts having unraveled in a few years.[57]

No other legislation ushered in school choice like the No Child Left Behind (NCLB) Act in 2001. Moving beyond proposals and lip service, NCLB legislated school choice as an alternative to failing public schools. When Congress passed the act with strong bipartisan support, they enacted sweeping policy change that both legitimated privatization and sanctioned its place in educational policy discourse. It was President George W. Bush's signature education legislation and the crowning achievement for the school choice movement. The get-tough approach that capitalized on the "accountability movement" fit the bill of the Texan commander-in-chief. He provided a heavy hand to fix what by this time much of the nation believed to be a broken system. Drawing on if not co-opting civil rights ideals—such as focusing on the test scores of Black students and other students of color—NCLB also opened the door wider to competition through charter schools and vouchers while enforcing an unfunded mandate for test-based accountability. The legislation was an impressive feat and a milestone in the history of school choice.

The most expansive federal education policy since the Elementary and Secondary Education Act of 1965, the No Child Left Behind Act built on notions of accountability that had percolated since *A Nation at Risk*. It required states to build stringent accountability systems, annually testing students in grades 3–8 (and once in high school) in mathematics and reading. Tests were to be aligned with challenging state standards. Annual progress was to be reported, and the new law required disaggregated test score reporting: test results would be published by subgroups defined by race, ethnicity, class, ability, and proficiency in English. It was expected that all students would reach proficiency in math and reading by 2013–14 (which was twelve years from when the bill became law). The bill received fervent bipartisan support, passing easily by a vote of 381–40 in the House and 87–10 in the Senate. Senator Ted Kennedy, a leader and staunch advocate of the landmark legislation, remarked that education reform encapsulated in the bill was "a defining issue about the future of our nation and about the future of democracy, the future of liberty, and the future of the United States in leading the free world."[58]

In addition to its rigorous (albeit unrealistic) expectations, No Child Left Behind mandated a series of punitive measures for schools. Part of "leaving no child behind" meant holding, once and for all, failing schools accountable for their results. Authorizing and establishing guidelines for how the $12 billion spent annually through Title I funds—federal dollars first authorized by LBJ in 1965 and directed to schools that enrolled student populations of whom 40 percent or more lived in poverty—carried tremendous weight. The law was designed to push schools to ensure that all students would make adequate yearly progress. If schools failed to make yearly progress toward established proficiency goals, they would suffer consequences or "corrective action" under the new law. They were labeled—with wide press coverage in many instances—schools "in need of improvement." If a school continued to test below standards for a second year, that school had to cover the cost of transportation for students who elected to attend a different school of their choice or after-school tutoring. Persistently failing schools, or schools that did not meet progress goals for four or more years, were subject to closing or "restructuring" and a loss of federal funds.[59]

Popular with venture capitalists and choice advocates, NCLB drew the ire of teachers and their unions. It heightened the animosity harbored between teachers and legislators as policy ultimately blamed schools and reprimanded teachers for the failure of schools. With the threat of budget cuts and school closures, teachers were pressured to "teach to the test" in unprecedented ways. Educators consequently curtailed their teaching and curricula to align with the test. This led to rote memorization, scripted teaching, and cutting material that was deemed irrelevant if it was not on standardized tests.

Teachers were tasked with the impossible. With high expectations and little to no support to achieve it, teachers were expected to bring all students—regardless of background and previous educational experience—up to a level of proficiency. It was a daunting task for all teachers, but especially those with large classes, students with disabilities, students who were English-language learners, and other students who required additional support that was not forthcoming under the new legislation.[60]

The threat of punitive action spread to public schools themselves as well, not just their teachers who were expected to teach to the test or face the consequences. No Child Left Behind incorporated school choice into federal policy to an unprecedented degree. By law, if a school was failing its students, it was first expected to offer its pupils funding (including tuition, if applicable) to attend a different school of their choice. If the school was determined to be failing and had to be restructured, it faced several additional options. Staff, faculty, and administration could be replaced. The school could be converted to a charter, or a private entity could run the school. States could also open charter schools, and were encouraged to do so, to turn around failing public school districts. During the first year of No Child Left Behind, the Supreme Court ruled that public funding could be used for religious schools through voucher programs, which opened the door even further.

Stern repercussions for failing schools opened the door for school choice. By 2006, the Department of Education estimated that over 120,000 students had transferred to different schools, though nearly three million were eligible. By the same year, between nineteen thousand and twenty-five thousand schools—over 20 percent of all public schools in the nation—were identified as schools in need of improvement or restructuring. The number grew by 2008 to thirty thousand or over 35 percent of all public schools. Some estimates placed the number as high as nearly 40 percent.[61] The choice option was ready to be exploited because tens of thousands of schools were failing, and charters,

magnets, and private schools were viewed as a viable option among reformers to improve districts through competition or by enabling more
students to enroll in them. School choice made significant legislative
and ideological headway under the circumstances.

Unlike teachers, wealthy business executives and philanthropists
were both emboldened and courted by the Bush administration. A new
wave of philanthropists emerged as the financial backers of education
reform. The Bill and Melinda Gates Foundation and the Walton Family
Foundation alone were responsible for 25 percent of all funds contributed by top donors once the bill was signed into law. Another billionaire—Eli Broad, who founded the Eli and Edythe Broad Foundation
in 1999—joined the top contributors and became a significant player
in the education reform game. Diane Ravitch, education scholar and
former assistant secretary of education under George Bush, referred
to them as "venture philanthropists" as they integrated the practices of
venture capital finance and business management with education reform.[62] One such plan among major funders included the NewSchools
Venture Fund's Charter Accelerator Fund, intended to establish more
charters. The major donors collectively committed $40 million to edu-
cation entrepreneurs who sought to expand choice options.[63] Such ventures represented only the tip of the iceberg. Education was a lucrative
industry, offering the opportunity not only to generate profit but also
to significantly influence policy as well, if one had the means to do so.
A background in education or teacher certification was not required.

Federal support through No Child Left Behind and the *Zelman v.
Simmons-Harris* (2002) decision, which allowed public funding to fund
private school vouchers, inspired a national movement of wealthy donors who supported school choice legislation. Though vouchers never
proliferated to the extent that some predicted, voucher advocates across
the political spectrum were emboldened.[64] All Children Matter, one of
the groups to sprout up to support the new choice movement, was a
pro-voucher political action committee that raised millions to influence
state elections. Funding came from backers across the country, including the Walton Family Foundation and Betsy DeVos, who was at the
time an educational philanthropist from Michigan. The PAC helped
defeat an anti-voucher gubernatorial candidate in Utah and elected

pro-voucher candidates to the South Carolina legislature. The national Alliance for School Choice targeted legislation across the nation to promote pro-voucher and general choice options. Since the early 2000s, groups such as these cultivated a strong presence in states that eventually embraced strong choice models, including Florida, Indiana, Wisconsin, South Carolina, and Missouri.[65]

Though studies pointed toward mixed results, burgeoning federal support institutionalized the idea that choice was a solution to failing public education. Charter schools more than doubled during No Child Left Behind, and policymakers and philanthropists were authorized to implement other choice options in a further abandonment of public education.[66] Nearly fifty years after Milton Friedman had published his then-obscure ideas of market-based education reform, federal policymakers wrote his ideas into law with bipartisan and popular support.

Federal investment in school choice accelerated after No Child Left Behind. As divisive as some issues were, such as health care and access to the ballot, school choice remained a rare unifying issue that both parties could agree upon. President Barack Obama, who had run on a platform for change the nation could believe in, was poised to enact sweeping education reform as NCLB earned the scorn of educators for its punitive provisions based on high-stakes standardized testing. Though he had campaigned on a contagious message of hope, Obama did relatively little to alter the momentum of No Child Left Behind. During his 2008 campaign, Senator Obama was unabashedly supportive of charters, claiming: "I've consistently said, we need to support charter schools. I think it is important to experiment, by looking at how we can reward excellence in the classroom."[67] After his election in 2008, the core principles of school choice enjoyed even greater support and cultivation under Obama's administration. Yet education never moved beyond the backburner of his domestic agenda. In fact, Obama changed little except to greatly expand accessibility to choice and perpetuate our nation's ideological commitment to it. Additional moves made by the Department of Education cemented what critics had feared: a continued reliance on school choice.

Obama appointed as his secretary of education Arne Duncan, who served from 2009 until 2015. Duncan had known Obama in Chicago when Obama served as US senator for Illinois. Appointing Duncan was a powerful indicator that choice would remain a standard in education reform. As chief executive of the Chicago Public Schools system from 2001 to 2008, Duncan had earned experience in the trenches of education reform led by Chicago mayor Richard Daley. He had ushered in charter schools and used the rhetoric of choice to address the problem of failing public schools. He had supported public-private partnerships to improve schools too. He had developed a reputation as a renegade reformer, challenging teachers' unions, expanding charters, and closing traditional neighborhood schools.[68]

Duncan brought to the national level what he had learned on the ground in the Windy City. Duncan had been an integral part of Daley's Renaissance 2010 plan, which was announced in 2004 as an ambitious strategy to build one hundred new schools across the city that used "non-traditional" educational and management methods. This largely translated to building schools through charters and contracts granted to those who wanted to manage public schools, with or without credentials in education. Business and civic leaders pledged to raise $50 million to fund Daley's initiative. Demonstrating how reform would work with corporations outside the public system vested in choice, city and school district leaders founded the nonprofit organization New Schools for Chicago to assist in the public-private venture. The organization's language of reform reflected the larger choice movement, as the *Chicago Tribune* reported that it was seeking to hire "the most innovative, dedicated educators . . . to think, act and lead with creativity and autonomy" and issuing "performance contracts" that would provide the "freedom to innovate."[69]

Duncan shaped the platform for President Obama's education policy. Since it was a low priority for the Obama administration, Duncan exerted strong influence. Congress did not reauthorize the Elementary and Secondary Education Act (still known when Obama served as No Child Left Behind) during his first term in office, but the Obama administration then launched the Race to the Top Program. This was a competitive program that was part of a $5 billion education stimulus fund.

Of the larger economic stimulus package created in 2009, $100 billion was committed to offsetting the cost to state and local budgets for teacher salaries, 5 percent of which was devoted to Race to the Top. One of the requirements for grants under Race to the Top was the use of charters as a mechanism to turn around underperforming schools. The program also awarded partnerships and collaboration with charter school management companies and charter association members.[70] It was a program that harkened back to the Renaissance 2010 plan implemented in Chicago but on a national stage and with wider implications. As one of Duncan's spokespersons said two years into President Obama's administration, "Renaissance 2010 and Race to the Top both reflect a willingness to be bold, to hold yourself to higher standards and push for dramatic change, not incremental change." The Renaissance 2010 program in Chicago produced dismal results, however, with the "Renaissance" schools faring no better than their traditional public school counterparts.[71] The writing was on the wall that this reform would fail to live up to its promises of hope and change.

Arne Duncan and Barack Obama were not immune to venture philanthropy in education either. The Bill and Melinda Gates Foundation continued to invest in education reform. Duncan referred to one of the foundation's publications, *The Turnaround Challenge*—a report that touted charters and hybrid forms of charters—as a "bible" for restructuring schools.[72] And Duncan appointed Joanna Weiss as his chief of staff. Weiss had previously been the chief operating officer at the New-Schools Venture Fund—the multimillion-dollar investment in charters backed by top education philanthropists Bill and Melinda Gates, the Walton Foundation, and the Broad Foundation.[73] Duncan brought to the Obama administration an entrepreneurial style of education reform that crystallized a connection between corporate-driven school reform and public school improvement.

President Obama finally introduced education reform in the last year of his eight-year term and signed into law the Every Student Succeeds Act in 2015. The new act was the reauthorization of ESEA—and the renaming of No Child Left Behind—and it left choice and charter schools firmly entrenched. The law required states to submit specific plans for turning around the bottom 5 percent of school districts, granting greater authority and flexibility at the state and local level. Though the law would not be applied consistently across the United States, its gist was this: if a school failed to meet standards for four consecutive years, states had the option to take over a school, fire the principal, or convert the school into a charter. The law also created the federal Charter Schools Program, granting charters more authority and oversight by way of state grants and requiring individualized teacher recruitment and retention plans.[74]

A public-private relationship had been established in the field of education policy. The major philanthropic nonprofits such as the Walton Family Foundation and the Bill and Melinda Gates Foundation continued to spend hundreds of millions on education reform, from financing charters to instituting new merit pay assessments that tied teacher salaries to student test scores. Since starting their foundation in 1987, the Walton family had donated more than $1 billion in K–12 education reform through the Obama administration, over one-third going to charter school incubation.[75] In concert with research organizations like EdChoice (formerly the Friedman Foundation for Educational Choice), private entrepreneurs have invested billions of private dollars toward enacting choice across the nation and to actively court choice advocates at the local level in school board and district positions.[76] Business and private interests are fueling the choice agenda, successfully arguing that a corporate, privatized model will lead to better schools. Openly cultivating connections with businesses and wealthy benefactors, local and state governments—and the federal government—have increasingly embraced the movement and authorized private organizations to lead the way.

The school choice movement reached a new high-water mark in 2017. After a tumultuous election, President Donald Trump nominated Betsy DeVos to lead the Department of Education. With the vice president breaking a tie vote in a Republican-majority Senate, DeVos's appointment was one of the most contentious in congressional history. Her ideology and praxis were contrary to the values of public education. She was a billionaire who had never taught in or attended public school;

her children had also never attended public school. She had invested millions in voucher programs, which were arguably more controversial than charter schools.[77] In many ways, she represented the antithesis of public education. While critics decried her appointment, few highlighted the fact that her nomination signified a continuation of school choice policy rather than an abrupt shift. Secretary of Education DeVos was the culmination—not the origin—of the school choice movement.

CHAPTER FIVE

The School Choice Menu

WE CAN GET LOST in the school choices we have before us today. In fact, choice often necessitates that school districts commit resources simply to ensure we know our options. It is easy to forget that when the *Brown* decision was reached in 1954, American parents had only two options: the neighborhood public school or a private school if they so desired and could afford it. Today, parents face a multitude of options that resemble a menu. Particularly for those with the social and political capital to navigate a convoluted education landscape, choosing a school may be akin to dining out. Magnet schools, charter schools, voucher programs, homeschooling, online learning, and private options are all on the menu. As many choice advocates claim when discussing failing public schools, all options, or choices, are "on the table." After decades of struggle and disinvestment, traditional public education is often the least desirable item—but the other options often leave much to be desired.

Today's choice menu was created by policymakers who were either indifferent or hostile to desegregation. The education system was rebuilt around the ideology of choice in ways that spanned the political spectrum. It also obfuscated racism and classism that have historically limited educational access. Choice, on the surface of things, is not outwardly exclusive or racist. The options on the menu are theoretically available to everyone. Several school districts around the country use a "controlled choice" plan, where all families must rank the schools they want to attend, and the district then assigns each family a school.[1] In these cities—and in cities like New Orleans, converted to an all-charter school model—there is no choice but to choose.

To be sure, the private segregation academies that emerged in the first decade after *Brown* still persist across the country. But such privatization did not define the core features of school choice or the educational landscape it shaped. In fact, by the mid-1970s the Supreme Court had begun upholding the denial of tax-exempt status to private schools that practiced racial segregation in a series of cases that began with *Coit v. Green* in 1971. This continued until the culminating *Bob Jones University v. United States* (1983) decision, in which the court denied tax-exempt status to private institutions that practiced racial segregation or discrimination, putting an end to a blatant practice that originated with the rise of private segregation academies in the 1960s.[2] Such federal oversight struck a deep blow to intentional segregation in private schools. But while overt racial discrimination was largely stamped out, the mechanisms of privatization grew.

The claims to certain rights in education have defined policy since the 1970s. Since Whites protested that the federal government was interfering with *their* right to choose an education, the courts have upheld their claims to freedom of choice. Essentially, one's right to choose schools fell short of a new constitutional right, but local and state laws across the country have protected access to choice where it exists. The ideology of choice is now ingrained: Americans no longer demand choice; they assume it. A Democrats for Education Reform poll in 2018 revealed that about 65 percent of Americans think that access to charter and magnet schools—and other schools provided through a school choice model, regardless of zip code or income—is a top priority.[3] One could argue today—as many have from Donald Trump to Martin Luther King III—that the lack of a right to choose has been the defining civil rights issue of our time.[4]

The education market was open for business in the decades after *Brown*. Public education suffered during the full-scale desegregation efforts that began in the late 1960s as Whites moved out of cities and took with them the resources needed to sustain even an adequate public education system. Popular opinion about public education plummeted, further depleting the will to invest in it. Yet this disinvestment was accompanied by "innovation" in education reform. Reformers, Black and White, from across the political and economic spectrums imagined, developed, and offered enticing schooling options. Some of the reforms were explicitly antiracist or sought to directly address racial inequities.

Community-controlled schools in New York, Detroit, Chicago, and other northern cities carried out some of the more radical ideas of the era of desegregation and the civil rights movement. They inspired White progressives too. After decrying the "death at an early age" of American schoolchildren, education professor and reformer Jonathan Kozol advocated for a "free school" movement in the early 1970s that emboldened concerned parents, teachers, and advocates to establish their own schools. With the help of legal professionals and foundation funding, Kozol envisioned the establishment of "free schools": small neighborhood schools of less than one hundred students that were beyond the reach of the "public education apparatus" and outside the "White man's counter-culture." Kozol saw these situated primarily in American cities and catering to the needs of those historically underserved and victimized by traditional public education—namely poor Black and Brown communities.[5] Many reforms began with teachers who also drew from the ideology and work of the civil rights movement. Deborah Meier, a progenitor of the "small schools movement" that focused on locally, democratically governed and decentralized schools with small class sizes and founding director of Central Park East, an alternative public school in New York, wrote, "The kinds of change required by today's agenda can only be the work of thoughtful teachers . . . participants themselves in a climate of self-governance."[6] This type of ideology fueled an alternative school movement *esprit de résistance* among leftist educators that propagated the idea that *something* had to be done.[7]

These reformers collectively saw that achieving high-quality schools required change by any means necessary—including boycotts, strikes, and working outside the parameters of the traditional system. This alternative school movement shared some of the same urgency, methods, and discontent with public education as segregationists after *Brown*.

Everyone wanted choices. The movement for more choice therefore transcended any conservative or liberal label. Moreover, legislation from the local to the federal level supported alternatives to a broken system. There is much to order from the menu.

Magnet schools emerged as the first legitimate option on the menu of school choice after privatization and freedom of choice plans developed in the South post-*Brown*. Magnet schools originated in the 1970s to facilitate integration and to improve the quality of urban education after White flight. When Congress passed the Elementary and Secondary Education Act in 1965, it provided federal support for nonprofit, state-approved, local educational agencies committed to school improvement. This included federal and state grants where applicable for educational programming. The Emergency School Aid Act in 1972 expanded this, legislating various paths to school desegregation and alleviating racial unrest. The act included a federal competitive grants program to inspire efforts that would aid the desegregation process on less hostile terms than what the nation had seen in Little Rock. The program also sought to stymie the more subtle forms of resistance to integration, such as White flight. One such initiative was the Magnet School Assistance Program.[8] The courts supported the use of magnet schools to stimulate school desegregation on a voluntary basis in a series of decisions in Houston, Milwaukee, and Buffalo in 1975 and 1976. After the busing controversy in Boston, magnets were a welcomed alternative. Under the Reagan administration, courts permitted school districts to replace older mandatory desegregation plans—which were becoming increasingly unpopular—with voluntary magnet school plans.[9]

Magnet schools are public schools with highly specialized curricula, usually located in urban areas. They may focus on the sciences or the arts, administer academically rigorous programs such as the International Baccalaureate, or practice progressive pedagogies such as Montessori, which, as education scholar Mira Debs notes, "are a potentially ideal soil for creating intentionally diverse choice schools."[10] Magnets were designed to attract both families of color and White families. Even some prestigious academies across the country, such as

Boston Latin, converted to a magnet school status to gain funding and a more diverse student population.[11] Through high-quality, desirable programs, magnet schools compelled some Whites to voluntarily desegregate schools. They are unique because they have desegregation as a specific goal. Moreover, coupled with "controlled choice" policies, they have demonstrated potential to disrupt both school and residential segregation patterns.[12]

Magnet schools presented a compelling, attractive, and prized alternative to busing for the federal judges presiding over the desegregation cases of the late 1960s and early 1970s. In Michigan, federal judge Stephen Roth actively pushed a magnet school alternative before reluctantly settling on the busing option that resulted in the *Milliken* ruling. For Roth, magnets provided the best alternative because they were based on voluntary choice, not his orders. Moreover, promising to deliver high-quality instruction, magnets were also selective. They offered districts a means to meet desegregation mandates while allowing parents to choose to participate—an integral element of expanding choice ideology.[13] In this way magnets were the first attempts to co-opt choice with goals of integration, taking it out of the hands of diehard segregationists but leaving the structural system of racism intact.

Historian Nicholas Kryczka traces how magnet schools were incorporated into the first voluntary desegregation initiatives in Chicago's "Redmond Plan" in 1968, demonstrating how schools catered to and reinforced the privileges White and middle-class families enjoyed during desegregation. Magnets were part of a desegregation plan that created "educational parks," or pleasant campuses to attract White students from across the city. They were flush with science laboratories and state-of-the-art equipment that bolstered a specialized, rigorous curriculum that would draw in a critical mass of Whites to ensure racial "balance." Moreover, racial quotas promised a diverse student population with students of color that reflected proportional representation— but not to the extent where Whites were the minority. Such schools were also "anchors" and potential pillars of stability for White communities that could be used to prevent further White flight while projecting images of cosmopolitan, integrated spaces that upheld the values of the civil rights movement.[14]

While not all were successful, magnet schools gained academic distinction. Magnets were and still are common enough to generate widespread interest. Desired by parents who remain committed to public education, magnets allow parents control over where their children enroll and, in gentrified neighborhoods, communicate a message of success, innovation, and diversity. They also provide the flexibility to offer progressive, hands-on, student-centered, and project-based pedagogy, such as the magnets that operate as part of the public Montessori program.[15] Magnet schools represent some of the best that public education has to offer and are subject to the same public oversight as traditional public schools. Magnet schools and the controlled choice options they add to the menu connect to a view put forth by education researchers Gary Orfield and Erica Frankenberg. They argue that "there is a much richer and more beneficial practice of choice possible, deeply rooted in the experiences of the civil rights era, and there are ways to use its power for much more positive outcomes, for students, families, and our society." When school districts have structured choice and incorporated integration as a guide for choice, mutually beneficial results can occur.[16] The reality has often belied the potential, however.

The use of magnet schools in Charleston, South Carolina, is telling. Magnets in that city emerged as a solution to a desegregation case that persisted throughout the 1990s. The Department of Justice, joined by the NAACP Legal Defense Fund, sued the Charleston County School district for segregation and discrimination, alleging that the county had intentionally drawn district and attendance zones to maintain racial separation. Schools downtown were segregated, while the suburbs were mostly White.[17] The courts upheld that Charleston County was an example of de facto segregation, following the pattern established with the *Milliken v. Bradley* (1974) case, and consequently ruled that suburban schools that maintained a modicum of desegregation would not have to desegregate further.[18] In response to the trial, Charleston County constructed two downtown magnet schools, Academic Magnet High School (AMHS) and Buist Academy, an elementary school. Both were meant to foster integration, accept kids from across the county, and draw White families back downtown. The judge encouraged such programs to avoid busing and other "forced" desegregation methods.

Academic Magnet High School was initially housed in Burke High School, the oldest historically Black high school in the city that had never fully desegregated. At the start of the court case, only one of Burke's thirteen hundred students was White. Though the county was evenly split between the Black and White population, eighteen public schools were at least 90 percent Black.[19]

Magnets became a viable path toward integration in Charleston since courts there established a racial quota at the new magnets that reserved 60 percent of the total enrollment for White students and 40 percent for African American students.[20] Still, within the first few years of the program, at a time when 60 percent of the Charleston school system was African American, 68 percent of students at Academic Magnet were White.[21] Physically locating the magnet school within the premises of Burke High School, while maintaining separate teachers, staff, lunch hours, and students bodies, created an "us versus them" dichotomy and essentially segregated students by program—segregation that carried with it deep racial and class divisions.[22]

Then district officials moved AMHS to a different location, a site in North Charleston, and the school became increasingly White. Racial imbalance was addressed only after Charlestonians took issue that race was used as a factor in the admissions process. Larry Kobrovsky, a local attorney and former school board member, filed a suit to remove race from the admissions process at Buist. "In America, you deserve to be treated the same," Kobrovsky noted, drawing upon the pervasive color-blind rhetoric of the post-*Brown* era, "not depending on what you look like." Kobrovsky contended that maintaining a racial quota at Buist and other magnets was unconstitutional.[23] In response, the district eliminated all racial quotas, and the suit was dropped. More than a decade since the board reversed its race-based admission policy, the population at Buist in 2009 was over 75 percent White and only 10 percent African American.[24]

Academic Magnet High School and Buist Academy are highly valued and coveted schools among parents in Charleston County today. Admission is very competitive, and the waitlist is long. Students are required to take a difficult entrance exam and have a B average. Given the number of applicants and the sparse availability, admission into the

Charleston magnets has been likened to getting into our nation's prestigious Ivy League universities.[25] Like all freedom of choice plans, magnets have been and will continue to be about race. Like other choice plans, the burden is placed unduly on students of color and their families to get in. Moreover, the very concept of "magnet" here means attracting Whites—not students of color—back to the urban areas White families have fled. Whites, again, are privileged by this system, and it is their needs that are placated.[26]

Magnet schools can present one of the best options on the menu, but they also have problems. Successful magnets can be the first to sell out and fill up, access to them is severely limited, and genuine integration is not guaranteed. Magnet schools are an elusive option and, though they espouse the values of "diversity," do little to address the systemic nature of inequity that still defines the educational landscape today.

School vouchers are the most direct, if not the purest, application of school choice. They are also one of the most controversial options on the menu. School vouchers embody the idea that per-pupil allocation should be spent directly by individual families. Families, in turn, decide how and where to spend their school voucher. With families as consumers, vouchers provide the means to enact Friedman's ideal marketplace, as individuals can directly influence the market with their purchases. Whereas magnets are designed to attract middle-class white families back to the public school system, the purpose of vouchers is in some ways the exact opposite: to provide a way out for families who would like to choose private schools but would otherwise be encumbered by their tuition. The quintessential pro-choice organization EdChoice—founded as the Milton and Rose D. Friedman Foundation—defines vouchers as the mechanism to "give parents the freedom to choose a private school for their children, using all or part of the public funding set aside for their children's application."[27]

Like the concept of school choice in general, vouchers originated with racism and the politics of segregation in the aftermath of *Brown*. Vouchers were one of the earliest manifestations of choice and the first option selected by southern segregationists to avoid integration. As early as 1944, defenders of segregation in South Carolina had been calling for the complete abolition of public schools if they were going to be desegregated and replacing them with private school alternatives. Within months of the *Brown* decision, Georgia and Mississippi built upon the threat and passed legislation that earmarked public funding to cover the cost accrued by White families enrolling in private segregation academies. They were tantamount to tuition grants, or vouchers by another name.[28] Such legislation was permissible until the Supreme Court struck down "freedom of choice" plans in 1968 and the direct subsidization of private schools was stigmatized and eventually overruled by the 1980s. Yet the concept of vouchers was far from abandoned.

Vouchers enjoyed support outside the South among education reformers who sought to improve if not completely restructure public education. Christopher Jencks, an education professor at Harvard, and the Center for the Study of Public Policy in Cambridge drafted plans for federal vouchers, lending institutional weight. As opposed to the views of segregationists, Jencks's and others' support for vouchers was part of larger efforts to improve education for all students. Jonathan Kozol and the supporters of "free schools" saw vouchers as a way to support an alternative small school movement. State education officials in New Hampshire advocated for a statewide voucher system to foster a competitive statewide system of schools of choice—public, private, or magnets—that benefited rural areas.[29] Much of the rationale for vouchers in the North was built on a different sentiment than that of southern segregationists. Jencks, for instance, thought that reformers should "follow the Catholic precedent and allow nationalists [referring to Black advocates] to create their own private schools, outside the regular school system, and to encourage this by making such schools eligible for substantial tax support."[30] Seeking to empower African American calls for community control, vouchers presented the means to advance the ongoing civil rights struggle, drawing on the same methods of privatization but with very different goals. These advocates sought nothing less than the radical reorganization, community empowerment, and reconstruction of public education in the wake of *Brown*.

By "Catholic precedent," Jencks referred to Catholics' advocacy for vouchers in the 1950s to bolster their parochial schools. Rev. Richard Blum, a Catholic priest and professor at Marquette University in Wisconsin, published *Freedom of Choice in Education* in 1958, just three years after Milton Friedman published his work on the topic.[31] Blum helped popularize the argument for the subsidization of Catholic education in addition to vouchers outside the South. By the time of the *Brown* decision, Catholics had already established a strong network of parochial schools across the nation since the nineteenth century, embedding them in the education landscape. As historian Robert Gross notes in his analysis of school choice, Catholic schools transformed the education landscape to a marketplace, where private religious schools were an integral part of meeting larger public goals. These institutions received public support for their service, including property tax exemptions, which reduced the cost of enrolling in and maintaining private schools.[32] Alongside the common or public school system developed in the middle of the nineteenth century, Catholic parochial schools became a mainstay in the United States, and tax exemptions were critical to their founding and expansion across the country. Their presence was contested and controversial after *Brown*, however, as private religious schools endorsed the same voucher legislation as southern segregationists.

In spite of a professed commitment to the ideal of separation of church and state suggested by the First Amendment, Catholic schools were primed to advocate for vouchers to expand the educational services they had been providing. Two cities in particular, Milwaukee and Cleveland, became critical test sites for the constitutionality of voucher programs. In Milwaukee, White flight, failed desegregation attempts, community control experiments, and conservative Republican leadership at the state level coalesced to create a ripe ground for vouchers, which came to a head when Governor Tommy Thompson signed the Milwaukee Parental Choice Program into law in 1990.[33] In Ohio, White flight from the urban "crisis" depleted investment and resources for public education in Cleveland. The state had a long history of petitioning for public subsidies to support private education. With the rise of Republican leadership in the state legislature and governor's office in the 1990s—and some Democratic allies—vouchers enjoyed wide support. Legislators implemented the controversial Cleveland Scholarship and Tutoring Program that funded the vast majority of private school tuition for low-income families.[34]

Teachers' unions, civil rights organizations, and other traditional public education advocates across the nation bitterly opposed vouchers. Not only did the programs violate perceived understandings of the separation of church and state; they also circumvented traditional teacher licensure processes and undermined the viability of teachers' unions. The controversy came to a head in 2002, when the Supreme Court upheld the constitutionality of vouchers in a 5–4 vote in *Zelman v. Simmons-Harris*. The court found that the voucher programs as practiced in Ohio were constitutional because public funding was not going directly to religious schools. Rather, the money was going to individuals who then elected to invest in religious programs. Writing for the majority opinion, Chief Justice William H. Rehnquist wrote: "Entirely neutral with respect to religion, it provides benefits directly to a wide spectrum of individuals, defined only by financial need and residence in a particular school district. It permits such individuals to exercise genuine choice among options public and private, secular and religious. The program is therefore a program of true private choice."[35] Voucher advocates received a morale boost with the decision, and the boundaries of the educational marketplace expanded.

Though vouchers unnerved the most ardent defenders of public education across the nation—not to mention the teachers' unions— the *Zelman* decision affirmed the fundamental right of parents to send their child to private schools or a constitutional claim to choose.[36] Since the test cities of Milwaukee and Cleveland were firmly outside Dixie and maintained minority-majority school systems, voucher advocates achieved a critical symbolic victory as well. Vouchers were no longer the tools of racist segregationists. Vouchers at the turn of the century, to the contrary, theoretically benefited those most in need. And in a largely Christian country, many still welcomed the idea of publicly supporting parochial schools, such as Catholic schools, that made it their mission to improve the education of disenfranchised students.

The *Zelman* decision opened the door for voucher support at the federal level. In 2003, President George W. Bush signed the Scholarships for Opportunity and Results (SOAR) Act, which designated $20 million for vouchers to be used in District of Columbia schools. It also established the groundwork for Betsy DeVos to advocate for a school choice agenda predicated on vouchers and federal support for religious schools. Prior to her role as secretary of education, DeVos developed political acumen through philanthropy to advance a choice agenda, a goal to which she remained faithfully committed in 2020. She donated millions of her and her husband's fortune—from the Amway Corporation, a "multilevel" marketing firm for health, beauty, and home-care products that in 2015 reported a $9.5 billion profit—to school voucher and private school scholarships. She served on the boards of two national nonprofit organizations—Children First America and the American Education Reform Council—devoted to expanding choice through vouchers and tax credits. Based in Michigan, DeVos and her husband financially supported and successfully lobbied for the state's first charter school bill in 1993, just two years after the first such law passed in Minnesota. In 2000, she was the impetus behind the attempt to change the state constitution to allow tax-credit scholarships and vouchers. When that was defeated, DeVos began the Great Lakes Education Project and chaired the Alliance for School Choice to preserve the fight to alter state constitutional language. In 2010, DeVos established the American Federation for Children, a 501(c)4 nonprofit organization (permitted to engage in political activity) that focuses on advancing school choice, school vouchers, and "scholarship tax plans."[37] The scholarship plans, like the Education Freedom Scholarships and Opportunity Act, seek to provide dollar-for-dollar tax credits for those who financially support groups or organizations that provide scholarships.[38] Federal and judicial support ensure that vouchers will remain on the school choice menu.

Vouchers pose some of the most serious challenges to public education. Under voucher plans, state legislatures and school districts shift scarce public dollars to private schools, and states incentivize enrolling in private schools by providing tax credits to parents who enroll in them. Voucher plans support the privatization of public education—all in the name of choice.

Charter schools, the most recent addition to the school choice menu, now epitomize it. Charter schools are public schools funded by tax-payers' dollars but privately run. The state grants a "charter" to an organization that seeks to manage its own school. Charter schools are nonsectarian and held accountable to the state, meaning they cannot discriminate based on race, class, gender, religion, or ability.

Ray Budde, a former teacher and education professor in Massachusetts, first proposed the idea of an education charter in the early 1970s. He proposed that school boards should "charter" teachers to launch a program or curriculum that they thought would improve the quality of education for all students. Lasting for a period of three to five years, teachers would have the autonomy to direct their classrooms and department as they wished. "No one—not the superintendent or the principal or any central office supervisors," Ray Budde wrote, "would stand between the school board and the teachers."[39] The idea was also grounded in community control, much like the alternative school movement, as was the larger critique of ineffective, unresponsive school districts.

Al Shanker, the teachers' union organizer and leader, endorsed Budde's idea. As president of the American Federation of Teachers, Shanker garnered union support for the idea and used his platform as a columnist with the *New York Times* to advance it.[40] He referenced Budde's work to name what he had in mind: charter schools. To illustrate the experimental yet critical nature of his vision, Shanker employed an apt analogy of risk and discovery. "Explorers got charters to seek new lands and resources," he noted. "Many of our most esteemed scientific and cultural institutions were authorized by charters."[41] At the brink of failure, teachers were going to find a way.

Shanker held that schools run by a handful of teachers—six to ten licensed educators—could work with parents, school boards, and, of course, teachers' unions, to implement charters. For Shanker, teachers' unions were integral to the concept, which centered on the relationships between teacher and student, including additional planning time for lessons, cooperative team teaching, and alternative forms of assessment, among other strategies to improve student learning. His plan called for "faculty decision making, for participative management; team teaching; a way for a teaching team to govern itself." He also called for teachers to "have the time to share ideas and talk to and with each other."[42] Whatever the pedagogical intervention, the plan called for teachers to implement their best ideas without red tape, restrictions, or interference from the top. He called for charters to run from five to ten years, which would provide ample time to test, revise, and demonstrate the quality of the schools. It was then expected that the good ideas could be incorporated back into the larger public school system.[43]

Another crucial part of the initial charter school proposal called for diversity. As Shanker noted, "We are not talking about a school where all the advantaged kids or all the white kids or any other group is segregated to one group. The school would have to reflect the whole group."[44] One of the first extensive charter school programs in the nation developed in Minnesota, where the Citizens League, a nonprofit that advocates for stronger civic engagement across the state, committed to implementing Shanker's vision. The Citizens League worked with Shanker and a progressive coalition of teachers and policymakers from across the state. The report they published, *Chartered Schools = Choices for Educators + Quality for All Students*, called for integration objectives that cultivated diversity along racial, cultural, and economic lines. It championed a "multicultural and gender fair curriculum" and a racially diverse faculty and staff. It even called for "an affirmative plan for promoting integration by ability level and race."[45]

The charter movement began to take hold, much to the excitement of Ray Budde. Minnesota passed charter school legislation in 1991, and California followed the following year. By 1994, sixteen additional states had proposed charter school legislation, often with political fanfare from state governors. It was the genesis of a much larger movement. Twenty-five years after the first charter legislation passed, over three million students were enrolled in nearly seven thousand charter schools by the fall of 2016.[46]

Yet at the very moment of exploration and discovery that Shanker articulated, troubling clouds were billowing on the horizon. The gathering storm all but destroyed the original intent of charter schools. When Minnesota legislators passed the first charter law in 1991, the plan that emerged did not place teachers in control of charters. It did not even mandate standard teaching requirements. It also precluded collective bargaining rights for charter school teachers. This severely undermined the agency of teachers envisioned by the original charter architects.[47] Additionally, the charters first implemented in Minnesota targeted specific communities of color, in this case Somali, Hmong, and Ethiopian immigrant and refugee communities.[48] This undercut the historic Black disenfranchisement that charter architects had sought to address through their schools.

State officials served a more integral role than the original proposals called for too. After the first schools were established in Minnesota, state boards of education and other public entities were permitted to apply for charters.[49] In the original conception, school boards were supposed to charter departments or programs within a school, not necessarily an entire school. Teachers were initially meant to govern charter schools too. But reformers saw the potential for "educators and citizens of a large community . . . to revitalize their schools and create the conditions for giant leaps in the quality of education."[50] Teachers' unions were consequently and deliberately excluded in charter legislation. Businesses were free to run charter schools, and credentials in teaching or the field of education were not required. Instead of empowering teachers and teachers' unions, charter legislation undercut them. Chester Finn, a conservative education policy analyst who served in the Reagan administration, noted, "The single most important form of freedom for charter schools is to hire and fire employees as they like and pay them as they see fit."[51] By 2015, only five of forty-two states required charter school teachers to be covered by district collective bargaining agreements. Only 7 percent of all charter schools were unionized, as a result of antiunion legislation governing charters.[52]

One of the most notable mutations from the original charter school idea was the shift in agency from educators to corporate for-profit and nonprofit entities. With competition spurred by choice that underpinned the "education market," the entrepreneurial spirit ran high, and federal legislation further opened the market and the ability to compete by supporting more charters. Charter schools, based on the logic of charter school reformers, should be run like a business, and their first two decades have been driven by for-profit initiatives. By 2013, thirty-three states granted legislative approval to allow for-profit organizations to run charter schools. In Betsy DeVos's home state of Michigan, for instance, 80 percent of all charter schools were for-profit.[53]

Illustrating the nature of for-profit charters, the tennis superstar Andre Agassi captured headlines in 2001 for his newfound prowess in the education market. He formed a partnership with an equity investing firm, raising $750 million to build a network of charter schools to serve at least forty thousand students. It was built on the logic of school reform through free-market ideology. "I'm interested in seeing this school duplicated and used as a blueprint, a model for how our education system should be in this country," Agassi informed the *New York Times* when he opened his first school. "You need a lot of private dollars so you don't have to play by the same set of rules, so to speak." Investment banker Bobby Turner noted that they wanted "to attract investors who realize that making money and making societal change don't have to be mutually exclusive."[54] Agassi illustrated how for-profit initiatives shaped school choice, and an athlete with no education background or teaching experience—arguably the polar opposite of what Shanker and Budde had in mind—emerged as a force behind charter schools.

Agassi's company was but one of many such entities in the growing realm of for-profit education. And most for-profit charter schools have produced dismal results. Since their founding, the largest for-profit charter groups, such as White Hat Management, Educational Alternatives Inc., and the Edison Project, have been investigated, reported for mismanagement and fraud, and justifiably accused of capitalizing profits by reducing the cost of instruction and teaching.[55]

This dire record has generated a retreat of sorts from the for-profit sector and spurred new investment in the nonprofit segment of the expanding charter school business, generating over $500 million by 2010. In 2019 the federal government invested over $200 million alone in two charter companies, KIPP and IDEA, to create or expand over one hundred schools.[56] Though legally retaining 501(c)3 nonprofit status, charter management organizations—incorporated associations that attain the charter to operate in a given state—can still produce a profit because state laws permit school boards to hire a for-profit organization to manage, construct, or oversee parts of its operation. A board member of a nonprofit organization may also enjoy direct advantages from connections to a for-profit organization. Legal scholar Derek Black found that one of the biggest loopholes in nonprofit charter management is in facility leases and real estate management. Charter schools sometimes pay exorbitantly high fees—in Ohio, charter managers have charged millions in excess of average costs—that are much higher than what the real estate market demands. Some charter schools willingly paid inflated prices to another entity that they owned or governed, especially when compensated by tax dollars. They accepted public money and paid themselves a handsome fee for running the facilities. Other nonprofit organizations that manage charters are free to charge disproportionate administrative fees to the state and the public. Some founders of charter school chains have been awarded by charter management organizations they contracted with an annual salary and bonuses in excess of $400,000 for managing their schools. Exempt from the transparency typically imposed on public schools, charter schools have been largely free to exploit such profitable loopholes.[57]

Charter schools are often touted as a silver bullet for families ensnared in a failing school system, and the media regularly highlights high-performing charter schools. Plagued by decades of neglect, public schools in America were in desperate need of reform, and charters provided a quick means to do it. The free market ideology that supports charter development resonates with much of America too. So does the opportunity to address failing schools. In fact, "saving" disenfranchised students has become a civil rights issue.

The National Civil Rights Museum awarded Harlem Children's Zone founder Geoffrey Canada the National Freedom Award in 2013. The Harlem Children's Zone—a charter network in New York that focused on providing underperforming schools with wraparound services, which provide holistic student support (including counseling and familial support), and high academic expectations—was the inspiration behind President Obama's "Promise Neighborhoods" program in 2010. Appropriating $10 million to replicate Canada's school in twenty cities, the program illustrated integral federal investment and support for the charter model.[58] The Harlem Children's Zone, and the recognition and support Geoffrey Canada has received for it, demonstrate the popularity of the charter school idea in effecting change among marginalized communities.

Budde and Shanker did not foresee—and perhaps could not, given the high tide of teacher unionism—the support for charter schools among private, for-profit, and corporate entities. The rhetoric surrounding charters can be appealing and the ideas inspiring. Yet, in practice, charter schools, like every other option on the menu, have been controversial. In addition to having a record of fiscal malfeasance and profit exploitation, some charters push low-performing students out of school or otherwise restrict access. Unencumbered by state regulations, charters are free to hire non-unionized teachers, resulting in an underpaid and overworked teaching force. As such, charters constitute one of the gravest threats to public education. Not only do they steer public dollars away from traditional public schools; they also privatize the governance of schools, limiting public oversight and eliminating professional teachers' input.

At the same time, and in spite of lackluster or mixed results, charter schools remain one of the most tempting options on the menu.[59] Films like the blockbuster 2010 documentary *Waiting for Superman* have heightened the urgency so many Americans feel about education. The film, by Davis Guggenheim, chronicled the heart-wrenching stories of five students trapped in failing schools across the nation. Their only hope is to enter the lottery to win a seat in a high-performing charter school—the film's silver bullet for failing public schools. When the film concludes with parents and their children crying, grasping a ticket, waiting for numbers to be called, the solution seems clear: just open more charters. Not supporting charters is tantamount to standing in the way of children who need them the most.[60]

Another option on the menu is to completely sever ties with any formal schooling, private or public, and teach children at home. Over 1.6 million students are now taught in the confines of their own homes. This number has dropped slightly in recent years, but the number of home-schooled children doubled between 2000 and 2010, alongside significant charter school growth. The overall growth in homeschooling still marks a dramatic spike since the 1970s, when the movement began with only ten thousand to twenty thousand students.[61] With more parents opting to pull their kids out of the system altogether rather than enrolling in a public, private, or choice school, the homeschooling movement speaks volumes to the lack of faith or interest in public education. The United States has consistently sanctioned homeschooling and private forms of education since the founding of the republic, enabling families to educate their children without government oversight or with very little of it. Convincing citizens to levy a property tax for public education has always been a more difficult pitch in a country resistant to taxation than allowing parents to teach their children at home.[62]

Homeschooling, like choice in general, grew during the 1960s and 1970s after the tumult inspired by full-scale desegregation attempts. As education historian Milton Gaither has pointed out, homeschooling was shaped by larger social and cultural shifts of the postwar era. During the 1960s and 1970s, suburbanization continued at the same time that counterculture grew, the latter sometimes entailing a back-to-the-land movement, with small, alternative communes and movement away from cities. In both cases parents, left and right, sought refuge from an encroaching government.[63] When it came to education, Americans were ready for something new.

Homeschooling, building on the work of Milton Friedman, represented a libertarian, if not radical, approach to education reform. Educator and author John Holt became emblematic of the movement.[64] His books, including *How Children Fail, No More Public School, Deschooling Society,* and *The 12-Year Sentence,* painted a clear portrait of educators and reformers fed up with a broken public system. His later work, such as *Freedom and Beyond* (1972), promulgated an ideology of pulling out of and abandoning public schools altogether. Publishing the magazine *Growing Without Schooling*—the first to focus on homeschooling—Holt communicated an evolving message that resonated with a small but influential core of parents, scholars, and policymakers: "My concern is not to improve 'education,' but to do away with it, to end the ugly and anti-human business of people-shaping and let people shape themselves."[65] Building on the larger libertarian shift in education and part of a larger intellectual movement that supported divestment from public education, Holt published *Teach Your Own: The John Holt Book of Homeschooling* in 1981.[66]

Organizations such as the National Homeschool Association, the Home School Legal Defense Association, and a score of state and local groups guided parents through the convoluted pathways to homeschooling. Though the surge in homeschooling after 2000 is in part grounded in a larger nonsectarian movement outside the church, homeschooling is largely perceived as a religious movement, and homeschooling parents are viewed as the "educational conscientious objectors."[67] The mission of the Home School Legal Defense Association—an organization founded in 1983 to provide legal counsel to and defense of homeschooling parents—is illustrative: "To preserve and advance the fundamental, God-given, constitutional right of parents and others legally responsible for their children to direct their education."[68] The states agreed that this was indeed a right. By the early 1990s, parents who wanted to homeschool their children were legally protected by every state. Public opinion supported them as well. By the mid-1990s, a Gallup poll revealed that 70 percent of Americans supported homeschooling, a near reversal from one decade earlier.[69]

No longer part of a marginal religious education movement, parents increasingly pursue homeschooling out of frustration with both the public school system and the private, free market alternatives. As education journalist Melinda Anderson and lawyer Paula Penn-Nabrit explain, homeschooling in the African American community is part of a long history of self-reliance, driven by determination to provide a quality education by any means necessary—including pulling out of the system altogether.[70]

Homeschooling also feeds into the current push for online education. Building on the ideology and rhetoric of choice, online or virtual education has grown markedly in the past decade. During the 2014–15 school year, approximately 2.7 million K–12 students, the majority of whom were enrolled full-time in traditional brick-and-mortar schools, enrolled in 4.5 million supplemental online courses. Of this number, over three hundred thousand students were enrolled full-time in virtual classes—and that number is growing, especially since the beginning of the COVID-19 pandemic. In 2014 alone, there were over 130 bills introduced in thirty-six states to expand the role of e-learning, and by the next school year Alabama, Arkansas, Florida, Michigan, and Virginia actually required students to take some online courses. In thirty states and the District of Columbia, full-time cyber schools are now readily available for parents and their kids who do not want to step inside a traditional brick-and-mortar school.[71] Wherever one can connect, one has access to a virtual education that meets the criteria of mandatory K–12 education laws. As nearly two million families look for homeschooling instructional support, online material and curricula are the most efficient way to get it.

To millions of students left behind by traditional public education, online learning understandably holds great appeal. It seems logical to incorporate the technology at our fingertips into how we deliver instruction and curricula. Virtual course offerings particularly thrive in rural areas, where traditional public schools fall short in providing a wide array of classes or qualified teachers to offer them. Due to the significance of the property tax in funding public education, rural schools simply cannot raise the capital necessary for high-quality instruction. Charters or other choice options are less feasible in rural areas due to a less concentrated student population. Increasingly, virtual programs are the first and only choice other than traditional public schools that rural parents have when selecting schools. They cover ground where traditional public schools do not have the resources to venture.

Of all the choices on the menu, this may be one of the most alluring to remotely located parents and families whose children have physical, emotional, or academic needs not met by rural school districts. As a result of the coronavirus pandemic, it has also become central to delivering an education nationwide, not just to rural students. Virtual education sometimes promises a self-paced, personalized curriculum, and specialized courses that appeal to the lived realities of struggling and working parents, and it puts technology front and center in a nation with an insatiable appetite for the newest innovations. But these promises have rarely translated into a quality education, as parents and children alike can attest. Students have sometimes been assigned teachers who were then rarely available to answer questions in real time. And class sizes have sometimes been impossibly large—as many as 250 students in a class—to the degree that teachers could not possibly respond to all of the students' and parents' questions.[72] The live chat functions that many use are painfully slow. To make matters worse, not every student received the technology or materials, such as their own computer, that were promised by the virtual school or the district that approved the program—such an obvious, integral part of virtual education. Some students have been marked absent as a result, and those children started school behind. Some have had to rely on a slow connection to download an abundance of material. Many turned to paper and pencil, the very means of education they had sought to avoid. The COVID-19 pandemic has accentuated extant problems, including the fact that nearly 20 percent of students lack the ability to reliably connect to online instruction, if at all. The pandemic has highlighted the fact that BIPOC families disproportionately suffer from the digital divide. All told, many students have become lost in the virtual shuffle, vexed by this education "choice."[73]

Virtual schooling is lucrative for investors, however. Federal support for school choice and the demands to improve education opened the floodgates. With exceedingly high student-teacher ratios, support for quality teaching could be undercut. Technology is poised to replace teaching altogether. K12 Inc., a publicly traded, for-profit company, has emerged as the leader of the virtual education market. Enrolling nearly one hundred thousand students across twenty-nine states, it demonstrated to investors the potential value of online schools. In 2018, the company reported over $238 million in revenue.[74] Much of this was funded by public tax dollars at local, state, and federal levels. As professor of African American studies and education Noliwe Rooks revealed in *Cutting School*, five Pennsylvania cyber charters received $200 million in tax money in 2010–11, and Agora Cyber Charter, which is run by K12, took in $31.6 million in 2013 alone from taxpayers in Philadelphia.[75] Online learning is good for big business.

The technology used in virtual education has proved indispensable during the pandemic. Schools committed to a fully online format remain resilient in spite of the mixed results and several investigations into fraud and corruption. Having received a boost during the pandemic, virtual schools remain popular and enjoy legal, financial, and political support at the federal level. Betsy DeVos was a financial backer of K12, Inc. Two organizations she founded prior to her appointment as secretary of education—the American Federation for Children and the Great Lakes Education Project—are highly supportive of online learning and virtual schools. As DeVos wrote to Senator Patty Murray of Washington: "High quality virtual charter schools provide valuable options to families."[76]

There is faith in the ideal that all options should remain on the table, with a full school choice menu available for all. The school choice menu is ever growing, both in popularity and criticism. The existence of so many options presents a vastly different picture than that of the schools the boomer generation attended. School choice today represents a new ideology that addresses the very nature of public education and has perhaps already eclipsed it. Consumers continue to demand more choice and, though some may argue it democratized public education, the reviews are mixed at best.

CHAPTER SIX

Race and a Civil Rights Claim to School Choice

HOWARD FULLER was born in Shreveport, Louisiana, on January 14, 1941. He grew up in the all-Black part of town, a space policed and terrorized through the mechanisms of White supremacy much like the rest of the Jim Crow South. He moved with his mother and stepfather to Milwaukee, Wisconsin, at the age of five. Attending both private Catholic and segregated all-Black public schools, Fuller experienced what was then the full spectrum of education in the United States. He also served in the civil rights movement and participated in the more revolutionary aspects of it in the South. Fuller first became involved in the struggle when he joined the Congress of Racial Equality (CORE) in 1964 as a graduate student at Case Western Reserve University in Cleveland. CORE gained notoriety for its integral role in organizing the Freedom Rides to desegregate bus terminals across the South in 1961. Fuller's work in Cleveland changed the course of his life. In protests surrounding the local demand to desegregate, Fuller witnessed firsthand the Reverend Bruce Klunder, a twenty-seven-year-old White Presbyterian minister, crushed to death by a bulldozer.[1]

After leaving Ohio, Fuller worked with Operation Breakthrough, a North Carolina–based antipoverty program that focused on empowering local Black communities. Conservatives branded Fuller and his comrades "outside agitators" and "dangerous extremists."[2] Fuller also worked with Black students at Duke University who took over the campus administrative building in 1969. Eventually, Fuller led Black students, community supporters, and movement leaders such as Stokely Carmichael and Cleveland Sellers in the establishment of Malcolm X Liberation University—a Black institution of higher education in North Carolina committed to the principles of Black Power.[3] He traveled with anticolonial freedom fighters in Kenya, Tanzania, and Mozambique. He adopted the name Owusu Sadaukai, a name bestowed by his students in North Carolina and reflecting the militant, pan-African ideology that he gained during the Black liberation movement.[4]

We can see the work of both Martin Luther King Jr. and Malcolm X in Fuller's struggle. He has actively resisted racism and poverty, and his commitment cannot be questioned. But many have raised eyebrows at the path he has taken in recent years. Fuller is on the front lines of the school choice movement, though obviously for very different reasons than southern Whites. For Fuller, choice was and remains revolutionary. Choice is empowering. It is an opportunity for poor families to escape, if not control and repair, a broken system. As he notes in his autobiography, published in 2014, "Giving low-income and working-class parents the power (and the money) to make choices about the schools their children attend will not only revolutionize education but provide the compass to a better life."[5]

Having earned a PhD in the sociology of education from Marquette University in 1986, Fuller is one of several civil rights activists turned education reformers who embraced school choice in the 1990s. He is also one who reached across the aisle in ways that seemingly belied his revolutionary work of the 1960s and 1970s. Fuller sat at the table with some of the most conservative education reformers, and forged alliances with school choice advocates. He counseled the Republican governor of Wisconsin, Tommy Thompson, as the state adopted a private school voucher plan. "Howard Fuller and myself are friends," Thompson stated, adding a comment that can be read as a racial microaggression: "He is a very astute and articulate individual."[6] Fuller advocated the idea of choice to George W. Bush when Bush was governor of Texas, a year before he became president of the United States. In his words, "A surprising thing happened: I connected with the dude."[7] The organization he founded in 2000, the Black Alliance for Educational Options (BAEO), received significant funding from conservative philanthropists and think tanks including the Friedman Foundation for Educational Choice, the Bradley Foundation, and the Walton Family Foundation.[8] Fuller continued down this path, working with Betsy DeVos years before her appointment to the Department of Education.

It was easy to wonder how Fuller—a radical Black activist—ended up in the company of conservative Whites. It was even easier to criticize him for it. Yet Fuller's trajectory illustrates an ironic development in the growth of school choice—it is fully embraced by some as a genuine civil right.

Dr. Fuller has much support. Americans have been hungry for education reform, and school choice is an appetizing option on the menu. A study released by the right-wing American Federation for Children found that 67 percent of Americans support school choice while only 27 percent oppose it. Of those who positively view choice, over 40 percent *strongly* support it. Moreover, 80 percent of Republicans support it, as do 56 percent of Democrats. A strong majority—71 percent—placed a high priority on families having "access to a variety of public school options no matter where they live or how much money they have."[9] Even if biased, the level of support of choice cannot be dismissed. This is tantamount to establishing it as a fundamental *right* to choose.

But support for choice has been racialized, and race shapes the nuances of school choice and the advocacy for it. The numbers behind school choice support reveal a racial divide—one that Fuller's story illustrates today. One poll estimated that 73 percent of Latinx families and 67 percent of African Americans support school choice. Another showed that over two-thirds of African Americans support private school vouchers.[10] A poll conducted by the Democrats for Education Reform showed that 58 percent of Black Democratic voters and 52 percent of Latinx Democratic voters supported charter schools. This number is all the more significant when looking at the fact that only 26 percent of Democratic voters overall supported the schools.[11] Organizations like the Hispanic Council for Reform and Educational Options (HCREO) and Howard Fuller's BAEO push for school choice legislation and organize support for it.[12]

Though school choice originated with racist resistance to desegregation, it understandably appeals to parents who feel trapped in a failing system. People of color who support choice also position it as part of the continuing trajectory of the civil rights movement. Choice has grown increasingly complicated and nuanced a half-century after its inception, and the movement behind it must be viewed as fluid and at times paradoxical.

Like Geoffrey Canada and Fuller, a member of Martin Luther King Jr.'s inner circle who embraced the principles of school choice later in life represents the politics of choice in Black communities and communities of color across the nation. Wyatt Tee Walker was chief of staff for Dr. King and a key organizer in King's Southern Christian Leadership Conference. With King, Walker shaped some integral civil rights campaigns of the movement, including the Children's Crusade and the movement in Birmingham in 1963, which demanded and eventually achieved desegregation of public spaces, including schools, in the cradle of the Confederacy. The Birmingham movement has grown in our collective memory into a tale of nearly insurmountable odds, of youth and nonviolent activists who nevertheless slayed the behemoth of segregation in the epic proportions of David and Goliath.

Like Fuller, Walker eventually took up the cause for school choice. From New York in 2014, Walker wrote that his efforts in organizing a charter school in 1999 were part of "another nonviolent revolution and march for justice." He asserted, "The effort to create great new charter schools now is another such story, requiring community leaders and educators to overcome many obstacles and much entrenched opposition." Walker looked on the struggle to create charter schools as tantamount to overcoming segregation in the United States. Quality of education and the desegregation of schools were consistent priorities of the movement in the 1960s, and they still were for Walker as a minister in Harlem a half-century later. "The movement for justice,"

Walker wrote, "taught me the importance of education. . . . In the charter school movement, I am continuing the work of Dr. King."[13]

By most accounts from those who lived through it, and from reports in the press, public schools were failing their students by the 1980s. The promises of the *Brown* decision remained unfulfilled. Critical race theorist and legal scholar Derrick Bell commented on the fiftieth anniversary of *Brown* that the edict had "gained in reputation as a measure of what law and society might be" but that massive resistance and weak enforcement had "transformed *Brown* into a magnificent mirage, the legal equivalent of that city on a hill to which all aspire without any serious thought that it will ever be attained."[14]

After the fallout of massive resistance to desegregation in the South, criticism of public education grew nationwide. Conservative academic and political advisor Chester Finn branded education reform efforts during the 1980s as meager at best. He described policy grounded in shallow thinking and research as an "epidemic of 'dumbth,'" labeling the system of education as "a very sick patient."[15] Jonathan Kozol, author of *Death at an Early Age* and a leader in the "free school" movement of the 1970s, continued his narrative of failing public education with his 1991 best-seller, *Savage Inequalities*. Using graphic imagery, he exposed the shocking conditions of public education in urban "death zones" across the United States. Children still suffered "death at an early age." In *Savage Inequalities* he wrote, "Looking around some of these inner-city schools, where filth and disrepair were worse than anything I'd seen in 1964, I often wondered why we would agree to let our children go to school in places where no politician, school board president, or business CEO would dream of working."[16]

In more ways than one, families of color felt the brunt of a failing public school system. By the 1990s, they had few places to turn for quality education. Communities of color were ready for alternatives.

Like many segregated neighborhoods across the country, the Harlem community served by Rev. Wyatt Tee Walker lived the awful realities of public school failure. In *Savage Inequalities*, describing abhorrent conditions in public schools, Kozol revealed that New York City schools received half of what the surrounding suburbs spent per pupil. The wealthiest districts in the state spent nearly three times more than schools in the city. Much like students in other cities Kozol investigated—East St. Louis, Chicago, Camden, and Washington, DC—students in New York suffered infested and dilapidated buildings, worn-out classrooms, unmanageable class sizes, and old textbooks, for starters, all comprising a defeated, morose atmosphere that deadened any real prospects of learning.[17]

P.S. 144 in Harlem was one of the poorest-rated schools in the city, with just 21.7 percent of students reading at or above grade level. Only 12.5 percent tested at grade level in math the year the school opened in 1999.[18] Valerie Banks sent her son to the school, noting, "When you're a poor person, public school is usually your only option."[19] And, as Wyatt Walker stated, "the public schools were not doing their jobs."[20] With the support of advocates like Walker who had strong links to a larger movement, parents like Banks demanded options. A flourishing school choice movement provided them.

Walker was not alone in connecting school choice to civil rights. White conservatives were part of a growing chorus of pro-choice advocates who took up the banner of civil rights across the nation in advance of Donald Trump, who called school choice the civil rights issue of today. Conservative groups including the Heritage Foundation, an influential think tank, and the Landmark Legal Foundation, a legal advocacy organization, adopted a civil rights platform in 1989. In it they articulated an agenda ostensibly promoting "'individual dignity and empowerment' for minorities, with an emphasis on lifting regulatory barriers that conservatives say prevent minorities from pursuing economic advancement."[21] A choice advocacy group, D.C. Parents for School Choice, which received funding from the Walton Family Foundation, assailed Senator Ted Kennedy for his opposition to vouchers. They compared him to arch-segregationist Bull Connor, who had unleashed police dogs on children marching with Dr. Martin Luther King Jr. and Wyatt Tee Walker in 1963.[22]

Other school choice advocacy groups interested in education reform sought to address the "achievement gap"—itself a construct based on racist discourse around intelligence and standardized tests—and other racial disparities in education as part of their overarching argument.[23] Clint Bolick gained prominence in Republican circles in the early 1990s as a cofounder of the Institute for Justice, the "nation's only libertarian public interest law firm," and quickly rose through the ranks as an ardent advocate of school choice. He then served as president of the Alliance for School Choice, symbolically founded on the fiftieth anniversary of the *Brown v. Board of Education* decision, in 2004, to emphasize the lingering "gaps" in education. As a lead litigator and defender of the voucher programs in Cleveland, Bolick successfully argued the landmark *Zelman v. Simmons-Harris* (2002) case, in which the Supreme Court upheld the use of publicly funded vouchers for private and religious schools. "We've tried everything," he stated on the anniversary of *Brown*, "except transferring power over basic educational decisions from bureaucrats to parents." In his words, choice offered "an educational life preserver to children who desperately need it." Bolick now serves in his highest position yet, sitting as an "activist" judge of the Arizona Supreme Court.[24]

School choice advocacy group American Alliance for Better Schools wanted to "promote equity by giving middle- and low-income families some choices of all schools—public, private, and religious—that wealthy families already enjoy."[25] The libertarian-influenced Citizens for Educational Freedom published a pamphlet in the early 1990s, *Tuition Tax Credits for Low-Income Families*, promoting its members' interest in providing more options to underserved communities.[26] School choice was indeed the new civil rights issue leading into the turn of the twenty-first century—and conservative Whites were some of its most ardent advocates.

Regardless of ideology, the deplorable conditions of public education disproportionately affected poor families and students of color. The reality of shameful conditions was difficult, if not unethical, to ignore. The promises made by choice advocates included a quality of education that had yet to be realized since the failed promises of the *Brown* decision and the civil rights movement. Not only that, some school choice advocates, like Wyatt Tee Walker and Howard Fuller, who were seasoned civil rights activists, successfully established deep rapport and trust with the communities they served. They inspired a large following that grew to include Black leaders such as TV talk show host Steve Perry, political commentator Roland Martin, Senator Cory Booker, and Representative Hakeem Jeffries. Support for charters even extended into the Black Lives Matter movement.[27] Such Black leaders legitimated school choice in ways that White corporate interests could not.

Thirty years after the *Brown* decision, the insidious history and politics of school choice made little difference to many who sought a better education for their children. Wisconsin state representative Polly Williams, a Black Democrat, worked with Howard Fuller in proposing school choice legislation to improve failing schools in Milwaukee through a controversial voucher program that built on the network of private and Catholic schools in the city. "If you're drowning and a hand is extended to you," she noted, "you don't ask if the hand is attached to a Democrat or a Republican. From the African American position—at the bottom, looking up—there's not much difference."[28] Howard Fuller noted, "I'm neither Democrat nor a Republican, and I don't believe in any of them. . . . I'm just out here and surviving and trying to help a community move forward."[29]

Times have changed since the civil rights movement. Activists grew weary of trying to attain desegregation—a remnant of the movement that was increasingly seen as outdated. The efforts to enforce it have been mired, and a narrative of failure generally describes the experiences of children of color in the public system. The fact that many Black children and other children of color do not do well in school today is used as evidence that desegregation does not work. One could also point out that desegregation has never really been achieved.

James Forman Jr.—a charter school cofounder and son of the Student Nonviolent Coordinating Committee organizer—noted that on the fiftieth anniversary of *Brown*, there were only 130 White students in the entire public middle school system in Washington, DC, out of nearly five thousand students. John Philip Sousa Middle School, which was part of the *Brown* decision in 1954, was fifty years later all-Black—with zero White students in attendance.[30] Sousa is part of a larger pattern. In the Northeast, the percentage of students in schools that were between 90 and 100 percent Black or Brown in 2004 had actually increased to nearly 50 percent, up from 40 percent in 1960. The North, in fact, was more segregated than the South, where only 26 percent of students attended schools that were 90–100 percent Black, Latinx, and other students of color in 1990. In the North, the "de facto segregation" defense meant that school integration never materialized in genuine ways, particularly after unpopular busing plans were rejected.[31]

The Supreme Court facilitated resegregation in the 1990s by rolling back school desegregation mandates from the 1950s and 1960s. It effectively ended judicial oversight of nearly all desegregation efforts. In 1991, the Supreme Court returned desegregation mandates to local control in *Board of Education of Oklahoma City Public Schools v. Dowell*. This meant that if local districts claimed that schools were desegregated and federal courts did not oppose them, a district could end desegregation mandates that had originated during the time of the civil rights movement. Any race-neutral or color-blind enrollment policy would be permissible, significantly restricting the ability of school districts to voluntarily redistrict or rezone to promote integration.[32] The Supreme Court in *Parents Involved in Community Schools v. Seattle School District* (2007) struck down voluntary desegregation plans that intentionally incorporated race. Drawing on a notion of de facto segregation and the idea that such segregation was caused by individual and private choice, not policy, Chief Justice John Roberts wrote, "The way to stop discrimination on the basis of race is to stop discriminating on the basis of race."[33] Not only did it become common practice to ignore racial diversity as a compelling interest, trying to legislate racial diversity could undermine the efforts to achieve it.[34]

Charter schools reflect how school choice perpetuates larger patterns of segregation in the public school system. The Civil Rights Project at UCLA reported in 2014, sixty years after the *Brown* decision, that nationally 70 percent of African American students in charter schools are attending "intensely segregated" minority charter schools that are 90–100 percent students of color, double the rate found in traditional public schools.[35] Another report from 2017 published federal data that revealed that 17 percent of charter schools were intensely segregated and had student populations that were 99 percent Black or Latinx. Only

4 percent of public schools reported such dramatic segregation. In cities that had charters, over 25 percent were intensely segregated, as compared to 10 percent of traditional public schools. As of the 2014–15 school year, more than one thousand of nearly sixty-five hundred charters across the nation were intensely segregated.[36] A few schools were founded with the specific intent of fostering an integrated student population, but most charter schools did not seek to establish integrated enrollment.

Let off by Supreme Court decisions and bolstered by a collective, national movement away from desegregation, U.S. schools remain segregated, and, by extension, so do charter schools. This is compounded by the fact that many people of color support school choice and charter schools. There is also the ideology of reform that fails to question segregation. As Nikole Hannah-Jones, the Pulitzer Prize–winning journalist and MacArthur Fellow, points out, "The logic around the achievement gap, the entire logic of every conversation we have about education[,] . . . is a logic of how do we take all these separate schools in which by and large white children and black children go to separate schools, how do we make those separate schools equal?" In other words, the "separate but equal logic" or "the conceptual bedrock of segregation and Jim Crow" undergirds reform today.[37]

To many charter school advocates of color, the documented segregation of charter schools does not matter and continues to remain a nonissue. In fact, the contemporary debate is nothing new to the Black community. As early as 1935, NAACP cofounder and civil rights warrior W. E. B. Du Bois publicly questioned the logic of desegregation, noting that "race prejudice in the United States today is such that most Negroes cannot receive proper education in white institutions." He went on to note, "The plain fact faces us, that either he will have separate schools or he will not be educated."[38] Howard Fuller agreed, stating in the midst of the Milwaukee choice movement, "It's a waste of time to talk about integration." Instead, Fuller has advocated choice as an answer to a question that supersedes integration: "How do these kids get the best education possible?"[39] Cardell Orrin, a member of the board that governs Freedom Preparatory Academy in Memphis, called into question the merits of the debate, arguing that criticisms of charter schools perpetuating segregation were unfair. Memphis had remained segregated after *Brown*. The outlying suburban districts had pulled away and seceded from the city, essentially creating a new district. Charters were simply trying to work with what was given to city students.[40] Much of what Du Bois prophesized has remained true well into the twenty-first century.

James Forman Jr. was right to note that desegregation attempts were all but over. With desegregation blocked by the courts and with waning support for desegregation plans across the country, there is no longer a compelling or critical interest to advocate for it. If all else has failed in the eyes of parents, charter schools and school choice present a logical means to regain control of their children's education and future. But the connection between school choice and the civil rights movement was not ephemeral. It was led by Black organizers like Howard Fuller who facilitated the transformation of school choice into a civil right.

Howard Fuller's narrative is part of a larger national story of education activism that strove toward justice, liberation, and community control. In 1969, he put into practice the ethos of the civil rights movement, establishing "an independent Black university that would be controlled totally by us," Malcolm X Liberation University in North Carolina.[41] The same concept of community control was germane to the idea of school choice but for a radically different purpose. For Fuller, school choice meant turning around failing schools and steering them toward the best interests of the Black community.

After Malcolm X University closed in 1973 due to fund-raising difficulty, Fuller also grew frustrated with union politics in his work in the Revolutionary Workers League, a Black Marxist group. He packed his bags and returned to Milwaukee in 1976.[42] There he would transform the city's school system and put forth the question—and puzzle—of Black school choice.

Fuller began working for the Educational Opportunity Program at Marquette University, and through this he became involved in the politics of his alma mater, North Division High School. North Division had become embroiled in school desegregation politics after Fuller left Wisconsin. In 1976, federal judge John Reynolds found the Milwaukee schools to be segregated and issued a ruling to integrate. Wishing to avoid "another Boston," district officials in Milwaukee used busing but emphasized a "voluntary choice" program. As part of the city's plan to voluntarily desegregate, the district implemented an open enrollment policy that eliminated traditional attendance zones and created a magnet school at North Division High as a way to attract White students to the Black neighborhood. This meant local African American students had to apply to attend the school that had replaced their old one, and their applications were likely to be denied. Students walked out, and alumni, including Howard Fuller, supported them.[43]

Fuller was an ideal organizer for the embattled, segregated school system in Milwaukee. In 1979, he led the "Coalition to Save North Division"—composed of alumni, students, families of students, and other advocates—to present an alternative to the school board's magnet school catering to White families. The coalition proposed a neighborhood school that was majority-Black and offered a specialized curriculum including vocational training in medical, health, and science.[44] The coalition drew support from and worked with the city's established civil rights organizations, including the Urban League and the NAACP. Together they filed suit with the US Office for Civil Rights, and in 1980, after a year of legal wrangling and intense local dissension they pressured the district to reverse its decision to convert North Division into a magnet school. North Division would remain a neighborhood school.[45]

The coalition and its allies were not against integration, but they sought desegregation (or, as historian Jack Dougherty put it, "fair integration") that led to marked improvement for Black communities. Fair integration relied on community engagement in decision-making and increased local economic opportunity in the Black community.[46] The coalition valued the ideals behind genuinely integrated schools but not at the expense of Black empowerment and self-determination. Black communities, they argued, should no longer shoulder the burden of desegregation. It was an idea that was germane to a growing sentiment in civil rights legal theory.

In 1980, during the midst of desegregation battles, Milwaukee hosted a conference on the topic: "Desegregation: A New Form of Discrimination." Derrick Bell, a leading civil rights scholar and lawyer, once a champion of school desegregation, provided a keynote address.

By the time of the conference, he had grown weary of school reform after the *Brown* decision. Bell publicly criticized education reform plans that maintained rigid commitment to racial "balance," which had the consequence of closing Black schools. Such plans were committed to abstract principles of "integration" over the tangible improvement of Black education. He also advocated for the effective education of students within all-Black schools, shifting focus from racial balance to improving learning. Desegregation was not producing the results desired by civil rights activists and the NAACP of the 1950s and 1960s, both of which Bell was personally and professionally acquainted with.[47]

Bell's ideas resonated with Fuller and families in Milwaukee who were ready for alternatives to subpar public schools. Fuller was proposing stronger community control of the schools—the same idea that shaped his influential work with Malcolm X Liberation University in North Carolina. In the context of fighting racist school board policy in Milwaukee, the idea remained radical.

Legal scholar and parent of color Robin D. Barnes captured the sentiment behind initiatives that—like those proposed by Fuller and others by the 1990s—connected a desire for control to the very essence of charter schools. She asserted that "out of all the public choice initiatives, charters provide the only viable means of local control" and further that choice could be "an effective arm of communities in transition as Black America faces a twenty-first century that looks all too similar to the nineteenth."[48] Since the 1960s, after the first attempts at desegregation generally failed, local control by African American communities has remained an integral goal of the Black school choice movement as exemplified by Howard Fuller and the growing army of advocates who have joined him.

The organizing in Milwaukee invigorated Fuller. As he noted, "The coalition victory brought back many good memories of my community organizing days in North Carolina, and reminded me of what can happen when people stand together to demand change and stick with it."[49] The coalition drew momentum from the student protest, building on a network of activism established during the city's long civil rights struggle. By the late 1980s, though, Fuller was growing increasingly disillusioned with the pace and rhetoric of school reform. In 1987, he and Michael Smith, a professor and education advocate in Milwaukee, drafted the "Manifesto for New Directions in the Education of Black Children." In it, they proposed a separate, nearly all-Black school district carved out from the public school district in Milwaukee. The modest-sized district of one high school, two middle schools, and seven elementary schools would serve nearly 6,500 students, and the district was to be controlled by Black community members and educators and geared toward students of color.[50] Polly Williams, a Democrat representing an all-Black district in Milwaukee and an alum of North Division High, submitted the plan to the state legislature. It mirrored the local control politics practiced twenty years earlier during the freedom struggle in which Fuller had taken part. And the plan gained traction. Derrick Bell wrote about the movement in Milwaukee, lending his support for creating racially segregated schools to improve education for Black students. Bell also connected the legislative proposal to the longer struggle for Black education: "The Milwaukee manifesto is simply the next logical step in the continuing effort by Black people to obtain effective schooling for their children."[51] In many ways, it was a relief from desegregation, which had been a heavy load on the backs and shoulders of Black communities. Bell found in the bold proposal "a legislative remedy . . . that [might], after a long struggle, enable them to do what can be achieved independently by those of a higher economic status."[52] Bell argued that such legislation could facilitate the placement and support of African Americans in positions of power over the schools and districts their children attended.[53]

The proposal immediately sparked controversy that exposed deep schisms. The Milwaukee branch of the NAACP condemned the plan, castigating it as "urban apartheid," unconstitutional, and a "giant step backward for Black people." One of the highest-ranking Black representatives in the Wisconsin legislature, state senator Gary George, opposed the plan, joining ranks with Black state representative Marcia Coggs. Walter Farrell, a popular Black professor at the University of Wisconsin-Milwaukee and president of the Milwaukee Afro-American Council, also spoke out against the plan. Farrell called it "ridiculous" and claimed it ran contrary to the essence of the *Brown* decision. Milwaukee city attorney Grant Langley issued an opinion that challenged the constitutionality of the proposal. Liberal Whites who supported the deseg-regation plans already in place also joined the chorus of opposition.[54]

To the charge that the plan perpetuated segregation, Fuller replied cynically: "There is no way that things could be worse."[55] Bell argued that the plan did not abandon the ideals of integration—it simply em-powered people of color long wronged by the system "by first putting administrators and faculty in place who are both accountable to the community and dedicated to improving the quality of schools now serv-ing Black children."[56] All could admit—and plainly see—that current administrators and faculty had largely failed to serve these children, as had teachers and administrators ever since the *Brown* decision.

Advocates for the plan included not just Polly Williams but also Black state representative G. Spencer Coggs, three Black Milwaukee aldermen, and one of the city's Black newspapers.[57] To the astonishment of many, the bill for a separate district passed the state assembly with a commanding majority, but it failed in the state senate.[58]

Though it failed to pass, the proposal highlighted a new direction in education. It also called attention to new leadership distinct from the civil rights movement era. For those behind the initiative, it was a movement intended to empower the Black community to educate their children themselves. The advocates were Black, determined, and in-formed by the insights of history and experience of how best to educate their children. As Polly Williams noted, "We have a new movement of Black people emerging. . . . This is not the 1960s."[59] The controversy they inspired and the political agency of choice advocates empowered by Fuller's grassroots organization set the stage for a national policy debate about publicly funded private voucher programs. The school voucher plan that emerged from Milwaukee would helped build mo-mentum for the *Zelman* case.[60]

The initial proposals for vouchers in Wisconsin—public money al-lotted for individuals to use for private schools— gained the support of Republican governor Tommy Thompson. After compromises that followed, Thompson signed the Milwaukee Parental Choice Program into law in 1990.[61] Polly Williams supported Thompson's new initia-tive, stating clearly and passionately: "The best educational program for children is the voucher program."[62] Howard Fuller signed off on it as well, noting that "choice can be the savior of public education."[63] Milwaukee showed how the Black freedom struggle shaped the very essence of privatization.

After Milwaukee, Memphis became another battleground for school choice in a beleaguered Black public school system. Based on analysis of national educational statistics, the US Chamber of Commerce gave the state of Tennessee an F for its dismal school assessments and public education accountability system. The chamber's 2010 "report card" found that 105 Memphis schools—nearly half the schools in the city—had failed to meet federal academic standards. Following such scathing reports, the state relied on authorizing charters to improve education and also catered to and relied on private philanthropic funding, including a $90 million grant from the Bill and Melinda Gates Foundation to improve teaching. State legislators also passed a "First to the Top" law that granted the state authority to take over the lowest-performing schools in Tennessee to turn them around. Under the watchful eye of President Obama's new education secretary, Arne Duncan, the state became a blank slate for new school reform through "turnaround districts." In 2010, Tennessee became one of the first states to be awarded a "Race to the Top" federal grant of $500 million.[64]

Reform in Tennessee had all the hallmarks of the new era of choice ushered in under President Obama. As part of the Race to the Top initiative, the state created an "Achievement School District" comprising the bottom 5 percent of failing schools in the state, the majority of which were in Memphis. The goal was to take those schools and raise them to the top 25 percent in just five years. Thirty-one schools comprised the Achievement School District, serving over eleven thousand students, over 90 percent of whom were Black, or just over 10 percent of the city's student population.[65] The Achievement School District drew on the competitive logic of school choice. The state could take over failing schools and hand them over to charter school operators who, in turn, promised to turn the schools around.

The state was open to choice advocates, charter school operators, and philanthropists. *Everyone* was welcome. According to Stephine Love, a school board member in Memphis, it was the "Wild, Wild West."[66] The state hired Chris Barbic of Houston to serve as superintendent of the Achievement School District. Barbic was the founder of Yes Prep Public Schools, a charter conglomerate across the Houston metro area that served over four thousand students. A former Teach for America educator, Barbic received $1 million from Oprah Winfrey in 2010 as part of her philanthropic efforts in education. Charter management companies from across the nation submitted applications to run schools in Memphis.[67] Other options were on the table as well, including the faith-based Cornerstone Preparatory School at Christ United Methodist Church in Memphis. The executive director of Cornerstone, Drew Sippel, had learned about school administration by attending a six-week crash course on the topic in Boston. Though Cornerstone was openly religious, it operated as a public school.[68]

Charter school and public school officials alike called for grassroots support. Barbic noted to a roomful of parents, organizers, and activists, "I see what we are doing as community transformation work. . . . We see this as a collaboration, not a takeover."[69] Kriner Cash, the superintendent of Memphis City Schools, had publicly opined in 2010 that the times were "like the civil rights movement of the 1960s." "Communities across our state must step up," Cash had added. "We need grassroots advocates from the classroom to the board room."[70]

Once the new district was in operation, education reformers embraced the rhetoric, names, and ideals of the civil rights movement. One school in the district was named after civil rights leader Maxine Smith. The Soulsville Foundation, dedicated to promoting the legacy of the city's famous Stax Records, organized the Soulsville Charter School as a college preparatory school featuring an "academically rich, music-rich environment."[71] Other charter schools in the district included the Martin Luther King Jr. College Preparatory High School and Freedom Preparatory Academy.[72] Connections to the civil rights movement were made through curricula as well. One district-sponsored event took a handful of Memphis students to Birmingham, Alabama, to study the role of young activists in the historic struggles there.[73]

Beneath the thin veneer of civil rights rhetoric and nomenclature, Memphis has a rich history of resistance to slavery and segregation. It has been home to critical junctures of the Underground Railroad, the activist journalism of Ida B. Wells, and sit-ins and Black Power struggles of the civil rights movement. And the city was the site of Martin Luther King Jr.'s assassination in 1968.[74]

The grassroots organization behind charter schools was compelling to parents who had experienced or at least bought into the narrative of public school failure. The process of restructuring schools through a choice model created possibilities for people in Memphis to work for the children of the city, through "single-site," mom-and-pop charter schools. As opposed to charters organized by corporations, these schools were organized and governed by local activists and advocates. Unlike the big charter networks like KIPP, the Memphis model allowed the community to organize schools tailored specifically to the needs of their children and in turn generate buy-in from the community. Stax Records, as noted, built on its legacy to offer a unique charter school specific to the historic city.[75] Black Memphian Dr. Bobby White, a proud alumnus of Memphis public schools, founded Martin Luther King Jr. College Preparatory High School in 2014. He was different from the first school reformers like Chris Barbic who had entered the scene after the Race to the Top grant was announced. White was from the city—he'd graduated with pride from Frayser High School and the city's historically Black college, LeMoyne-Owen. After working in the Tennessee Charter School Resource Center—a support center for charters in the state—he later founded Frayser Community Schools, a three-school charter school network that includes MLK Prep. White took great pains to speak with the community as he planned the school.[76]

The single-site charters in Memphis are part of a larger national network. The National Charter Collaborative, a nonprofit with a mission to support and connect charter school leaders of color, has identified more than five hundred single-site schools around the country in which people of color lead the school's administration and make up at least 30 percent of the board. Representing nearly one-quarter of all charter schools, these schools serve over 335,000 students.[77]

Working for the Shelby County School District in Memphis, La-Tricea Adams gained perspective overseeing charters through community organization. Looking at schools like Granville T. Woods Academy, Memphis Business Academy, and Freedom Preparatory Academy, Adams emphasized, "It's empowering to see grassroots organization in action and inspirational to see them."[78] In some respects, these Memphians were carrying forth the work of Howard Fuller and realizing some promises for quality education that the longer civil rights movement had yet to fulfill. Local Black advocates were in control of schools in their community—at least in some instances.

Single-site charters have also opened other avenues of empowerment. Cardill Orrin, the Memphis-based executive director of Stand for Children in Tennessee—a choice advocacy group—spoke about the economic empowerment that can come through school choice. Some schools in Memphis—such as Freedom Preparatory Academy, MLK Preparatory, and Granville T. Woods—were founded and managed by people of color, and some have annual budgets of $20 million or more.[79] As Orrin noted, charter networks can stipulate the contracting of Black-owned businesses—from information technology to landscaping—to serve schools governed by Black communities. Memphis charter school founder Roblin Webb noted that charters can help "lift and change" Black business to compete for bids and to provide business.[80] The economic opportunity is enticing. Few other fields, even in majority-minority cities like Memphis, so effectively support Black-owned businesses or Black wealth.

Still, school choice is fiercely contested in the broader Black community nationwide. As in the past, the NAACP remains a central part of the debate. The organization again stirred controversy when it issued a call for a moratorium on charters at its 107th national convention in 2016. The call followed the organization's historic resistance to charters. Nearly twenty years earlier, in 1998, the NAACP had opposed charter schools that were "not subject to the same accountability and standardization of qualifications/certification of teachers as public schools and divert already-limited funds from public schools." In 2014, the NAACP issued a report, *School Privatization: Threat to Public Education*, that staunchly opposed the privatization of public education and the use of public funds to subsidize charter schools.[81] Derrick Johnson, then president of the NAACP, situated the moratorium along with ten thousand lawsuits initiated by the association in the interests of improving the quality of public education.[82] As noted in the moratorium statement, "It is a concern that charter schools have had a larger influence on the national conversation about how to improve education in communities of color than these other well-researched educational investments."[83]

The statement was met with swift protest, and Memphis became a focal point for the ensuing melee. Protests organized there by charter supporters shaped the national debate. Members of Memphis Lift, a pro–charter school organization, drove to Cincinnati to disrupt an NAACP meeting there after the NAACP announced the moratorium. Police responded and threatened to arrest the group.[84] Sarah Carpenter, a Black founding member of Memphis Lift, mother of three, and grandmother of thirteen, stated, "We are not against public schools. We want good schools of any type. Where was the NAACP when so many public schools were failing our children?"[85] Rev. Keith Norman, president of the Memphis branch of the NAACP, praised the group.[86]

The following year, the NAACP softened its language around charters but did not retract the call for a moratorium. Its narrowed opposition focused only on for-profit charter schools. National NAACP leaders demanded more stringent requirements for charter school authorizers, whom they wanted to limit to local school districts. They also demanded that districts impose on charters the same accountability measures in place for public schools.[87]

Memphis Lift was founded during the rapid growth of charters in the city and it had the strong support of Chris Barbic during the Achievement School District's first administration. The group gained distinction through the NAACP protest in Cincinnati, and it also sent representatives to lobby for choice at the state and federal levels in Nashville and Washington, DC. After the NAACP revised its moratorium, Carpenter noted, "I'm happy about it but I also think they should call for a moratorium on bad schools, period."[88] Even though connected to a pro-charter agenda, the group maintained a critical position on all schools. Moreover, it was a group that spoke to issues of self-determination. "We're starting a movement to demand better," Carpenter said. "We believe that the people from our community should lead this movement. This movement should be for parents, by parents."[89] Carpenter continues to push the group forward. During the buildup to the 2020 presidential election, she and Memphis Lift continued to protest anti–charter school stances taken by the Democratic candidates, notably disrupting a speech by Elizabeth Warren.[90]

Likening herself to Harriet Tubman and a modern-day Rosa Parks, Carpenter continues to advocate for choice, work that she places on the same arc toward justice represented by the nation's ongoing civil rights movement. The stance becomes complicated when her advocacy overlaps with the rhetoric of Donald Trump and Betsy Devos, who promote school choice and call it the civil rights issue of our time. On the campaign trail in 2016, Donald Trump regularly vowed to "fight to make sure every single African American child in this country is fully included in the American dream." For Trump, school choice was "the new civil rights issue of our time." Secretary of Education DeVos, the controversial advocate of religious school vouchers, supported choice by similarly invoking civil rights ideology. DeVos claimed that historically Black colleges and universities demonstrated how choice benefited African Americans. Trump and DeVos connected school choice to race again in commenting on the rebellion that followed the death of George Floyd at the hands of Minneapolis police in 2020.[91]

School choice remains a rare issue that inspires bipartisan support. Democratic US senator Cory Booker recalled his work as mayor of Newark, New Jersey, saying, "[I] had a Republican governor, [and] I could write a dissertation on [our] disagreements, but he and I found common ground to help transform Newark schools, to actually create a contract that got our teachers union and [the] governor sitting around a table and agreeing to raise teachers' salaries."[92]

Anchoring the public rhetoric that unites both sides of the aisle and traverses racial divides is the common belief in a fundamental right to choice in education. When Keith Norman expressed skepticism about how public funds were expended on charters, he conceded "that does not negate a parent's right to choose."[93] Shelby County School Board member Stephanie Love, parent and graduate of the Memphis public school system, noted, "My position is that I'm advocating to provide the best education for our children, and I can't tell a parent to not exercise their right to choice . . . what I can say is 'make sure you know what that choice means.'"[94] The claim that choice is a fundamental right is not uniquely Black, however. It's the same rhetoric as conservative-branded education reformers such as Chester Finn, who claimed, "We *all* have the right to meddle here, to turn ourselves into informed, demanding, persnickety consumers" of education.[95] As illustrated in numerous iterations since Milton Friedman's first articulation of choice in the 1950s, all were equal in the marketplace of school reform. Finn believed that the "revolution" began with conceptualizing the system for the "benefit of consumers" and that such consumers must "have the right to choose how they will do this."[96] By ignoring deeper structural issues and the persistence of segregation, the rhetoric of choice is appealing to many indeed.[97] The field remains open—and the debate often rancorous.

The whirlwinds at the intersection of race and school continue to churn. After the flash of reform, the thunderclap that followed reverberated across the nation. This was most evident in New Orleans after Hurricane Katrina. Prior to the 2005 storm, the public school system there was racially segregated. In a city that was 67 percent African American, over 90 percent of students enrolled in New Orleans public schools were Black, and 77 percent were eligible for free or reduced-cost lunch.[98] Conservative reformers viewed the disaster as an opportunity to rebuild and, in the process, implement changes that benefited them. In 2017, the US Congress created "Opportunity Zones" as part of tax code revision that contravened the Clean Air Act, increased oil drilling and production, and gave tax incentives to investors. Education was a part of it. Plans included enhancing school choice and encouraging "investment and entrepreneurs" and "private-sector creativity . . . in which capital gains tax on investments is eliminated and regulations eliminated or simplified."[99] When Congress created such zones, they enacted one of the greatest experiments on students of color initiated by a partnership between private industries and the federal government by opening the door to widespread charter schools and a new teaching force under the auspices of choice. It was a dream unrealized even by the bold Howard Fuller.

Opportunity Zones decimated public schools in New Orleans. Local administrators and Louisiana legislators worked with the support of conservative think tanks and Congress to carry out the new policies with far-reaching and devasting impact. In 2005 state legislators passed Act 35, which transferred authority for all failing public schools to the state-run district, the Recovery School District, which legislators also expanded after the storm to manage all schools that they determined were "failing." Expanding the criteria for failure, state legislators authorized themselves to take over 112 of 128 schools in the district. Elected representatives used federal funding to build charter schools and recruited teachers from outside the district using federal funding originally earmarked to pay teachers and staff who were out of work—a move that cut out the local union, the United Teachers of New Orleans. Louisiana legislators later passed a bill that fired all New Orleans public school teachers and staff without pay—approximately 7,500 in total, including approximately 4,300 teachers—claiming the district no longer had funds for schools after the state created the Recovery School District. Fourteen years after the storm, New Orleans became the first sizable city in the United States to turn its public schools entirely to charters, earning the moniker "Charter School City."[100]

Howard Fuller entered the fray as well, reminding the nation that school choice without empowerment mattered little. He noted that New Orleans was wholly unique in that school choice governed the entire district—an ideal scenario for launching a choice program—and that there was unprecedented investment in the city. Still, Fuller was concerned with what he saw as a prevailing notion among people of color that "reform was done to me and not with me." As Fuller elaborated, "I want to imagine a world where parents are sought after to serve on charter school boards and other decision-making bodies; whose perspectives are valued enough to produce policy recommendations . . . ; where they have the collective power to hold these districts accountable. These are the actions that will sustain education reform."[101] As part of his work empowering communities of color, he helped found Black Education for New Orleans, which assists families of color in choosing their best school options and staying informed about the decisions most affecting them.[102]

The entire nation's system of education was caught up in Katrina's deadly wake. New Orleans was the new experimental site for all sides to study, examine, and stake claims. Charter School City demonstrated to the rest of the nation the potential—and risks—of school choice on a grand scale. As organizer and educator Raynard Sanders noted, "Black and Brown families and children have, once again, been left out in this new equation, and those in most severe need are least likely to receive quality education."[103]

Howard Fuller stands tall and jovial above his students in the single-site charter in Milwaukee that now bears his name, the Dr. Howard Fuller Collegiate Academy. "There are so many issues [when it comes to educating] poor Black children," he sighed in an interview, yet another conversation for a battered veteran to clarify his stance—one that remains perplexing to White progressives. "I only have so much time, and I'm worried about my school, that these three-hundred-plus kids get the best education possible."[104] Fuller is forced to constantly fend off allegations of working with the worst of the worst. In one interview, exasperated, Fuller said, "[If you are] saying I'm trying to help Donald Trump, you're insane. I'm not the person that you ought to be talking to." Instead, he pushes the blame on those who take choice away: "Tell Elizabeth Warren and Bernie Sanders or any of these other people, tell them to quit attacking us."[105] To Fuller, standing against choice—which many see as not only a solution to failing schools but also as the path to a long-promised opportunity at self-determination—is a violation of a fundamental right.

Civil rights organizers like Howard Fuller, Wyatt Tee Walker, and more recently Sarah Carpenter illustrate a direct link between the civil rights movement and school choice, an intersection that makes or could make many liberal reformers uneasy. The rhetoric too closely aligned with the unscrupulous privatization agenda and zealous ethos of Donald Trump and Betsy DeVos.

Yet Howard Fuller's work illustrates how the term "school choice" is mostly rhetorical and without clear political alliance. Black support for school choice shows how choice is connected to more than one agenda. As Howard Fuller noted to me: "'Freedom of choice,' 'integration' . . . all of these terms have different meaning dependent upon who's using it and the context . . . and so concepts or terms like 'choice' [are] sort of neutral in a certain sense. But it's all in how people use them and for what purposes. And what [is] clear is that . . . two people who have diametrically different ideas for what they're doing can use the same terms to define it."[106]

For many Black choice advocates, other people of color, and their allies, choice represents community control, autonomy, and the best means given the reality of public education in the twenty-first century. Though articulated in a wildly different context—post-*Brown*, post-MLK, and "post-racial"—such arguments support the essence of W. E. B. Du Bois's assertion that Black education is best left in the hands of Black educators.

This is a far cry from the maligned agendas of Donald Trump and billionaire education reformers, however. Trump and Betsy DeVos never had to rely on the public schools in this country and do not inherit the same history as Howard Fuller, yet they still refer to school choice as the pressing civil rights issue of our time. The paradox behind a simple or narrow definition of "choice" obfuscates the complexity of the term and how it has failed to meet the ideals of those who need it the most.

CHAPTER SEVEN

The Sinking Ship of Public Education and the Failure of Choice

MILTON FRIEDMAN HAS WON, even beyond the economic theory that earned him a Nobel Prize. His greatest legacy is advancing school choice and inspiring one of the most comprehensive reform movements in educational history. For the last ten years of his life, he and his wife, Rose, committed themselves to privatization and school choice. As he noted in their joint autobiography, "Rose and I feel so strongly about the importance of privatizing the school system that we have established the Milton and Rose D. Friedman Foundation with the sole mission of promoting public understanding and support of the measures necessary to achieve that objective."[1] With their foundation—now called EdChoice—the Friedmans worked to steer the school choice movement into the safe harbor we know today. As the conservative pundit Cal Thomas opined after Friedman's passing in 2006, "If school choice becomes the norm in America, it will be Milton Friedman's real legacy and every poor child who is liberated from a failed government school will owe him a lasting debt of gratitude."[2] The choice movement is forever indebted to its savior.

Friedman's ideas have eclipsed and surpassed in popularity the desegregation movement that defined the era of his first foray into school reform politics in the 1950s. Yet his ideas remain supported by an unchanging systemic racism that undercuts the righteous demands of advocates connected to a longer struggle like Howard Fuller and Sarah Carpenter. A structurally racist system will never give real power to historically marginalized communities and, therefore, a fair chance at success.

Millions of families of color, as well as poor Whites, stand to lose, as they truly have no choice but to enroll their children in underfunded, segregated schools—public, private, or charter. Choice has provided a safety net for some, but the majority are in peril. Dave Dennis, a civil rights activist who led CORE in Mississippi during the 1960s, mobilizes communities to demand quality education as a constitutional right today. He employs the apt analogy that school choice provides a life raft for the few who can escape the sinking ship of public education. The remaining families—majority-Black, -Brown, and poor—are left on the ship as the nation watches, critiques, and largely refuses to extend a helping hand.

The theoretical edifice of school choice crumbles under the crushing weight of racism in the United States. Race is the key to understanding how school choice has failed to deliver its promises in any equitable way. The forces of racism, which Friedman relegated to a footnote in his seminal essay, now dominate the implementation of school choice. Choice is essentially all about race. Historically, all of American public education has been shaped by race. In the antebellum era, since education for slaves was explicitly forbidden, Whites excluded Africans and African Americans at the advent of public education during the mid-nineteenth century.[3] After the Civil War, education was racially segregated by law in the South through the 1950s. The tumultuous period of desegregation from the 1950s to the 1980s then shaped education policy, affecting the experiences of millions of students since then. If choice works according to Friedman's economic theory, then race is not supposed to motivate decision-making. Yet it does. It also illustrates the toxicity of the very culture around choice.

W. E. B. Du Bois's argument from 1935—that our society does not permit the genuine integration necessary for a democratic education of all students, particularly Black students—remains painfully true. His observation that "race prejudice in the United States today is such that most Negroes cannot receive proper education in White institutions" is still experienced daily. Such institutional racism precludes what DuBois called "that sort of public education which will create the intelligent basis of a real democracy."[4]

The strict economic argument for choice is that competition, the market, and the "invisible hand" will improve schools, but one cannot assume that corporate interests seek to empower Black communities, communities of color, and people living in poverty. If society cannot integrate its schools, it cannot integrate the very institutions of capitalism founded on the backs of enslaved people and their descendants. Nor will the individual advocates and captains of industry willingly share decision-making power and wealth generated by that same system. A few families of color or families in poverty may benefit, to be sure. However, the masses of those dependent on public education will not be integrated into the for-profit governing system.

Reports on resegregation in choice districts and schools illustrate the depths to which the system remains controlled by wealth and White supremacy. In essence, BIPOC families and families living in poverty remain segregated and excluded from the genuine privileges and benefits that choice is supposed to provide. In New York City, over 13 percent of the student population is enrolled in a charter school. Of this number over 90 percent are Black or Latinx students as compared to their being 68 percent of the total public school population. Washington, DC—one of the first cities ordered to desegregate after the *Brown* decision—enrolls nearly 50 percent of its total student population in a charter school. At the same time, 70 percent of students of color attend segregated schools in which 90 to 100 percent of the student body is Black or Latinx. Chicago, the ideological birthplace of school choice, shows similar trends. Studies have reported that only 20 percent of traditional public schools and only 7 percent of charter schools are racially diverse.[5] As education scholars Erica Frankenberg, Gary Orfield, and other researchers at the Civil Rights Project at UCLA concluded, "Charter schools are more racially isolated than traditional public schools in virtually every state and large metropolitan area in the nation."[6]

There are situations where choice has in fact reversed desegregation trends. Duke University researchers found that North Carolina, after rolling back the busing mandate and implementing choice in the early 2000s, showed signs of White flight and resegregation. After fifteen years of choice, public schools became nearly 15 percent less White while the state's charter enrollment grew to over 62 percent White.[7] In Indianapolis, a city that embraced choice under Mike Pence's 2013–17 tenure as Indiana governor, 80 percent of the student population is Black or Latinx, yet magnet schools there are over 80 percent White.[8] In cases such as these, when choice is available, it is largely driven by the interests of White parents, not by Black demand. As Nikole Hannah-Jones noted, "White communities want neighborhood schools if their neighborhood school is White. . . . If their neighborhood school is Black, they want choice."[9]

The inherent racism of the system is apparent in cases where choice has been leveraged as a way to improve public education, like in Memphis. Federal education officials and choice advocates alike viewed the city as a model site for reform. The ambitious plans to turn around schools in the Achievement School District there entailed many of the factors that attracted parents to choice—not just the right to choose a school but also new management, innovative ideas, and a promise of quick, transformative change.

Whites, however, wanted nothing to do with it. In 2014, not even five years after Tennessee launched its ambitious takeover through choice policies—with hefty federal support under President Obama as well as investment from philanthropists like Bill and Melinda Gates—six outlying suburban towns seceded from the Memphis school district. With assistance from the state legislature, the suburban districts had begun to talk of secession at the same moment that the state merged the city school district with the surrounding suburbs. They seceded one year later.[10] The move was clearly driven by race and class. The city district served a population that was overwhelmingly Black—over 90 percent of the students were people of color. Nearly one-third of families served by the city district lived below the poverty line, compared to only 11 percent of the areas that seceded. Segregation persisted, and economic fissures deepened. Memphis schools were forced to cut their budgets—a reported $90 million the first year after secession—as they lost tax revenue from the districts that seceded. They were also pressured to close dozens of schools, and they laid off or pushed out more than five hundred teachers. At the same time, one of the new suburban districts, Collierville, began charging tuition to families from outside the attendance zones to maintain a "neighborhood school." The same district also approved $95 million in bonds to fund a new high school and athletic facilities.[11]

Just as it had at the height of desegregation and the civil rights movement, secession occurred across Dixie. The most glaring example occurred in 2010 in Jefferson County, Alabama, where one town, Gardendale City, proposed to separate itself from the majority-Black district. A group of suburban parents organized to achieve this aim. They called themselves FOCUS (Future of Our Community Utilizing Schools). Incidentally, it was the same acronym used in Mississippi over forty years earlier for Freedom of Choice in the United States—the segregationist, pro–school choice group founded in Jackson.[12] In both cases, parents for secession used coded race-neutral language to stoke fear. Addressing a small crowd, David Salters, one of the founders of FOCUS, said, "It likely will not turn out well for Gardendale if we don't do this. We don't want to become what [Center Point] has."[13] The reference was clear. Center Point, a formerly all-White town outside Birmingham, Alabama, had become majority-Black after desegregation occurred in the 1970s. The federal courts denied the city's motion to secede.[14]

Dating from 2000, 128 communities across the country have attempted to secede from their public school districts. Of these attempts, 73 have been successful, 27—including the case in Gardendale—have been defeated, 17 are ongoing, and 11 have become inactive.[15] Though small in number, such attempts indicate dissatisfaction with education reform and also validate Du Bois's assertion from a century ago: the system does not provide the equity and support needed for Black children and other children of color. The wave of attempts to secede from majority-Black and -Latinx school districts merely reifies the sanctity of the "suburban veto."[16]

Some Black advocates like Howard Fuller have continued to argue that persistent segregation does not matter or it does not matter enough to shape educational reform initiatives—that it merely conforms to a racist, unchanging history. Yet, to many, integration is important. We know that integration promotes Black achievement, particularly if it is consciously incorporated into education policy. Despite fierce resistance to it, desegregation after the 1954 *Brown* decision cut the "achievement gap" by half across the nation, boosting the test scores of millions of students. Particularly when placed in a wider historical context that measures scores over time and through an intergenerational perspective, integration and the federal policies supporting it were effective in improving education for *all* students.[17]

The problem of race and school choice is confounded by the assertation that we are not supposed to see color. Our Constitution, we are told, is color-blind. As Justice John Harlan expressed in dissent to the *Plessy v. Ferguson* decision in 1896 that is often praised: "Our constitution is color-blind, and neither knows nor tolerates classes among citizens. In respect of civil rights, all citizens are equal before the law." This color-blind lens continues to filter the way we see education policy. Particularly after the election of President Barack Obama, many Americans subscribed to the notion that race no longer determined educational destiny or the access children have to good schools—and that race should not determine one's destiny. The latter idea was enshrined in the *Brown v. Board of Education* decision. According to prevailing legal and popular opinion, to not see color is the ultimate goal, and by the turn of the twenty-first century, the courts had determined that we were there.

A color-blind ideology drives racism deeper below the surface of a society that wants a quick fix to broken schools. Color-blindness allows school choice to function in menacing ways that mask the persistence of historic racial inequality. Choice gives all Americans the rhetoric to safely distance themselves from racist policy even as they support it. White families use race-neutral rhetoric to defend their avoidance of all-Black schools—much like Whites in the 1960s who claimed a right to choose and avoided discussions of racial segregation. They point to failing test scores, the "achievement gap," or the lack of foreign language and college preparatory courses. On the surface, race is not a factor.

Color-blind ideology and the craving for quantifiable data muddy some of the more comprehensive findings about school choice. Take, for instance, the 2013 and 2015 studies published by the Center for Research on Education Outcomes (CREDO) at Stanford University. All sides of the choice debate reference this comprehensive study, which reported that less than 30 percent of charter schools on average outperformed traditional public schools in 2013. The follow-up report two years later found higher performance in math and reading in urban charters when compared to the overall charter sample. Funded by the Walton Family Foundation, this study touts that—when looking at racial and class-based subgroups of charter school students—poor families and parents of color benefit from choice and, to an extent, this is true. Several of the highest-performing charter schools across the nation are majority-Black or -Latinx, such as the Knowledge Is Power Program (KIPP). Charter schools and voucher programs often target poor families and students of color. Therefore, when choice programs do excel, underserved students do too.

However, the claims put forth by charter school skeptics are equally valid. The same report shows us that most students do not benefit from choice: 70 percent of students in choice schools perform similarly to or worse than their traditional public school counterparts. Statistics are pliable, but facts are stubborn things. Race and racism cannot be quantified.

Race is not the only determining factor in the implementation of school choice, to be sure. Class and wealth operate stealthily in a system that theoretically does not see color. Given that choice is grounded in an economic theory that eschews governmental "interference," individuals, corporations, and other organized entities can all participate in the education market, but individuals do not have equal means. Corporate interests—not the public or elected officials—are providing the options on the school choice menu, shaping public education with undue influence. Wealthy donors can redesign the system in their own favor according to the logic of a free market. Since the 1990s, the Walton Family Foundation, the Bill and Melinda Gates Foundation, the Los Angeles–based Eli and Edythe Broad Foundation, and others garnered influence in the federal government through unprecedented donations to school choice. These exclusively White benefactors invested nearly $2 billion through grants and direct donations to school reform initiatives that emphasized school choice and charter schools, including the campaigns of choice advocates.[18] The Gates and Broad Foundations—sometimes in partnership and often in overlapping initiatives—invested more than $60 million in the 2008 presidential election–with large donations to both major parties–to push issues such as national standards and merit pay to improve teaching. They promised $1.7 billion more in the next five years.[19] With their connections to the school choice movement, they bought significant federal influence.

Choice advocates have been explicit in how they connect school choice advocacy and charter school development to profit. At the Harvard Club in Manhattan, the Walton Family Foundation, in conjunction with the Bill and Melinda Gates Foundation, hosted a symposium in 2015 entitled "Bonds and Blackboards: Investing in Charter Schools." Tailored to hedge fund investors interested in broadening their portfolios, the meeting was intended to inform investors about the new, growing revenue stream fed by state and federal investment in schools that on the surface operated like public schools but were not regulated like them. With terms such as "very stable business, very recession resistant" and "high demand product," the language and rhetoric of schools for profit could not be more clear.[20] The posh New York meeting fit into what education researchers Michael Fabricant and Michelle Fine identified as "layers of interlocking powers [that] have dedicated a substantial part of their economic and political capital to building a charter movement."[21]

School choice is open for business, and no one person illustrates this more than the curiously unqualified, laughably incompetent, unabashedly wealthy, and unequivocally evangelist Betsy DeVos. Chosen by

Donald Trump, DeVos was the first secretary of education whose background and ideology stood wholly counter to public education. Her rise to lead US public schools was not inevitable, but she stands out among her predecessors. Indeed, much of the nation seems to have enjoyed casting harsh judgment on her nomination, and the media rightfully made a spectacle of her public gaffes. A conservative billionaire who has liberally funded school vouchers, she has never attended, much less taught in, a public school. Her own children were either homeschooled or attended private Christian academies.

Despite the controversy of her appointment as secretary of education, DeVos was poised to carry the choice movement to new heights. Fitting neatly with Trump's "drain the swamp" mentality, she explicitly promised school choice and privatization as a solution to failing public schools. She reinvigorated the debate around choice and carried unprecedented fervor for it. She possessed the networks, wealth, and the faith to push the choice movement forward in unprecedented ways.

By far the wealthiest member of a wealthy cabinet, DeVos inherited the money and networks it takes to shape policy in the United States. Her father, Edgar Prince, was a billionaire businessman who founded the Prince Corporation, a supplier of automobile parts. After his death, the family sold his business for over $1 billion, catapulting DeVos beyond the "one percent"—a tremendously influential, seemingly untouchable network of wealthy stakeholders—to the top .01 percent of Americans in terms of wealth.[22] In addition to this wealth, which put her in the same league as Bill and Melinda Gates and Eli Broad—comprising a collectively well-funded network that paved the way for choice—DeVos was deeply entrenched in the GOP. She served as chair of the Michigan Republican Party and as the Republican National Committee representative for Michigan. Her husband ran for governor in 2006.[23] Though unsuccessful, his run paved the way for additional Republican connections. These relationships helped the Devos family deliver the state's electoral votes to the Republican Party in 2016, a crucial win on Trump's path to the White House.

Though choice was never a critical issue in the presidential campaign—in fact, it was a rare point of commonality between Trump and his Democratic opponent, Hillary Clinton—DeVos's presence in the cabinet provided a national platform to expand it. With her roots in Michigan, she was a vocal partner outside the South to work with states like Mississippi and South Carolina that had fiercely advocated for choice since the 1960s.

Another barrier to the equitable implementation of choice is the budget shortfall it perpetuates. The greatest peril schools face today is the staggering financial toll triggered by choice. Many view the capital investment of major philanthropists as helpful. Money is needed, after all, and such a capital infusion is nothing short of a godsend to cash-strapped districts across the nation. However, the money is not dispersed equally. Much of a school budget is based on student expenditures, so that each school receives funding based on the number of students it has. For instance, when approximately fourteen million parents opted out of traditional public schools in 2010 for charters, voucher programs, or other publicly funded schools of choice—a number that has subsequently increased each year—they triggered a shortfall of approximately $171 billion for students still enrolled in those public schools.[24] The money that would have gone into traditional public schools followed students into other schools instead. One study highlighted school funding in California, which has more charter schools than any other state and nearly 20 percent of all charters in the country. California faced a crisis after legislation defunded traditional public schools in the wake of the charter movement. In Oakland, charter schools precipitated a loss of over $57 million for traditional public schools, and in San Diego the loss climbed to over $65 million. As the report found, the fiscal pressure mounted by charter schools in California "intensifies fiscal pressure to cut core services like counseling, libraries, and special education, and increase class sizes at neighborhood schools."[25]

Beyond the siphoning of school funds, there is the direct economic exploitation and profit generated by this grand educational experiment. Questionable business practices allow charter operators to profit within a "nonprofit" framework. Some charter operators sign contracts with their subsidiaries in order to turn a profit. These subsidiaries are on paper separate and distinct from the board that manages the day-to-day operations, but they work with charter management companies to provide services. In the process they charge exorbitant prices for land purchases and leasing school facilities. These unseemly tabs are paid by the charter operators that are, in turn, paid by state and local taxpayer money.[26] One of the most egregious cases was revealed in a report from Ohio that a charter operator in Cincinnati paid $867,000 to lease its school buildings. Another in Cleveland paid over $500,000 above market value to retain its facilities.[27] Due to the largely unregulated nature of charter school operation, many of these dealings go undetected. The "nonprofit" façade of charter schools covers their connection to for-profit initiatives. Keith Benson, the president of the Camden Education Association, a teachers' union in New Jersey, on the front lines against privatization of schools, notes that such audacious profiteering is nothing more than a "land grab."[28]

These scams steal from taxpayers and families who depend on public schools. A report jointly authored by the Center for Public Democracy and Integrity for Education—a coalition of grassroots organizations, organizing alliances, and progressive unions in New York—found and tallied reports of fraud, waste, and abuse that extended across corporate charter networks in fifteen states and amounted to more than $100 million. The malfeasance was so extensive that the report broke down the different categories of crimes: public funds used for personal gain; public revenue used for charter mismanagement that endangered children; and misreporting enrollment numbers for increased revenue.[29]

Comedian John Oliver put it in these terms:

> The problem with letting the free market decide when it comes to kids is that kids change faster than the market. And by the time it's obvious the school is failing, futures may have been ruined. So if we are going to treat charter schools like pizza shops, we should monitor them at least as well as we do pizzerias. It's like the old saying, "Give a kid a [shit] pizza, you've [fucked] up their day. Treat a kid like a [shit] pizza, you could [fuck] up their entire life."[30]

The scandal fits into the larger scheme of what African American studies scholar Noliwe Rooks calls "segrenomics," defining it as "the business of profiting specifically from high levels of racial and economic segregation." There is a long history of White philanthropists and business owners who saw opportunity in the education of Black students and people of color through vocational education to shape a workforce they desired to maximize profit.[31] With charter schools, this maligned form of economics has continued by ensuring that corporate, largely White interests control or significantly shape the choice movement. It is the inverse of what Howard Fuller, Sarah Carpenter, and other grassroots choice advocates have demanded—full control of their own schools.

Since school choice theory as enshrined in economic arguments since Milton Friedman dictates direct governmental subsidies to families so that they may choose charter or private schools, traditional public schools are seriously shortchanged, if not financially exploited. Providing more options has depleted the coffers of public schools still operating, siphoned off by new schools of choice. With fewer resources at hand, failing public schools that lose students due to competition are forced to make difficult budget cuts. This, in turn, makes it nearly impossible to compete.

School choice is based on an exclusionary foundation of free market logic, color-blind rhetoric, and a blatant denial of systemic inequality. As millions of parents celebrate school choice, the traditional public school system is a shadow of its former self. Public schools are essentially as segregated as they were in the 1950s and 1960s. They are regularly cited as failing in a never-ending public education crisis. Billions of dollars raised for public education through taxation have been diverted to schools of choice. Though highly popular and lauded as an inherent right, school choice presents a grave threat to the very existence of public education.

Choice and traditional school advocates alike will reference a failure of public education as the reason why all options are needed. However, without the equitable funding that choice precludes, traditional public schools are continually slashing services and jettisoning quality to pay the bills.

Somehow, traditional public schools are expected to compete for students, or at least maintain a sizable enough enrollment to better serve students left behind. They must educate those who have no other school to attend or do not have the means to take advantage of choice. According to Friedman's free market logic, bad businesses simply close to make way for stronger, better ones. Likewise bad schools will close, good schools will thrive, and the overall educational market will improve as a result—in theory. But schools that take in disadvantaged students are not businesses. They are not run for profit. They are tasked with educating, protecting, and in many instances, supporting children who may be displaced, disabled, or marginalized. Public schools cannot shut their doors because our laws compel all children to attend.

Unfortunately, school choice does not require corporate entities to address the systemic issues of racial segregation, poverty, and inequitable funding. No matter how well-intentioned corporate reformers may be, the Institute on Race and Policy found that the most desirable choice schools use sorting mechanisms such as interviews, required contracts for parental involvement, or zero-tolerance disciplinary policies to selectively enroll or handpick elite students. When choice advocates point to a few Black or Latinx students who manage to excel in the choice environment, their exemplars are far from representative of the larger populations still in need of a quality education.

Those motivated by profit in the United States will not concede to those seeking genuine community empowerment. Scraps will be shared, but there is no genuine, widespread empowerment. Simply providing more choice or removing the barriers to equal school choice does not help those dependent on the public education system. In theory, choice relies on competition, which is supposed to drive traditional public schools to excel or at least improve. But many American politicians, capitalists, scholars, and educators invested in choice are unwilling to invest the resources that these public schools need in order to make improvements. They would rather invest in the "solution" of choice. Public schools are caught in a perpetual vicious cycle.

Even if local and state governments expanded options for everyone, taking advantage of choice requires social and economic capital that poor and working-class families do not possess. They must overcome a multitude of barriers to make choice work. Transportation is needed to take kids to school outside of your neighborhood. Understanding the convoluted choice procedures requires that parents do an abundance of research, which is very difficult for those struggling to make ends meet. Additionally, getting into some charter programs requires self-selection and active application—one has to consciously do the work of enrolling in an alternative program beyond the traditional neighborhood public schools. This separates parents who are able from others who do not have the ability or capital to apply or maintain contractual obligations to the school. If parents do make it over these hurdles, choice schools are not required by law to accept their children. Enrollment in some schools requires parents to enter contracts that mandate regular meetings and other obligations that, if not met, can result in their children's dismissal. Even then, it is a gamble as to whether that school will outperform the traditional public school. The charter and magnet schools that effectively provide exemplary education have waiting lists. Many Whites and middle- to upper-class families of color can fly over the hurdles. Poor and working-class families do not find the going so easy.

Poor families and students of color that do benefit from school choice are the exception yet often touted as evidence that school choice works for all. Choice advocates are quick to highlight that some students of color do succeed—just as "freedom of choice" advocates in the South pointed to the fact that a token number of Black students desegregated White schools.

School choice is also predicated on the assumption that "consumers" have equal access to all schools in their area, including the information needed to identify and apply to them. Such access is rarely equal, however.

Twenty years after the founding of the KIPP charter school network in 1992, after nearly one hundred charter schools were founded across the United States, serious concerns were raised about the schools and the sorting mechanisms that excluded some families. Admission to premier choice schools is determined by the social or cultural capital that parents possess. Social capital consists of the networks of relationships one has established, the knowledge one has accumulated, and the skills one has acquired over time. Though acquired and expended individually, social capital is structurally determined through race and class. The networks formed, knowledge accumulated, and skills developed by poor Latinx families will be very different from those of wealthy Whites, for example. To be expected, the capital acquired by wealthy Whites is more likely to lead to the knowledge and relationships needed to gain entry into the best schools of choice.[32] Forms of capital that mediate a family's access may also involve language barriers, access to technology, or transportation. One's previous educational history and experience shape one's choice as well.[33]

The process itself is convoluted, cumbersome, and stressful to those unfamiliar with the system. Aiko Kojima was raised in Japan and came to the United States for graduate school. It was not until her son was ready for school that she confronted the labyrinth of school choice in Chicago. It was a process that she referred to as "shopping for a school"—an intricate procedure that required visiting schools and meeting principals, who, feeling pressure to attract students sold a bill of goods that was unrealistic. It required filling out applications, taking a test, and waiting. Her sheer intellect was not enough to provide for an education she felt comfortable with, but, luckily for Kojima, she acquired the social capital through relationships forged while attending the University of Chicago.[34]

Many others are not so lucky. The system of choice is stacked against those without the social capital to successfully navigate the system. Moreover, students who bring special needs or require extra resources are discouraged from shopping for choice schools.

Beneath the promising veneer of school choice is an unsettling truth that, in spite of its purported objectivity, promised neutrality, and popular appeal, it is anything but equitable in its application. School choice continues to benefit a select few as it jeopardizes the entire public school system.

Choice undermines community empowerment—the very thing demanded by Black activists like Howard Fuller. Memphis school board member Stephanie Love noted that a "Wild, Wild West" atmosphere pervaded the city after the onslaught of school choice entrepreneurs.

School choice led to a lot of paternalism and condescension. From her perspective, the situation was tantamount to Whites telling communities of color what was best for their children. There was no cultural sensitivity, no connection to the area, no sense of history among outsiders who moved into Memphis to set up charter schools. There was also no genuine inclusiveness in the decision-making processes. In Memphis, many charters that were part of a corporate chain replaced the single-site or mom-and-pop charters that were controlled by local people of color. As Love laments, "No one asked us." Love and others view the increase in charters as a hostile takeover instead of a process of building on what was already there. It was akin to an "experiment [with] guinea pigs," she says. "Our children lost."[35] The ideas pushed in Memphis and across the nation—vouchers, charters, online programs—amounted to a huge experiment on poor communities and many families of color. Yet these solutions, as Noliwe Rooks points out, are "rarely if ever prescribed as an educational panacea for White students, or for those with wealth."[36]

As school choice advocates gained or, rather, purchased entrée at the federal level, corporate interests at the local level became emboldened to influence and at times directly control public education policy. Scores of for-profit organizations such as Charter Schools USA, Connections Academy, and K12 Inc. manage charter schools across the nation. Though for-profits account for less than 20 percent of all charter schools, their ongoing presence perpetuates a favorable climate for choice. When families, irrespective of race and class, accept that private business models are better than public schools, they implicitly trust that for-profit endeavors have their best interests in mind. Within this environment, private interests ultimately control our options.

Terrenda White, a scholar-activist in New York, noted that the corporatization of charters has transferred power and control away from mom-and-pop charters to massive chains. Though the choice movement appropriated the rhetoric of the freedom struggle and involved a few of its stalwart leaders, like Rev. Wyatt Tee Walker—the battle has shifted away from genuine empowerment for those without it. There are no "formidable battles against a charter sector that offered hope and the promise of change but instead has taught bitter lessons," writes education scholar and activist David Stovall. There is an inherent "contradiction of capital." Successfully managing a charter school requires forms of capital that alienate families or engender a "politics of desperation" where the silver bullet of school choice reform attracts people of color to the ranks of the movement.[37]

Deborah Meier, one of the founders of Central Park East, a network of independent choice schools in East Harlem, sums up the issue. Like many educators who led alternative schools, Meier by the early 1990s saw school choice as a natural extension of her work. As she noted in 1991, "By using choice judiciously, we can have the virtues of the marketplace without some of its vices."[38] However, choice has not been used wisely, and the intersections with race and class point to serious concerns about the underlying economic theory. The critique is not merely abstract—there is a dismal track record that justifies the concern.

Available statistical data do not decisively prove that choice has failed, but the results of choice after five decades are lackluster at best. Many choice advocates claim success based on the 2015 CREDO report from Stanford University, which stated that about 43 percent of charter schools outperformed traditional public schools in math and 38 percent outperformed in reading. The report also noted that this constituted a rise of more than 10 percent in both categories from the figures in a CREDO publication of 2013. The same report (and a follow-up in 2015) could point to cities like Boston, in which 92 percent of charters performed better than their traditional public counterparts in math and 81 percent in reading. In Newark, students in 77 percent of charters outperformed their peers in math, and 69 percent did so in reading.[39] Widely recognized as one of the most comprehensive reports on the topic, it was heralded by the Bill and Melinda Gates Foundation as proof that urban charters were making a "significant positive impact."[40]

From the perspective of those left behind, however, the more significant takeaway is one of caution. A more prudent interpretation emphasizes that about 60 percent of choice programs do *not* perform better than traditional public schools, as the CREDO report shows in analyzing twenty-five years of charter schools. As skeptics can point to in the same report, while northern cities like Boston or Newark are celebrated, other cities have experienced disastrous results. In Mesa, Arizona, 91 percent of traditional public schools outperformed or tested at the same level as charter schools in math and reading. In Orlando, 83 percent of traditional public schools outperformed charters in math and 84 percent did so in reading.[41]

The opposing readings of the CREDO report reveal a troubling truth. The data itself and the reliance on numbers to "prove" the effectiveness of a program obfuscate how we use research to evaluate school choice. Parents consistently look for an easy solution and statistical data may seem to point toward one. Claims based on quantitative data in relation to school choice can be problematic, however. As education researchers Erica Frankenburg, Genevieve Siegel-Hawley, and Jia Wang note, such studies are prone to methodological critique from numerous angles. Important factors to consider in assessing the overall effectiveness of choice include the length of a longitudinal study, the extent to which English language learners are included in the study—if at all—and whether the study seeks to delineate national or state-by-state trends.[42] Careful critique illustrates just how untenable are grand claims by the likes of the Bill and Melinda Gates Foundation that cite reports like CREDO's.

What the CREDO report does tell us is that enough numbers exist for us to state with conviction that school choice has not lived up to its promise. Viewed from a larger historical context centered on race, the system of choice is far from equal. In Detroit, a city that has converted nearly its entire public school system to charters or voucher programs, only 10 percent of choice schools outperform traditional public schools. Education Trust-Midwest, a nonpartisan research and advocacy group, found in 2017 that over 70 percent of Michigan's charter schools were in the bottom half of the state's school system.[43] A 2014 report issued by the Network for Public Education, a public education advocacy group, found that the New Orleans public school system, which was replaced by a choice model after Hurricane Katrina, was one of the worst performing in the nation.[44] In 2011, the Center on Education Policy, an independent organization committed to public education, found that students of color across the country whose parents used vouchers to enroll in private schools performed no better than traditional public school students. The Education Policy Program at New America, a think tank committed to solving pressing issues in education, was even less optimistic in its 2017 report, which concluded that vouchers' impact on poor students and students of color was detrimental—some students' reading scores dropped over 25 percent in just one year.[45]

Beyond statistical malleability, the funding and advocacy of school choice ideas remain corrupted by wealth and influence. Several examples illustrate the depth to which this corruption goes on behind closed doors and beyond the public gaze.

In some poignant cases, money associated with school choice networks has been implicated in elections pushing school choice advocates. In 2003, Richard and Betsy DeVos founded All Children Matter, which was billed as a "bi-partisan, non-profit advocacy organization supporting quality choices in public education for all Michigan students to improve academic achievement, increase accountability and empower parental choice in our public schools."[46] The organization in its first year spent over $7 million to support school choice advocates.[47] In 2008, the Ohio Elections Commission fined All Children Matter over $5 million for campaign finance violations—improperly channeling $870,000 in contributions from a Virginia-based political action committee, steering it to candidates who embraced a pro-choice agenda as part of their platforms.[48] The fines remained uncollected and the ruling unenforced at the time of DeVos's appointment as secretary of education.

The contributions from choice advocates have held significant sway in many communities, as exemplified in Charleston, South Carolina. Charleston has been deeply immersed in the politics of school choice since 2018, when the Coalition for Kids—a well-funded 501(c)4 committed to improving education—entered the local scene. The organization's rhetoric of "serving all children" carries with it a pro-choice message, and the slogan eased the way to putting all options on the table in South Carolina: magnets, public-private partnerships, and charter schools. Coalition for Kids has ties to Teach for America, an organization known to support charters and to undermine teachers' unions. Coalition for Kids supported local Charleston school board candidates without teaching experience and seemed to place a premium on business acumen as opposed to experience in education policymaking. The coalition also funneled untraceable or "dark" money into local school board elections—the nerve center of education policy in the United States—and enabled "progressive" philanthropists of various political hues to flex their muscles and exercise undue influence locally.[49]

The powerful network of school choice advocates not only passed legislation that enabled the choice movement to prosper. It also successfully mounted a legislative and ideological assault on the staunchest defenders of traditional public education: teachers' unions.

Teachers' unions have long been understood to strengthen education. Unionized teachers improve the profession through higher salaries and better working conditions. This is often evident in higher test scores, not to mention stronger systems of traditional public education.[50] Yet teachers' unions have inspired controversy. Historically calling for robust spending on public education, higher salaries, and better working conditions, unions have rallied against school choice once it was clear that private, corporate entities controlled it—and choice advocates and the private sector have retaliated. Union resistance has increasingly been funded and led by the same powerful elites who supported, led, and otherwise influenced the school choice movement. Milton Friedman wrote of the antagonism directly in 1998, "Public dissatisfaction with the present school system is growing rapidly. Sooner or later pressure for free parental choice will succeed in breaking the hold of the union monopoly."[51] Facing increasing hostility, teachers' unions have borne the brunt of public critique. This was on full display in 2011, as anti-union sentiment inspired new laws in states like Wisconsin and Ohio that all but eradicated collective bargaining, the right to strike, and publicly supported, comprehensive insurance plans.[52]

School choice advocates aligned with anti-union education reformers. One of the most visible, influential, and therefore controversial figureheads of the movement has been Michelle Rhee, who appeared on the cover of *Time* magazine in December 2008. Then the head of Washington, DC, public schools, Rhee stood defiantly in a classroom, holding a broom, with pursed lips and a serious gaze. The cover line reads: "How To Fix America's Schools."[53] As the photo deftly captures,

Rhee was billed as a no-nonsense reformer. Her uncompromising, gruff tactics were popular and welcomed by a public that had pegged public education as a sinking ship. In the last months of 2008—at the height of the optimism ushered in with the election of President Obama— Michelle Rhee symbolized radical reform. As a Teach for America alum, Rhee presented a popular solution of cleaning house, which she fully intended to do in Washington, DC. There she sought to abolish teacher tenure—the ultimate job security—in exchange for greater pay. It earned the scorn of teachers' unions nationwide. Though tenure was protected in the compromise that followed, teachers were subject to a "pay-for-performance" plan, a program that financially rewarded those who improved their students' test scores.[54] Rhee's work also included partnering with Teach for America as its leaders increasingly supported school choice. Charter schools, free from the regulations of traditional public schools, were often free to "break the mold" and hire teachers without traditional certification.[55]

In New Orleans—ground zero of school choice—a different narrative emerged. Choice advocates and reformers implemented brash new school choice policies there in the wake of Hurricane Katrina. One move, the widespread dismissal of seventy-five hundred traditionally licensed teachers—without pay or the promise of back pay—was the most controversial and sent a biting message.[56] It was clear that veteran teachers had been diagnosed as a cancer on the progress of reform and had been targeted for removal.

Many of the dubious policies supporting school choice operations unfolded in Los Angeles, the second-largest school district in the country. After Minnesota, California was the next state to pass legislation that opened charter schools in 1992. The initial bill called for founding between fifty and one hundred schools. It also stated that teachers would not have to hold credentials and would not be granted tenure, and collective bargaining would only be used if written into the contract. The bill also provided the ability for a charter to secede from public school districts. It was the blueprint that many union-friendly states used, further entrenching the schism between teachers' unions and choice advocates.

Since the passing of the legislation, California has been gripped by deadlock, unable to make changes to a charter bill that many legislators across the aisle agree need to be reformed. As California became home to more charter schools than any other state, the gridlock became all the more pronounced. According to *Los Angeles Times* reporter Anna Phillips, state legislators are "torn between allegiances to pro-charter philanthropists and the powerful teachers union."[57] The most recent manifestation of the charter school conflict was evident in the 2018 gubernatorial race. Democratic primary candidate Antonio Villaraigosa had been a vocal critic of teachers' unions while mayor of Los Angeles from 2005 to 2013. He called unions "the loudest opponent and the largest obstacle to creating quality schools." As mayor, Villaraigosa unsuccessfully attempted to take control of the Los Angeles Unified School District, putting forth plans to replace the elected school board with a committee led by himself, school choice supporters, and choice philanthropists. He also formed a nonprofit that took control of eighteen low-performing schools in the district.[58]

Because of Villaraigosa's candidacy, the primary election in California's 2018 gubernatorial race became a focal point for choice advocates. Reed Hastings, Netflix CEO, donated a massive $7 million to Villaraigosa's campaign. Philanthropist Eli Broad donated $2.5 million. Former New York City mayor Michael Bloomberg donated $1.5 million. Bill Oberndorf, the hedge fund manager and Republican donor who succeeded Betsy DeVos as chair of the American Federation for Children, donated $2 million. And Walmart heiress and charter school philanthropist Alice Walton contributed $750,000. In all, charter supporters raised $23 million to support Villaraigosa's bid for governor, compared to the totals raised by Gavin Newsom, $58 million, and his opponent, John Cox, just under $17 million.[59] Despite this massive backing, Villaraigosa came in third in the primary and thus did not achieve a spot on the ballot in November, but deep divisions remained.

The nexus of campaign funding and education policy in California was troubled in 2017 when the president of the Los Angeles Board of Education pled guilty to felony charges and resigned his office. Refugio "Ref" Rodriquez was charged with three felonies and twenty-five misdemeanors mostly stemming from campaign finance violations but also including perjury and conspiracy to commit assumed name contribution.[60] Prior to his fall from public office, he had been a spokesperson for the choice movement. In 2000, he started a nonprofit "social venture investment fund," the Partnerships to Uplift Communities Schools network, seeking to financially support educators of color interested in founding and governing charter schools, using funds from the Walton Family Foundation, the Bill and Melinda Gates Foundation, and other philanthropic donors. Their investment, in hindsight, was unsound. Rodriguez cut checks for $265,000 for professional training, but it was unclear whether the funds had then been used for the stated purpose.[61]

Beyond the scandals and mixed statistics on test scores, school choice also challenges one of the essential premises of education in the United States, which is that our schools are open to all. Enshrined in the current Individuals with Disabilities Education Act, which originated as Public Law 94–142 in 1975, is the principle that all students, regardless of ability, will be welcome in the public schools. Theoretically, school choice is available to all. Yet concerns were raised, beginning in the first years of the charter movement, that disabled children were being shut out. Initial reports indicated that charters were not enrolling students with disabilities to the same extent as traditional public schools. A study revealed that only 4 percent of charter students in Arizona received special education services, compared to a national sample of 10 to 12 percent. In California, one-quarter of all charter schools in California reported *no* students with special needs. The inequity had lessened by 2014, but charters still enrolled proportionally fewer students with disabilities nationally, 8 to 10 percent as compared to the 13 percent of students in traditional public schools, amounting to a difference of about two hundred thousand students. Some states provided additional funding for charters enrolling students with disabilities, and approximately fifty charters have existed nationally that catered specifically to this population. However, many have not provided services to meet the needs of children and students with learning or physical disabilities.[62]

Parents of students with disabilities may be discouraged from applying to enroll their children in charter schools or other schools of choice. One study, which covered nearly 6,500 schools in twenty-nine states, found that charter schools responded with less frequency to parents who posed questions indicating that their children had special needs. These practices effectively manipulate the applicant pool, excluding those who need specialized instruction.

When students with disabilities *are* enrolled in charters, they are more likely than others to be pushed out of school. When the Knowledge Is Power Program (KIPP) popularized its "no excuses" model to critical acclaim beginning in 1992 and generous funding followed from the Gates Foundation and other prestigious donors, strict discipline became the signature feature of many successful charters that graduated their students and placed many in college. This dovetailed neatly with the no-excuses, get-tough rhetoric behind President George W. Bush's signature No Child Left Behind policy, which ushered in more charters.[63] As appealing as the rhetoric was to many, troubling studies on KIPP emerged as it was being touted as a panacea. The results were detrimental to those children who did not fit the mold or meet charter school leaders' expectations regarding punctuality and "grit." In short order, they were suspended or expelled. One particularly damning report released by the Civil Rights Project at UCLA found that charter school administrators nationwide suspended students at a rate that was 16 percent higher than traditional public schools. Of a sample of 5,250 charter schools, the study reported, 374—or over 7 percent—suspended one-quarter of their students at least once. Nearly 10 percent of schools suspended Black students at a rate at least 10 percentage points higher than Whites. Further, the study noted that over 20 percent of charters suspended students with disabilities at a rate that was 10 or more percentage points higher than nondisabled students.[64] These results are telling, because students with disabilities are twice as expensive as nondisabled students to educate, and students with severe disabilities, in which one's performance in major life skills is limited, are eight to fourteen times more costly.[65] Though some studies from KIPP and charter school associations reference attrition rates, and others are comparable to traditional public schools in the same district, another study showed significant differences in attrition rates and Black students.[66]

Results are mixed. With other exclusionary factors—like self-selection and pushing out challenging students—programs like KIPP and other charters do not serve the same student population as tra-ditional public schools. If the highest-performing charter schools do not accept students that require special education, then comparisons are skewed.

Studies like those from KIPP and charter school associations con-firm the suspicions of many skeptics who charge that school choice does not provide equal access. Students who require specialized in-struction—including bilingual instruction or differentiated instruction for emotional or behavioral needs—need more one-on-one time with qualified teachers, individualized education plans with a team of educa-tors and social workers, and other resources, including alternative and more costly forms of assessment, among others, all of which are difficult to provide in any financially strapped school. By excluding and pushing out such students, selective schools can bolster their test scores.

Any way one cuts the statistical cake, racism remains baked into our education system. As in the early era of the freedom of choice plans in the 1960s, the vast majority of disadvantaged students remain stranded in an inherently unequal system. But some parents, educators, and ac-tivists are resisting.

CHAPTER EIGHT

Resisting School Choice Through Counternarratives and Coalitions

AS MUCH AS I LEARNED about the history and complexity of school choice in the board rooms, media centers, city auditoriums, and school cafeterias across Charleston, South Carolina, I also learned that there is resistance to the attack on what remains of public education. Though the choice movement has grown in scope and power, a national movement and a counternarrative have begun to emerge to challenge it, including an educational justice movement in Chicago, a city that was earlier critical to the advent and explosive growth of school choice. It is this conflict—from Charleston to Chicago—that comprises the struggle for educational equity and "civil rights" today.

Charleston is a microcosm of the larger fight to prevent school choice from closing or converting the last remaining traditional public high schools, starving public schools of desperately needed funds, and empowering entrepreneurs instead of Black and Brown families. The struggle in Charleston communicates that resisting school choice is a much more difficult sell than choice itself and signifies how local context reigns supreme. The United States is the only wealthy nation on earth that does not mention education in its constitution, which means that education policy is largely relegated to and therefore fiercely debated at the state and local level. The parameters of these fights are not equal: federal funding supports charters, state governments allow vouchers, and philanthropist dollars back pro-school-choice politicians. The fight, then, must be proximate to the local centers of power—school district boardrooms and administrative offices, the schools our children attend, and the cafeterias or auditoriums where parent organizations meet. In education, thinking locally is a brutal reality. Without a firm grounding at the local level, organizers face nearly insurmountable challenges when trying to tackle problems at the state and federal levels.

Ronsha Dickerson of Camden, New Jersey, a parent, public school advocate, and activist, demonstrates how the struggle to preserve education begins locally. Born and raised in Camden in a community in the central part of the city that, in her words, "took care of itself," Dickerson was a proud graduate of Camden High School in 1995. As she looks back on what she feels was a strong education, Dickerson remembers that families and neighbors were involved in the schooling of their children. She was taught by Black teachers who lived in the neighborhood and knew her family. Nearly a statistical impossibility today, Dickerson did not have a White teacher until she was in the fifth grade, and this teacher understood the life of his students from Camden. Today, as a mother, Dickerson remains fully invested in the same school system, having chosen to send each of her six children to local public schools.[1]

But after twenty years of enrolling her kids in public schools, Dickerson noticed that things had changed. New Jersey's Urban Hope Act, signed into law in 2012, created "Renaissance schools" in the state's worst-performing areas, which included Camden. Championed by Republican governor Chris Christie and following the blueprint established under Richard Daley and Arne Duncan in Chicago, the act opened the door for charter schools, with state per-student expenditures on charters nearly equaling spending on traditional public schools (95 percent). Then, in 2013, Christie took over the Camden school district, wresting control from the local district by appointing a school board and canceling the local elections that traditionally determined who occupied the seats.[2] Christie appointed Paymon Rouhanifard as the new superintendent of Camden schools. A thirty-two-year-old "reformer" of the likes of Michelle Rhee, and someone who had spent more time on Wall Street than in the classroom, Rouhanifard ran the district according to the principles of school choice. He grew the number of charters, many of which included "hybrids" or co-located charters, where a charter coexisted in the same space as a traditional school. In many cases these coexisting schools were essentially segregated—with different entrances, different class periods, and different teachers. In many instances, these charters were then in a position to "take over" the school. In a brazen move, Rouhanifard proposed and oversaw the demolition of the city's oldest public high school and replaced it with four smaller magnet schools run by a charter organizer. He fired over two hundred teachers, and other experienced and unionized teachers were pushed out, only to be replaced by an influx of teachers who were not unionized. Connected to Teach for America and embracing the prevailing corporate mindset for reform, newly hired teachers in Camden were largely White women who did not live in the community. By the end of Rouhanifard's controversial tenure, 8,200 students, more than half of all students in the city, were in over two dozen charter or "hybrid" schools, compared to 6,800 remaining in traditional public schools. Keith Benson described it as demoralizing reform "forced" on the community. The result was a very different educational landscape than what Dickerson and Benson knew from childhood and their work in the community.[3] It was much more of a "market," and those running it did not check in with locals.

For Dickerson, it was too much. At the same time of Rouhanifard's reforms, in May 2013, students across the Delaware River in Philadelphia used social media and organized a series of walkouts. Striking less than one year after massive teacher strikes in Chicago, the Philadelphia students protested over $800 million in state budget cuts that had resulted in proposals to shut down over forty schools, with the concomitant loss of 1,600 teachers. The walkout took place on the fifty-ninth anniversary of the *Brown* decision, and thousands of students from twenty-seven schools marched and shut down traffic outside Philadelphia's city hall and the school district office.[4] In Camden the following year, students called "Momma Ronsha" (Dickerson) who came and marched in solidarity as hundreds protested massive budget cuts in New Jersey that reflected the trends in Philadelphia and across the country.[5] As a fervor of resistance grew across New Jersey, Dickerson began organizing at the local level with greater intensity and frequency, forging a coalition with the local teachers' union and others. In drawing the lines for a protracted struggle in this embattled city, Dickerson opened another local front in a much larger battle.

Encountering misinformation at every turn, grassroots education organizations are forced to combat ignorance—willful or otherwise—with research and debate. Since school choice is often understood as a right, most parents are not aware of the negative implications of choice or the fact that choice is not an immutable policy. Parents and advocates locally must engage in conversations and raise awareness about school choice. Research and published statements critiquing school choice can be shared through social media, published in local print media, brought to school boards in public hearings, and discussed in social settings. Taking a page out of choice advocates' playbook, defenders of public education must confront the spread of choice with research and education about the privatization of public education.

Troy LaRaviere, an activist school administrator in Chicago, illustrates how resistance grows from sharing information about education with communities and families. Chicago also demonstrates how a city central to the development of choice remains a critical site of resistance to it. In 2011, LaRaviere accepted a position as principal at Blaine Elementary School, one of the city's best-performing traditional public schools, located on the predominantly White North Side. That same year, Rahm Emanuel became mayor of Chicago. Emanuel, having served as President Obama's chief of staff from 2009 to 2010, brought a lot of fanfare—and criticism. With his appointment came the corporate, get-tough policies of his predecessors. It was a similar move to what unfolded in Camden and Memphis. Inheriting the school choice plans of Arne Duncan, who served as CEO of Chicago Public Schools before his appointment as secretary of education under Obama, and former mayor Richard Daley, education became a thorn in Emanuel's side.

LaRaviere spoke out against charter schools and the Rahm administration, drawing attention to unjust budget cuts and misuse of education funding across the public school system. He spoke against the culture of fear, one that LaRaviere felt suppressed criticism of policy making that was detrimental to students. It was an environment that LaRaviere scathingly identified as "annoying micromanaging and finger-pointing without the slightest bit of intelligent conversation and support." One principal referenced a "gag order" that prevented administrators and teachers from voicing concerns.[6] LaRaviere's criticism was published both locally and nationally and became a lightning rod for spirited debate.[7]

The timing was critical for Chicago principals to speak up. With the city school board's consent, Emanuel authorized the closure of fifty schools in 2013 as part of their solution to turning around failing schools.[8] It inspired a costly campaign that ultimately contributed to Emanuel deciding not to seek reelection in 2018. LaRaviere and others drew attention to other serious problems in the district under the flawed leadership of Emanuel and Duncan. According to research LaRaviere conducted, charter schools and the "turnaround" schools—failing schools rebranded, reorganized, and put under new management—were not only failing but also overrepresented among schools with the poorest academic performance. Traditional public schools, meanwhile, had the highest growth of student enrollment. "I did research about the situation, and I got the *Washington Post* and *Chicago Sun Times*, the *Chicago Tribune*, all the local places," LaRaviere says. "I fed the data to them. I compelled principals into talking to reporters and got that issue on the front page."[9]

Ronsha Dickerson and Keith Benson likewise used the press in Camden to counter the narrative put forth by the harsh school choice policies implemented under Chris Christie and Paymon Rouhanifard. In the midst of rampant school closures, teacher layoffs, and what they identified as false narratives of progress, Benson and Dickerson proffered a scathing critique. In their commentary in the local *Courier Post*, they asserted that Rouhanifard lacked "the requisite education, practical experience and certification qualifying him" to lead the struggling district. Based on their research, their experience in the district as parents, educators, and organizers, they found that Rouhanifard's disruptive reforms "under the falsehood of school choice" led to nothing but "an explosion of test-centric, equity-denying, 'no-excuse' charters that are forced into low-income minority communities exclusively, for low-income minority children specifically; understaffed and under-resourced public schools; and an expanded perception that Camden's public schools are inherently inferior places to learn."[10]

The message was not well-received. New Jersey state representative Arthur Barclay and school board member Felisha Reyes Morton issued a blistering rebuttal, defending the work of the superintendent and the school choice policies he pushed and chastising what they saw as a "personal attack strategy." They quoted former first lady Michelle Obama: "When they go low, we go high."[11]

Sharing our findings and criticism of school choice is critical to grassroots public education advocacy across the United States. Though these views are often unpopular, we can create counternarratives and document the institutional racism through the voices of those who experience it firsthand.[12] As David Stovall wrote from the front lines in Chicago, where he observed resistance to the charter movement on the ground, "a combination of firsthand accounts—as more students, families, and former teachers share stories about their experiences with charters—and awareness of the realities of broad-based oppression have great potential for galvanizing resistance."[13] This was exactly what Ronsha Dickerson had in mind. Dickerson and other parents, educators, and advocates saw that the reforms around New Jersey's Urban Hope Act and the privatization agenda it entailed were put forth as if "ordained that way," as if there were no alternatives.[14] For Dickerson, it was a matter of organizing and amplifying a counternarrative to demonstrate that choice was not the only or even the right solution. Counternarratives can lead to a revolution of sorts or sustained, critical community engagement and praxis, putting theory into practice on the ground. The "alternative account" of the impacts of charter schools, alongside the numbers published by critical educators in the movement, like Dickerson and LaRaviere, inspired resistance.

Ronsha Dickerson grew up in the Gateway neighborhood of central Camden. She attended John Greenleaf Whittier School through eighth grade and graduated from Camden High School in 1995. Later, both her former elementary and high schools were closed, torn down, rebuilt, and reopened as a charter and a magnet school, etched out of the school choice theory supported across the city and state by Democrats and Republicans alike. As Dickerson enrolled her children in the public schools, she learned firsthand the impact of privatization.[15] For Dickerson, it was critical for parents and community members to regain control at the local level. After observing the segregation perpetuated by choice, the dismissal of Black teachers who lived in the communities where they taught, and feeling the frustrations of students harmed by such policies, Dickerson decided to act. After organizing walkouts and convening with other organizers, they decided to gain back citizens' vote for school board candidates.

Teaming up with the American Civil Liberties Union, the National Education Association, and the Camden Education Association, Dickerson joined a coalition called Save Camden Public Schools—which included collaboration with the NAACP led by Keith Benson—to take back the vote through the courts. Eventually a state appellate court ruled in their favor, effectively placing the issue on the ballot of whether to maintain or overturn mayoral appointment of the school board of Camden. Then they organized locally to get the ballot initiative passed, with volunteers working twelve-hour days, canvassing the community door-to-door to convince voters to vote to restore elections. In a city often regarded as one of the poorest and most dangerous in the United States, BIPOC voters turned out in numbers unseen since the election of President Barack Obama. A majority of Camden voters let it be known that they wanted to elect their own school board.[16] In Chicago, Troy LaRaviere—who grew up in the South Side's Bronzeville neighborhood and was educated in the Chicago Public School System—understood the city, his students, and the needs of his community too. After his own schooling he had joined the US Navy and ultimately enrolled at the state flagship university, the University of Illinois at Urbana-Champaign.[17] He was the quintessential advocate for traditional public education. As he noted:

> Those of us who know better must lift our voices to persuade the residents of Illinois to reject these backward ideas and to oust the politicians who peddle them. We must work together to build our own system-wide improvement effort. The future of public education is at stake. . . . We must lift our voices and be heard.[18]

Like Dickerson, LaRaviere was formidable. He had begun his teaching career as a supporter of the school choice movement. He had submitted a proposal in 2004 for a Black charter school on the South Side, where he was from. It was part of the comprehensive choice program ushered in under Duncan and Daley's ambitious "Renaissance 2010" school choice reform agenda. He served as an assistant principal at a "turnaround school" and also as a principal at a private school. "I've shown a willingness to experiment and to try things out," LaRaviere says.[19]

LaRaviere sampled from the menu of choice, taking part in the options it had to offer. "But at some point," LaRaviere notes, "you have to start paying attention to results. At some point the experimentation tells you something and you have to sit back and look at what it tells you. And when I sat back, that was the beginning of it all, and charters aren't doing the same as the public schools. That was the beginning of the questioning for me."[20] It was at this point that he began advocating for public education, protesting Emanuel's policies and the false narratives and harm perpetuated by school choice.

LaRaviere joined the chorus of critics challenging Emanuel, including Chicago Teachers Union president Karen Lewis. LaRaviere amplified his critique through the media, at one point even appearing on a TV ad for Bernie Sanders in 2016 assailing the mayor: "We have endured a corrupt political system, and the chief politician standing in our way for us getting good schools is our mayor."[21]

As many teachers might have predicted, the city fired LaRaviere. In a letter that outlined the causes for his dismissal, the district noted, "As a principal of a Chicago Public School, you owe a duty of loyalty to the [school] board, the CEO and their designees." The district found LaRaviere's actions—speaking publicly against the mayor, engaging in public criticism of district policy, and refusing to follow the district's standardized test protocol—to be "reckless, critical and insubordinate."[22] LaRaviere's dismissal was a controversial move. David Moore, a Chicago alderman from the South Side, heavily criticized the decision on social media: "All I hear is, stay in your place . . . and don't dare challenge the DICTATORIAL AUTHORITY designed to put corporate profits over effective public education." Sanders called the termination a "politically motivated retaliation because he dared to stand up to the mayor of Chicago."[23]

Like Chicago and Camden, community members in Charleston, South Carolina, mobilized in 2015 to block initiatives to convert Burke High School into a charter school.[24] Resistance inspired confrontational public comments, signs, a student march and protest, and a proposed moratorium against conversion, all of which coalesced into a grassroots organization, the Quality Education Project.[25] Five years later, Burke remains a traditional public high school—for the moment.

Similar success occurred in Memphis, where direct community involvement derailed several attempts by charter management organizations to take over traditional public schools. One community-led effort blocked Green Dot Public Schools, a national charter chain, from taking over Raleigh Egypt High School in 2014. Parents and community activists—citing a fear of losing control of a local school, expressing support for a principal they trusted, and calling the attempt by Green Dot a "hostile takeover"—successfully organized to block the move.[26] Spurred by fierce resistance, the Houston-based YES Prep Public School organization announced plans to withdraw from Memphis altogether, and the national KIPP chain scaled back its efforts there as well, though it has remained in the city. Such resistance included parents, community organizers, teachers, and school board member Stephanie Love, who fought for the families in her district to be informed and stay informed about proposed charters.[27]

Parents in Chicago organized to defeat the school board's plan there to close the National Teaching Academy (NTA), an elementary school that originally educated children who lived in the Harold Ickes Homes, a public housing development. As White parents began to gentrify this area of the city, referred to as the South Loop, they refused to send their kids to the school. Though the school was performing well according to city standards, the school board proposed to close it and repurpose it as a high school to accommodate the growing demands of White parents. Local parents such as Elisabeth Greer organized to keep NTA a neighborhood elementary school. After sustained pressure on the board and city council, and after pursuing legal action, parents organized under the name We Are NTA and protected the school from closure. It remained open as a neighborhood elementary school, serving children who continued to live in the area.[28]

Protests like this across the nation effected a modest retreat from the frontal assault on traditional public schools. When met with such fierce resistance locally, charter organizers backed off. Such resistance requires disruptive politics: protests, signs, sharp questioning of charter representatives, and some heckles and boos.

These victories may be few in number, but they are significant as a demonstration of community organization and strength. They also make state leaders think twice about trying to control community schools. In some cases, resistance to school choice has restored some local control to the community.

Coalition building is a critical part of the education justice movement, and there are several organizations that form the foundation of a critical alliance. Journey for Justice (J4J) is one that fights the privatization of public schools as part of a larger struggle for educational equity. Its goals include twenty-five thousand sustainable, high-quality, community-based public schools across the country by 2025, ending "zero tolerance" policies that punish students for infractions, equity mandates for public education at the state and local level, protection of Black teachers, ending state takeovers and mayoral control, and eliminating overreliance on standardized tests. Started in 2012 as a national organization, with members from Chicago, Detroit, Newark, New York, Baltimore, and Philadelphia, among other cities, J4J has organized marches and a protest outside the Department of Education that attracted over five thousand participants. In one protest that drew national attention in 2015, Jitu Brown and other organizers went on a thirty-four-day hunger strike in order to reopen Chicago's Dyett High School in ways that followed the interests and demands of the local community. And they won.[29]

The organization's platform against school privatization calls for a moratorium on privatization under school choice. Their platform states:

> School privatization has failed in improving the education outcomes for young people. There is no such thing as "school choice" in Black and Brown communities in this country. We want the choice of a world class neighborhood school within safe walking distance of our homes. We want an end to school closings, turnarounds, phase-outs, and charter expansion. We have an evidence-based solution for America's struggling, neglected schools.[30]

The national director of Journey for Justice, Jitu Brown, notes: "J4J operates in the spirit of Ella Baker and Septima Clark: we trust and believe in the brilliance of human beings, regardless of whether they're a PhD or a no D."[31]

Ronsha Dickerson organized Camden in the tradition of such civil rights activists as Baker and Clark and was asked to join Journey for Justice to serve as its national director. Dickerson in essence became a full-time organizer for justice. While working with J4J across the country, she continued to organize locally in Camden and across New Jersey, applying the same strategies the organization used across the nation. After forming Camden We Choose in 2019, engaging in a legal struggle in the courts and then registering voters, Dickerson maintained a fierce level of commitment. She helped organize an "equity walk" from Camden to Beverly to Willingboro to Trenton for people to talk with state representatives about the dire situation of public education in New Jersey. She then organized an "equity bus tour" that showed legislators around Camden to illustrate how a controversial tax break of over $1 billion did not benefit or empower Black and Latinx communities.[32]

Dickerson's work also illustrates how coalition building necessarily entails connecting education to larger issues. As Keith Benson notes, you have to "connect what's happening on the outside to what is happening on the inside."[33] Through connections to Chicago, Pittsburgh, Washington, DC, and other organizations in New Jersey, Dickerson shaped movements from the local to the national level. For her, the coalition was an effective way to "fight the machine back."[34]

Organizing leads to more organizing. In a similar fashion, Chicago parents and community advocates formed Raise Your Hand and the Chicago United for Equity, both of which were connected to and supportive of efforts to combat budget cuts, school closings, and the politics of "Renaissance schools" in the city. These organizations are grassroots and local, led by and for those closest to the front lines. They also represent the local coalition efforts to push back and defend public education.[35]

Alongside Journey 4 Justice, the Network for Public Education (NPE) is another organization that leads national efforts to build a broad base of resistance against choice. Education reform stalwarts Diane Ravitch and Anthony Cody formed the network in 2013. Their mission is to "preserve, promote, improve and strengthen public schools for both current and future generations of students" by connecting reformers across the nation who are committed to quality public education reform. With chapters in 139 cities, the NPE is one of the largest grassroots organizations committed to public education advocacy. Like other advocates, the NPE has shared irrefutable evidence about the failure and wasteful spending of charter schools. In its 2019 publication *Asleep at the Wheel*, the NPE reported that nearly one-third of recipients of federal aid for charter schools either never opened or were forced to shut down, amounting to nearly $1 billion in wasted public spending.[36]

For Marla Kilfoyle, the grassroots liaison for NPE, coalitions formed by her organization and J4J indicate the growing strength of the movement to preserve and invigorate public education. As Kilfoyle observed, many coalitions—she counts just under 140, including organizations such as Save Our Schools, Rethinking Schools, Badass Teachers Association, and the Alliance to Reclaim Our Schools—are working together as opposed to "in silos."[37]

Building alliances harkens back to Martin Luther King Jr.'s Poor People's Campaign of 1968, a campaign cut tragically short yet inspiring North Carolina–based Rev. William J. Barber II today. As Barber reflects:

> In 1968, the idea—a Poor People's Campaign to unite activists from across the nation and bring them to Washington to shut down the government, to bring the issue of poverty compellingly to the fore—looked impossible. Except there was no other way. . . . Only by joining together and asserting our authority as children of God can we shift the moral narrative in this nation and create a movement that will challenge those in power to form the "more perfect union" to which we aspire. Now as in 1968, this notion looks impossible. Except, again, there is no other way.[38]

The urgent need for a broad coalition continues today. Jitu Brown has reached out to national organizations—such as the Network for Public Education, Save Our Schools, and the NAACP—to organize around a common education platform. As Brown elaborated: "Alone in our local groups, we can't beat the highly organized infrastructure behind school privatization. That's like throwing rocks at tanks. We have to organize strong membership-based grassroots community organizations and link them together to win education equity in our time. . . . Our main priority is advancing community voices in public education."[39]

The coalition exemplifies how resistance operates on the front lines of the debate over choice. In some cases, people resist choice in order to keep historically Black or Latinx schools open. In others, parents resist choice to pressure district officials to identify better solutions for traditional public schools. Without the financial backing of leading philanthropists, local resisters depend on moral and rational appeals to parents who seek to leave the public system. Outnumbered and underfunded, school choice resisters often constitute the last line of defense for public education. Keith Benson draws a distinction between grassroots organizers who fight choice and those who advocate for it. He notes, "There are, however, real Black leaders out here working to improve education for our next generation while upholding their commitment to our history and protecting our communities." Yet "most folks will never know their names because they're too busy working, not given a corporate-subsidized platform, and too strapped for cash to host anything."[40] Cognizant of the serious issues they face, advocates have demanded political power—and they have gained it.

The power of local organizing, or what Chicago-based activist scholar David Stovall referenced as *poder popular*, or "popular power," cannot be underestimated. The productive efforts it yielded in Chicago literally took a village. Stovall—alongside parent advocates of La Villita, or Little Village, a West Side neighborhood—inquired into the funding Mayor Richard Daley had promised for a new high school during his 1997 mayoral campaign. The grassroots coalition with Stovall and La Villita renewed efforts after the city built two selective-admission high schools—Walter Payton and Northside College Prep—to attract students from across the city. Both required entrance exams, and together they did not alleviate the overcrowding of students in Little Village. They were part of Daley's Renaissance 2010 plan and opened at the turn of the millennium just before Arne Duncan was appointed head of Chicago Public Schools (CPS). Unhappy with the situation, Little Village parents used confrontational politics and applied direct pressure on the Chicago Board of Education and Chicago Public Schools, organizing a nineteen-day hunger strike and establishing a vibrant tent city they called Camp Cesar Chavez. Under pressure, Paul Vallas, CEO of Chicago Public Schools, and Gary Chico, president of the school board, resigned. More significantly, under Arne Duncan, plans were started for the creation of the Greater Lawndale High School for Social Justice as part of the larger Little Village Lawndale High School, a $60 million city initiative that matched the aspirations of parents and community organizers: a 282,000-square-foot facility with two gyms, a swimming pool, and four separate schools on one campus—a school for world languages, a school for math and science, a school for the arts, and a school committed to social justice.[41]

Concerned parents are not the only organizers for better schools. So are youth who are victims of negligent, racist school reform. Students associated with the Baltimore branch of the Algebra Project—a grassroots national education reform initiative founded by Bob Moses—used the grassroots organizing, nonviolent ethos, and political consciousness of the civil rights movement to address a failing public and private school system. Students under the age of twenty-three run the Algebra Project in Baltimore. They have also participated in nonviolent demonstrations aimed at raising money for failing public schools and disrupting the State of Maryland's plans to build a juvenile detention center, designed to house minors charged as adults. For a week in January 2012, students occupied the site of what was slotted to become the detention center until they were dispersed by police (and some arrested). When Maryland soon afterward released its 2013 budget, it did not include funding for the prison.[42]

These students may not have been addressing privatization or charter schools directly. But they were well aware of historic disparities within public education and the debt accrued through the school choice movement: that which is owed to communities who still lack access to quality education. They also demonstrate that disruptive politics can effect change quickly. Sociologist Charles Payne labeled the Baltimore youth activists "Miss Baker's Grandchildren," referencing grassroots civil rights movement organizer Ella Baker, who was an advisor and mentor to the Student Nonviolent Coordinating Committee (SNCC) in the 1960s. Payne called the Baltimore Algebra Project "part of one of the most thoughtful, self-aware and other-aware traditions of American activism."[43]

Protests in Baltimore and Chicago illustrate the effectiveness of school protests in effecting real change, including more equitable funding.

Grassroots, local organizing and coalition building comprise a historically grounded strategy of resistance that entails—or should entail—direct action. Chicago, a battleground of school choice, exemplified this in 2012 when approximately twenty-six thousand members of the

Chicago Teachers Union voted to strike. They walked off the job and picketed for traditional bread-and-butter issues such as higher pay, better support staffing, stronger benefits, protection for teachers laid off in school closures, and reduced weight of standardized testing in teacher evaluations. The union won key provisions, including a raise of over 10 percent over four years, additional teaching staff, and other measures of modest job security (though not enough to prevent the massive closure of schools the following year).[44] The strike also connected to issues of corporate reform that included bringing in charters to turn around schools—a hallmark of Arne Duncan (by 2012 secretary of education) and President Obama's educational reform strategy. Given the complex issues of poverty and trauma intensified by decades of residential segregation, students in Chicago public schools presented serious challenges to an under-resourced teaching force. Phil Cantor, a strike captain, noted that the use of standardized tests to evaluate teachers and schools nearly guaranteed failure. When schools failed, they would be turned over to a charter organizer, or the city would close them. As Cantor said, "There's this constant threat over teachers that if you don't get test scores up, your school will be privatized into a charter, you'll lose your job, your community will lose a community-based school."[45] The strike was a significant demonstration of teacher strength, especially since it took place just two years after neighboring states Wisconsin and Michigan all but eradicated teachers' unions.

It also established precedent for the nation's first charter school strike. In December 2018, hundreds of teachers working in a fifteen-school charter chain in Chicago walked off the job. Like their public school teacher counterparts, charter teachers in the Windy City struck for better class sizes, salary, and a longer school day and school year.[46] The charter school was part of the "Red for Ed" movement that shook the nation in 2018 and 2019. Nearly four hundred thousand public school teachers in West Virginia, Oklahoma, Colorado, Arizona, North Carolina, Kentucky, and South Carolina went on strike as part of carefully coordinated movements in "red" or "purple" states.[47] They fought against right-to-work legislation, a privatization movement marked by charter school expansion, and budget-cutting austerity measures taken by conservative legislatures during the recession leading to losses that have not been recovered after economic growth and recovery.[48] The Red for Ed movement invigorated the teaching profession, particularly in states that have antiunion laws.

With the rising tide of teacher protests, some educators see themselves more and more as critical political actors. Keith Benson and Troy La-Raviere are exemplars. Keith Benson was born and raised in Camden. He attended college at the Rutgers campus there and later pursued his doctoral degree from the Graduate School of Education at Rutgers. While studying the history and politics of education as a teacher at Camden High School—a traditional public high school slated to be torn down to make way for charters—Benson decided to become more active. Seeing the big picture and the need to connect teachers to larger conversations and the community, Benson accepted an invitation to run for the presidency of the Camden Education Association, the local teachers' union. Wanting to "bridge the gap between the union and the community," Benson reached out to Ronsha Dickerson, who helped spread the word. He was elected in 2017.[49]

After LaRaviere was dismissed from his administrative post in Chicago, he decided to run for mayor of the city. In 2018, he was the first to openly challenge the incumbent, Rahm Emanuel, and one of ten early candidates. (Emanuel would eventually decide not to run for reelection, LaRaviere would also withdraw, and the city would choose Lori Lightfoot in January 2019 in a runoff between two Black women candidates.) Having experienced the corruption of local education politics, LaRaviere knew from firsthand experience what issues had to be addressed. School funding, school closures, and school choice were the issues that inspired him to run. He connected these to the larger structural and institutional problems of racism and segregation that pushed Black and Latinx residents from the city through gentrification and perpetuated inequality. Running on a fundamentally progressive agenda, LaRaviere called for the hiring of ten thousand more teachers and support staff, drawing attention to the fact that CPS was the most understaffed district in the state.[50] Though he did not succeed electorally, LaRaviere was a critical part of a rising wave of educators who sought public office to stem the attack on public education. By focusing on the issues that hit closest to home for teachers, he represented a significant departure from the policies of Emanuel, Duncan, and President Obama.[51]

Benson and LaRaviere pushed the field and their respective cities to at least momentarily consider genuinely progressive arguments. They demonstrated how education and school reform could—and should— become a central topic in local elections. Promoting elected school boards (as opposed to ones appointed by the mayor), "wraparound services" (including medical, psychological, and social services for students), and more and better-paid teachers, they placed education on the agenda in ways other candidates did not.

Defense of public education led to decisive shifts in the New York state legislature in 2016. Voters elected Todd Kaminsky to office, a Democrat, over Republican Christopher McGrath. School choice became an important and divisive issue. A business-oriented, pro-charter advocacy group, New Yorkers for a Balanced Albany, which was funded by groups like StudentsFirstNY—an offshoot of Teach for America— ran attack ads against Kaminsky, who earned the support of teachers' unions as an advocate for traditional public schools. "Teachers for Todd," an independent group supported by the teachers' union, backed Kaminsky. The election not only flipped the seat but also tipped the state senate to a Democratic majority. For Marla Kilfoyle, who worked on the campaign to elect Kaminsky and is involved with NPE, "When we get people to run who understand privatization and we really put boots on the ground, [we can defeat candidates financed by Broad and Gates]."[52]

With grassroots mobilization and the right candidate, results can be achieved. Moreover, with education increasingly viewed as a critical issue, Kaminsky illustrates the extent to which debate on education can shape integral elections.

By 2018, the context had shifted. More seemed to be listening to the concerns of our teachers. That year, when education emerged as a significant issue in the midterm elections, over 1,800 educators ran for office. At least 177 educators ran for state legislator seats, and 43 current teachers won election. Teachers in states with an active Red for Ed movement forced education funding to be addressed in several critical

races. It was part of the largest teacher movement since the unionization of northern teachers in the late 1960s and early 1970s. "In the wake
of historic walkouts and school actions," NEA president Lily Eskelsen
García noted, "we have a chance to leave our mark and elect to office
public education champions who will raise their voices and fight for our
students and public education."[53]

Oklahoma, with one of the most visible strikes of the Red For Ed
movement, advanced a bevy of educators in the state primaries, challenging incumbent Republicans who had spoken out against teachers
and voted against measures that supported the strikes. The Oklahoma
Education Association advocated a group it called the "education caucus," a bipartisan legislative coalition with direct ties to the field of education. Sixteen out of nearly fifty teacher candidates won, increasing the
legislative caucus to twenty-five members. Though that number was
small, the Oklahoma Education Association claimed in a press release,
"There are now more educators in the state legislature than ever before.
No matter how you look at it, public education won."[54] One of those
sixteen elected, John Waldron, a social studies teacher in Tulsa who
won a seat in the state house of representatives, said, "Once you look at
what's going on, you can't just return to your classroom and pretend it's
all right. You get up, and you fight for it."[55]

In the 2018 Wisconsin gubernatorial race, educators proved decisive. Tony Evers began his career as a science teacher in high school
in Tomah, a small town in the western part of the state. After teaching
and then serving as a principal, school district superintendent, and finally state superintendent in 2009, today he serves as governor. In 2018
he defeated Republican incumbent Scott Walker, who had dismantled
teachers' unions. Evers, with a PhD in educational administration from
the state's flagship university, billed himself as the education candidate
and made education a central issue, proposing pre-kindergarten programs and increasing annual special education funding by $600 mil-
lion. The majority of Wisconsin voters supported increasing spending
over reducing property taxes—a direct rejection of the conservative,
budget-cutting austerity and privatization measures enacted by Walker
that had led to teacher pay cuts and loss of benefits.[56] Evers had a track
record of consistently siding with the interests of educators, having

participated in the massive teacher walkouts that shook the state in 2011. As he noted in an interview with the *New Yorker* when he was still the Wisconsin superintendent of education: "I realized that if I really wanted to make a difference for these kids in the state, I couldn't rely on this position to do it. The governor is the one who sets the tone."[57]

That same year, in California's gubernatorial race, Democratic candidate Gavin Newsom defeated Republican nominee John Cox. Newsom gained the support of more unions than any other candidate in the state, including the California Teachers Association (CTA) and the California Federation of Teachers. In the midst of the Red for Ed movement and the school board scandal in Los Angeles involving Ref Rodriquez, Newsom's campaign offered strong support for teachers, but it faced stiff opposition from charter and privatization backers. In a statement released after Newsom's victory, the president of the CTA noted, "As educators who care deeply for our students, we stood in unity with Gavin. His election sends a clear message that in California we care about free public education for all students."[58]

School choice can also be resisted through legal channels where precedent has already been established. The moment the first voucher programs surfaced in Wisconsin and Ohio in the mid-1990s, lawsuits were filed to question their constitutionality.[59] Spirited legal resistance continues today that challenges the essence of school choice, including the role of charters in perpetuating segregation. A lawsuit in Minnesota, unresolved as of the publication of this book, challenges the segregation of schools there—the first state in the country to create a charter school. Civil rights lawyers and NAACP lawyers filed suit in North Carolina to challenge legislation that permits the creation of separate, tax-supported charter schools in Mecklenburg County—the site of the once-successful busing program where schools have resegregated.[60]

The litigation tactic of resistance has sometimes been successful. Public Funds Public Schools (PFPS) is a national campaign to ensure that public funds are used for the maintenance of public schools rather than going to charter schools. The organization uses litigation, advocacy, and research toward this aim. Targeting private school vouchers—including

traditional private, tax credit, and education savings account vouchers—
PFPS works with partners such as the National Education Association
and state teacher associations across the country to file amicus cur-
iae briefs—legal documents submitted to inform (and persuade) the
judges hearing cases—and mount direct legal challenges to vouchers.
They have filed briefs in Montana, Michigan, and US district courts.[61]

Successful cases include *Cain v. Horne* (2009) in Arizona, where
voucher programs were found to violate an aid clause prohibiting the
use of public funds to support private or sectarian schools. The 2016
Schwartz v. Lopez decision in Nevada terminated the operation of an
educational savings account plan, finding such funds to be unconstitutional as they used public monies intended to pay for K–12 education.
In Louisiana, the courts struck down a voucher program in 2013 because it violated the state constitution by using public funds for private
schools.[62] The Education Law Center, a legal advocacy group in New
Jersey, filed a suit in 2016 that challenges the state commissioner of
education's decision to expand enrollment in charter schools.[63] School
districts in Indiana filed suit in 2019 challenging the constitutionality of
state laws governing the sale of public school buildings. The law allows
charter schools first claim to occupy closed school buildings while also
allowing charters to purchase the property for $1, clearly benefiting the
person or corporation that buys it and then governs the school. For real
estate valued in the millions, charter management organizations would
stand to gain millions at the expense of taxpayers.[64]

There may be a right to choose that is protected by the courts, but
arguably the public and those elected to work in their interest cannot facilitate that choice at the expense of traditional public schools.
State constitutions outline and promise the right to a public education.
This constitutional guarantee places limitations on school choice when
magnets, charters, and other choice schools receive priority over traditional public schools. When choice schools violate a state's constitutional commitment to public education, limitation or regulation should
be applied.[65]

Advocates have been involved in other ways. Save Our Schools Arizona collected over one hundred thousand signatures to challenge a
statewide voucher proposal. The petition drive placed the issue on the

ballot as Proposition 305 in 2018. As the voucher proposal was widely framed and seen as pulling the plug on public schools and giving advantages to the rich, voters soundly defeated the plan.[66] Indeed, as PFPS has cited, voters across the country since 1966 have defeated thirty state referendum proposals, by wide margins, that would have diverted public education funds to private schools.[67]

Using the courts draws on a long history of efforts to build the public school system and improve it. Since the Civil War, public education advocates have litigated to provide, improve, and ultimately desegregate public schools.[68] The judicial system remains a critical institution in this fight.

It is of the utmost importance to listen to and prioritize the recommendations of people of color who advocate for school choice from a civil rights perspective. As Dave Dennis, civil rights activist and director of the Southern Initiative of the Algebra Project, has said, charters and school choice advocates are here to stay. Working with them is a new reality. When listening to those most proximate to public education and those advocating for choice in ways that empower Black and Brown communities, common solutions become more apparent. In 1990, Polly Williams—the Black Wisconsin state representative and school choice advocate from Milwaukee—worked with Howard Fuller to put forth guidelines in a house bill that, when combined with the principles of the NAACP charter moratorium, provided for an ethical, empowering compromise. As she wrote, conditions for equitable parental choice include "the restriction of private school choice options" to local students, "the encouragement of parents to participate fully in the governance structure of the schools they select for their children . . . autonomy in the development of curricula, extracurricular activities, and rules of conduct . . . the provision of transportation to students in need of it. . . . the annual comparison of the academic achievement; daily attendance; dropout, suspension, and expulsion percentages . . . and parental involvement of participating private schools' students with their Milwaukee public school counterparts." For Williams, such guidelines would ensure that school choice "not produce any wrenching and devastating impact on public education" and, moreover, include "only those participating private schools with a history of effectiveness in educating poor, multiracial populations."[69]

Understanding the rationale of earlier choice advocates grounded in the civil rights movement tradition—and Al Shanker's original vision for charter schools as a tool of the teachers' unions—presents a compromise. It allows and learns from more ethical charters. It resonates with Terrenda White, who suggested that activists must challenge any charter reform effort that is "gripped by competitive rationales of schooling" while they "simultaneously recover less dominant visions of charter schools." The alternative conceptions of Black-led choice proposals since the 1990s push us to re-envision what achievement means and how we measure it, while reconceptualizing just how schools relate to the state and the very raison d'être of public education.[70]

The actions we take at the individual level are critically important. Beyond joining the call to publicize the inherent danger posed by school choice, there are values around which to organize—integration, for one.

The arguments made by those who downplay desegregation do not speak for everyone. Research demonstrates that the overall attempt to desegregate schools has been beneficial. Black students have made significant gains in math and reading since National Assessment of Educational Progress began compiling test scores in 1969—the same time that federal courts ratcheted up plans to enforce widescale desegregation. Some studies estimate that the "achievement gap" has decreased by nearly one-half during the period of concentrated desegregation from the early 1970s through 1990. UC Berkeley economist Rucker C. Johnson found in 2019 that exposure to an integrated environment through all twelve years of school was effective enough to eliminate the achievement gap altogether. Academic gains occurred alongside other benefits, including increased high school graduation rates, increased college attendance and graduation rates, and a reduction in incarceration rates. Other studies point toward less tangible gains such as problem-solving and critical thinking skills. Quite notably, research also proves that desegregated education leads to social values that support integration, collaboration, and empathy.[71] When seen in historic context—recalling that schools were legally segregated by race until 1954 and widescale desegregation did not occur until the early 1970s—these achievements are remarkable.[72] In the words of education researcher Richard Rothstein, the gains made after desegregation "in a single generation represents an improvement rate rarely encountered in any area of human performance."[73]

Johnson tracked children in schools during the *Brown* decision through a longitudinal study across multiple generations. Though what he reported was not directly attributable to school desegregation alone, Johnson found an increase in the likelihood of living in excellent or very good health, and lower incidents of conditions such as hypertension, cardiovascular disease, and obesity. He noted that when desegregation was enacted beginning in the late 1960s, which marked a period of concentrated attempts to desegregate schools and invest in public education, the country "witnessed the greatest racial convergence of achievement gaps, educational attainment, earnings and health status."[74] Not only did desegregation raise test scores, it elevated the standard of living for children by improving access to health care and the labor market.

Johnson also points out that the gains for students of color did not come at the expense of Whites. The fact that Whites did not experience adverse consequences due to desegregation and, in fact, have continued to experience academic growth "flies in the face of the fears that many whites held about integration as they predicted it would have negative effects for white children," Johnson writes. "Those negative effects simply never occurred."[75] In the present, when many White parents and teachers still say that some students (i.e., White students), will suffer if schools are integrated, it is a crucial point to make. Schools may have been desegregated to a degree, but racism has never been eliminated.

Beyond integration, we know what works, and there are public school administrators and teachers who know how to do it. Troy LaRaviere took notes from his successful instruction and leadership at James Weldon Johnson Elementary, an all-Black school on Chicago's economically depressed West Side. When he later began as principal at Blaine Elementary, he candidly remarked, "The same shit that worked for Black kids—guess what, it works for White kids too. It wasn't a big change—culture, climate, instruction, curriculum, building a culture of staff collaboration, and focused professional development. I mean, we just did what the research said to do."[76] In order to attract parents to public schools, the merits of an educational environment open to *all* students—in an environment with diverse classrooms, public oversight, opportunities for engagement and influence over the curriculum, and access to college and future employment—must be communicated.

Simply sending children to public schools is one of the clearest solutions to stemming the scourge of choice. It is the most difficult choice, but one that has pricked our national consciousness. When Nikole Hannah-Jones published her piece in the *New York Times Magazine* about enrolling her daughter, she outlined the turmoil all parents feel when signing their children up for public school.[77] She also posed the most serious challenge to all families.

Enrolling in public schools is a difficult choice. But choosing traditional public schools and following, uplifting, and empowering the work of BIPOC parents and students who prioritize Black students and students of color improves education for all. Far from perfect, public schools need radical change too. But supporting change agents such as Ronsha Dickerson, Troy LaRaviere, and others who have already identified solutions will improve the education of all students. By following their lead, and organizing to improve the quality of teaching, curricula, and discipline policies, the overall educational experience will improve. Through our investment in these solutions, the scope of conversation would change toward improving traditional public schools, not providing a way out.

Investment in traditional public education must also mean empowering parents, teachers, and local school improvement committees. Rather than coming in with "new" choice-based solutions, it is critically important to invest in BIPOC advocates in our schools and neighborhoods and support those already invested in improving education. There is a historic commitment and constitutional obligation to public education. To abandon it now only facilitates its demise.

Reengaging with public schools, enrolling children in public schools, and working to improve traditional public schools will ultimately reframe the debate. A bottom-up approach to reform will transform the way we as a nation view education. Rather than an individualized, private endeavor, education will truly become an institution for a public, shared, and common good. The fight will not be for my children but for our children.

The choice we face is ours to make.

ACKNOWLEDGMENTS

THIS BOOK BEGAN in Charleston, South Carolina, while working with Dave Dennis, Millicent Brown, Minerva King, Kendall Deas, Thomas Dixon, Smurf, Patricia Wright, Dan Ryan, Daron Calhoun, Jesse Williams, Jeremy Rutledge, Meta Van Sickle, and other stalwart defenders of and advocates for public education. Their insights, experience, and commitment to the fight are real and humbling. Their ability to push and push back leaves me in awe.

John Brown and Tom Thumb provided the motivation, strategic direction, and Heaven's Door to muster the courage, manage the stress, and pursue a vision.

Alia Habib helped breathe life into my research and writing at the beginning. Brilliant critiques and encouragement from Rachael Marks and the incredible team at Beacon Press were instrumental in finishing the book.

Derek Black offered invaluable feedback and a sharp eye while writing his own books. I am indebted to his generosity, counsel, friendship, and standard of excellence.

It was a privilege to revise parts of this manuscript with Candace Livingston, a rising scholar-activist who keeps the struggle going and the fire lit.

Speaking with teachers, parents, and organizers on the front lines has been a true honor and a learning experience for which I am forever grateful. Ronsha Dickerson, Hymethia Thompson, Keith Benson, Dave Stovall, Cardell Orrin, Stephanie Love, LaTricea Adams, Roblin

Webb, Aiko Kojima, Elisabeth Greer, Natasha Irskine, Marla Kilfoyle, Howard Fuller, Troy LaRaviere, and Charlisa Pugh—thank you!

Many friends and scholars took the time to read my manuscript and impart insights that still illuminate my path. Thank you, Kara Brown, Derrick Alridge, Chris Span, James Anderson, Mira Debs, Carol Singletary, Stan Thangaraj, Allison Anders, Payal Shah, Gloria Boutte, Bobby Donaldson, Christine Finnan, David Martinez, Eddie Cole, Tondra Loder-Jackson, Jennifer Birkshire, and Nick Covington.

NOTES

INTRODUCTION: THE CHOICE WE FACE

1. Peter H. Wood, *Black Majority: Negroes in Colonial South Carolina from 1670 Through the Stono Rebellion* (New York: Knopf, 1974); Bernard E. Powers Jr., *Black Charlestonians: A Social History, 1822–1885* (Fayetteville: University of Arkansas Press, 1994); "Burke High School," Public School Review, https://www.publicschoolreview.com/burke-high-school-profile/29403.

2. Paul Bowers, "Odds of Getting into Buist Academy? A Little Worse Than Getting into Harvard," *Post and Courier*, May 19, 2018; "Porter-Gaud School Rankings," Niche, https://www.niche.com/k12/porter-gaud-school-charleston-sc/rankings.

3. Robert N. Gross, *Public vs. Private: The Early History of School Choice in America* (Oxford: Oxford University Press, 2018); Sigal R. Ben-Porath and Michael C. Johanek, *Making up Our Mind: What School Choice Is Really About* (Chicago: University of Chicago Press, 2019); Antony Flew, "History of the Voucher Idea," Foundation for Economic Education, June 1, 1995, https://fee.org/articles/history-of-the-voucher-idea; Frank Heller, "Lessons from Maine: Education Vouchers for Students since 1873," *Cato Briefing Papers*, no. 66 (September 10, 2001), https://www.cato.org/sites/cato.org/files/pubs/pdf/bp66.pdf; Phillip W. Magness, "Myth: School Choice Has Racist Origins," in *School Choice Myths: Setting the Record Straight on Education Freedom*, ed. Corey A. DeAngelis and Neal P. McCluskey (Washington, DC: Cato Institute, 2020), 21–38; on Black private education in Chicago, see Worth Kamili Hayes, *Schools of Our Own: Chicago's Golden Age of Black Private Education* (Evanston, IL: Northwestern University Press, 2020).

4. Matt Barnum and Gabrielle LaMarr LeMee, "Looking for a Home? You've Seen GreatSchools Ratings. Here's How They Nudge Families Toward Schools with Fewer Black and Hispanic Students," *Chalkbeat*, December 5, 2019, https://www.chalkbeat.org/2019/12/5/21121858/looking-for-a-home-you-ve-seen-greatschools-ratings-here-s-how-they-nudge-families-toward-schools-wi; Jack Schneider, "What Makes a Great School?," Harvard Graduate School of Education, October 23, 2017, https://www.gse.harvard.edu/news/uk/17/10/what-makes-great-school.

5. Richard D. Kahlenberg, "From All Walks of Life: New Hope for School Integration," *American Educator* 36, no. 4 (Winter 2012–13): 2–14; Charles Willie, Ralph Edwards, and Michael Alves, *Student Diversity, Choice and School Improvement* (Westport, CT: Greenwood Press, 2002), 12–14, 21–31; Charles Willie and Michael Alves, *Controlled Choice: A New Approach to School Desegregated Education and School Improvement* (Providence: New England Desegregation Assistance Center for Equity in Education, 1996).

6. *Estimated Charter Public School Enrollment, 2016–17*, National Alliance for Public Charter Schools, http://www.publiccharters.org/sites/default/files /migrated/wp-content/uploads/2017/01/EER_Report_V5.pdf; "Types of School Choice," EdChoice, https://www.edchoice.org/school-choice/types-of -school-choice; "Public Charter School Enrollment," National Center for Education Statistics, March 2018, https://nces.ed.gov/programs/coe/indicator _cgb.asp; Thomas Snyder, Cristobal de Brey, and Sally A. Dillow, *Digest of Education Statistics, 2017* (National Center for Education Statistics, 2019), 67, https://nces.ed.gov/pubs2018/2018070.pdf; Ben-Porath and Johanek, *Making Up Our Mind*, 3–10.

7. Vinny Badolato, "Getting Past CREDO," ChalkBeat, November 21, 2011, https://www.chalkbeat.org/posts/co/2011/11/21/getting-past-credo; "Charter Schools: Finding Out the Facts," Center for Public Education, n.d., https://www.nsba.org/Services/Center-for-Public-Education; William Bushaw and Valerie Calderon, "Try It Again, Uncle Sam: The 46th Annual PDK/ Gallop Poll of the Public's Attitudes Toward the Public Schools," *Kappan Magazine* 96, no. 1 (September 2014): 9–20.

8. *A Nation at Risk* (Washington, DC: US Department of Education, April 1983), https://www2.ed.gov/pubs/NatAtRisk/risk.html; Valerie Straus, "'A Nation at Risk' Demanded Education Reform 35 Years Ago. Here's How It's Been Bungled Ever Since," *Washington Post*, April 26, 2018.

9. Joe Heim, "On the World Stage, U.S. Students Fall Behind," *Washington Post*, December 6, 2016; Drew DeSilver, "U.S. Students' Academic Achievement Still Lags That of Their Peers in Many Other Countries," Pew Research Center, February 15, 2017, http://www.pewresearch.org/fact-tank/2017/02/15 /u-s-students-internationally-math-science; Sophia Faridi, "Happy Teaching, Happy Learning: 13 Secrets to Finland's Success," *Education Week*, June 24, 2014, https://www.edweek.org/tm/articles/2014/06/24/ctq_faridi_finland.html. The Finnish phenomenon is challenged as well; see Joe Heim, "Finland's Schools Were Once the Envy of the World. Now, They're Slipping," *Washington Post*, December 8, 2016.

10. David Tyack and Larry Cuban, *Tinkering Toward Utopia: A Century of Public School Reform* (Cambridge, MA: Harvard University Press, 1995), 13.

11. Brian D. Ray, "Homeschooling Growing: Multiple Data Points Show Increase 2012 to 2016 and Later," National Home Education Research Institute, https://www.nheri.org/homeschool-population-size-growing; "Private School Enrollment," National Center for Education Statistics, https://nces .ed.gov/programs/coe/indicator_cgc.asp; *Estimated Charter Public School Enrollment, 2016–2017*.

12. This conservative number is based on the finding that charter school students receive, in 2011 terms, $6,500 per student. This number does not account for the $3 billion spent on charter schools since 1995 and the $1.1 billion increase Donald Trump proposed to Congress. Caroline Cournoyer, "Trump Proposes Unprecedented Expansion of School Choice," *Governing*, February 12, 2018, http://www.governing.com/topics/education/gov-trump-doe-education-budget-schools-states.html; Jonas Pearson, "Feds Spent $3.3 Billion on Charter Schools, with Few Controls," PR Watch, May 12, 2015, https://www.prwatch.org/news/2015/05/12830/federal-billions-fuel-charter-school-industry.

13. National Center for Education Statistics, "Status and Trends in the Education of Racial and Ethnic Groups," July 2017, https://nces.ed.gov/programs/raceindicators/indicator_rbb.asp.

14. Buddy Moorehouse, "National Poll: Support for Charter Schools Shows Sharp Increase among All Demographics," *MI Charters* (MAPSA, Michigan's Charter School Association), August 26, 2018, https://www.charterschools.org/blog/national-poll-support-for-charter-schools-shows-sharp-increase-among-all-demographics.

15. Danielle Douglas-Gabriel and Tracy Jan, "DeVos Called HBCUs 'Pioneers' of 'School Choice.' It Didn't Go over Well," *Washington Post*, February 28, 2017; Yamiche Alcindor, "Trump's Call for School Vouchers Is a Return to a Campaign Pledge," *New York Times*, March 1, 2017; Morgan Phillips, "Trump Calls School Choice the Civil Rights Issue of 'All-Time in This Country,'" Fox News, June 16, 2020.

16. Kristen Clark, "Thousands Rally in Support of Program Opposed by Union," *Miami Herald*, January 19, 2016; Allen Tullos, ed., "Southern Segregationist Origins of School 'Choice,'" *Southern Spaces* 3 (in possession of the author).

17. Southern Poverty Law Center, "SPLC Lawsuit: Mississippi Charter School Funding Violates State Constitution," July 2016, https://www.splcenter.org/news/2016/07/11/splc-lawsuit-mississippi-charter-school-funding-violates-state-constitution; Kristen Anderson, "Stories from the Field: Alabama's School 'Choice' Law Offer No Real Choice for Many Disadvantaged Children," Southern Poverty Law Center, March 30, 2014, https://www.splcenter.org/; Valerie Strauss, "NAACP Sticks by Its Call for Charter School Moratorium," *Washington Post*, July 26, 2017.

18. Noliwe Rooks, *Cutting School: Privatization, Segregation, and the End of Public Education* (New York: New Press, 2017); Michael Fabricant and Michelle Fine, *Charter Schools and the Corporate Makeover of Public Education* (New York: Teachers College Press, 2012); Raynard Sanders, David Stovall, and Terrenda White, *Twenty-First-Century Jim Crow Schools: The Impact of Charters on Public Education* (Boston: Beacon Press, 2018).

19. Paula S. Rothenberg, *White Privilege: Essential Readings on the Other Side of Racism* (New York: Worth Publishers, 2004); Jasmin Collins et al., "Longitudinal Leadership Capacity Growth Among Participants of a Leadership Immersion Program: How Much Does Structural Diversity Matter?,"

Journal of Leadership Education 17, no. 3 (July 2018): 175–94; Danielle L. Tate, "White People Need Diversity, Too," *Diverse Issues in Higher Education*, June 19, 2018, https://diverseeducation.com/article/118431.

20. Emily Deruy, "A Tale of Two Betsy DeVoses," *Atlantic*, March 8, 2017, https://www.theatlantic.com/education/archive/2017/03/a-tale-of-two-betsy -devoses/518952; Áine Cain, "Billionaire Betsy Devos Is the Richest Member of Trump's Cabinet—and Most of Her Wealth Came from a Company That Has Been Called a 'Pyramid Scheme,'" *Business Insider*, February 15, 2018, https://www.businessinsider.com/trump-education-secretary-betsy-devos -billionaire-net-worth-2018-2; Abram Van Engren, "Advancing God's King- dom: Calvinism, Calvin College, and Betsy DeVos," *Religion and Politics*, Janu- ary 30, 2017, https://religionandpolitics.org/2017/01/30/advancing-gods -kingdom-calvinism-calvin-college-and-betsy-devos; Laura Meckler, "The Education of Betsy DeVos: Why Her School Choice Agenda Has Not Ad- vanced," *Washington Post*, September 4, 2018.

21. Charles Barone and Marianne Lombardo, "Pre-CNN/Facebook Dem- ocratic Debate: K–12 Quotes from Hillary Clinton and Bernie Sanders," Edu- cation Reform Now, October 8, 2015, http://edreformnow.org/accountability /pre-cnnfacebook-democratic-debate-k-12-education-quotes-from-hillary -clinton-bernie-sanders.

22. Adam Laats, *The Other School Reformers: Conservative Activism in Amer- ican Education* (Cambridge, MA: Harvard University Press, 2015); and Jack Schneider and Jennifer Berkshire, *Wolf at the Schoolhouse Door: The Dismantling of Public Education and the Future of School* (New York: New Press, 2020).

CHAPTER ONE: THE "DIVINE RIGHT" AND OUR FREEDOM OF CHOICE IN EDUCATION

1. John Lewis and Michael D'Orso, *Walking with the Wind: A Memoir of the Movement* (New York: Simon & Schuster, 1998), 51–52.

2. Colin Dwyer, "Colson Whitehead, Rep. John Lewis among National Book Award Winners," National Public Radio, November 16, 2016; Lewis and D'Orso, *Walking with the Wind*, 23–26, 52 (quote), 54–56; Heather Williams, *Self-Taught: African American Education in Slavery and Freedom* (Chapel Hill: University of North Carolina Press, 2005).

3. James Patterson, *Brown v. Board of Education: A Civil Rights Milestone and Its Troubled Legacy* (New York: Oxford University Press, 2001), xiv; "Editorial Excerpts from the Nation's Press on Segregation Ruling," *New York Times*, May 18, 1954; Lewis and D'Orso, *Walking with the Wind*, 54–55.

4. "Segregation Crisis Faces Us," *Clarion-Ledger* (Jackson, MS), May 18, 1954.

5. "Voice of the People," *Clarion-Ledger*, June 8, 1954.

6. "Private School System Setup Is Considered," *Vicksburg (MS) Evening Post*, December 9, 1953.

7. "Editorial Excerpts from the Nation's Press on Segregation Ruling," *New York Times*, May 18, 1954.

8. "Southern Manifesto," 102 Cong. Rec. 4515–16 (1956); Matthew Las- siter and Andrew B. Lewis, *The Moderates' Dilemma: Massive Resistance to School*

Desegregation in Virginia (Charlottesville: University Press of Virginia, 1998); Ronald L. Heinemann, *Harry Byrd of Virginia* (Charlottesville: University Press of Virginia, 1996).

9. Pamela Grundy, *Color and Character: West Charlotte High and the American Struggle over Educational Equality* (Chapel Hill: University of North Carolina Press, 2017), 33–58; Frye Gaillard, *The Dream Long Deferred: The Landmark Struggle for Desegregation in Charlotte, North Carolina* (Columbia: University of South Carolina Press, 2006), 3–22.

10. Melba Pattillo Beals, *Warriors Don't Cry: A Searing Memoir of the Battle to Integrate Little Rock's Central High* (New York: Pocket Books, 1994), 1; Daisy Bates, *The Long Shadow of Little Rock: A Memoir* (Fayetteville: University of Arkansas Press, 2007); David Margolick, *Elizabeth and Hazel: Two Women of Little Rock* (New Haven, CT: Yale University Press, 2011).

11. Lewis and D'Orso, *Walking with the Wind*, 55–56.

12. Byrnes quoted in "South Carolina," *Southern School News*, November 4, 1954.

13. Rebekah Dobrasko, "Architectural Survey of Charleston County's School Equalization Program, 1951–1955," University of South Carolina, Public History Program, April 2005, 8–12; Charles Bolton, *The Hardest Deal of All: The Battle over School Integration in Mississippi, 1870–1980* (Jackson: University Press of Mississippi, 2005), 33–60; Neil R. McMillen, "Development of Civil Rights, 1956–1970," in *A History of Mississippi*, vol. 2, ed. Richard Aubrey McLemore (Jackson: University Press of Mississippi, 1973), 154–57; "Mississippi," *Southern School News*, November 4, 1954; "Private School System Setup Is Considered," *Vicksburg Evening Post*, December 9, 1953.

14. On equalization in South Carolina and Mississippi, see Dobrasko, "Architectural Survey of Charleston County's School Equalization Program"; and Bolton, *The Hardest Deal of All*.

15. On the history of school choice and the role of southern segregationists, see Steve Suitts, *Overturning Brown: The Segregationist Legacy of the Modern School Choice Movement* (Montgomery, AL: NewSouth Books, 2020).

16. "South Carolina," *Southern School News*, April 7, 1955, May 4, 1955; John W. White, "Managed Compliance: White Resistance and Desegregation in South Carolina, 1950–1970" (PhD diss., University of Florida, 2006), 54–58.

17. "Georgia," *Southern School News*, September 3, 1954; "Mississippi," *Southern School News*, January 6, 1955, March 3, 1955; "Louisiana Legislature Busy with Bills to Maintain Segregation," *Southern School News*, July 1956.

18. "Alabama," *Southern School News*, August 1955.

19. Sondra Gordy, *Finding the Lost Year: What Happened When Little Rock Closed Its Public Schools* (Fayetteville: University of Arkansas Press, 2009); Benjamin Muse, *Virginia's Massive Resistance* (Bloomington: Indiana University Press, 1961); Andrew B. Lewis, "Emergency Mothers: Basement Schools and the Preservation of Public Education in Charlottesville," in Lassiter and Lewis, *The Moderates' Dilemma*, 72–103; Christopher Bonastia, *Southern Stalemate: Five Years Without Public Education in Prince Edward County, Virginia* (Chicago: University of Chicago Press, 2012); Jill Ogline Titus, *Brown's Battleground: Students, Segregationists, and the Struggle for Justice in Prince Edward*

County Virginia (Chapel Hill: University of North Carolina Press, 2011); Bob Smith, *They Closed Their Schools: Prince Edward County, VA, 1951–1964* (Farmville, VA: Robert Russa Moton Museum, 1996).

20. Neil R. McMillen, *Citizen's Council: Organized Resistance to the Second Reconstruction, 1954–64* (Urbana: University of Illinois Press, 1994), 11–16; John White, "The White Citizens Council of Orangeburg County," in *Toward the Meeting of the Waters: Currents in the Civil Rights Movement of South Carolina During the Twentieth Century*, ed. W. B. Moore Jr. and Vernon Burton (Columbia: University of South Carolina Press, 2008), 261–73; Bolton, *The Hardest Deal of All*, 74–75, 174–77; John Dittmer, *Local People: The Struggle for Civil Rights in Mississippi* (Urbana: University of Illinois Press, 1994), 45–48; White, "Managed Compliance," 181–88.

21. Dittmer, *Local People*, 50–52; Millicent Brown, "Civil Rights Activism in Charleston, 1940–1970" (PhD diss., University of Florida); Bolton, *The Hardest Deal of All*, 66–67, 73–75.

22. R. Scott Baker, *Paradoxes of Desegregation: African American Struggles for Educational Equity in Charleston, South Carolina, 1926–1972* (Columbia: University of South Carolina Press, 2006), 159–61; "Ordeal of Numbers," *News and Courier*, August 31, 1963; "Submissive South," *News and Courier* (Charleston, SC), February 16, 1944; "To Revolutionize Schools," *News and Courier*, June 12, 1944.

23. Byrnes quoted in White, "Managed Compliance," 44; *Address of James F. Byrnes, Governor of South Carolina, to the South Carolina Education Association* (Columbia, SC: 1951).

24. "South Carolina," *Southern School News*, April 7, 1955, May 4, 1955; White, "Managed Compliance," 54–58; "Byrnes Plans Study Before Commenting on Court Ruling" and "SC Leaders Adopt 'Wait-See' Attitude on Court Decision," *The State* (Columbia, SC), May 18, 1954; "SC Candidates Accent Separate School Issue," *The State*, May 19, 1954; "Virginia Lawmakers Overwhelmingly Approve Interposition," *Southern School News*, March 1956; "Georgia," *Southern School News*, September 3, 1954, November 4, 1954; Bolton, *The Hardest Deal of All*, 105; Suitts, *Overturning Brown*, 12–17.

25. Suitts, *Overturning Brown*, 12–47; Jim Leeson, "Private Schools Continue to Increase in the South," *Southern Education Report* (November 1966): 22–25; McMillen, *The Citizens' Council*, 297–304; Michael W. Fuquay, "Civil Rights and the Private School Movement in Mississippi, 1964–1971," *History of Education Quarterly* 42, no. 2 (Summer 2002): 159–80; White, "Managed Compliance," 389–91.

26. Suitts, *Overturning Brown*, 12–17; Leeson, "Private Schools Continue to Increase in the South," 22–25; McMillen, *The Citizens' Council*, 297–304; Fuquay, "Civil Rights and the Private School Movement in Mississippi," 159–80; White, "Managed Compliance," 389–91; Kitty Terjen, "White Flight: The Segregation Academy Movement," in *The South and Her Children: School Desegregation 1970–1971*, ed. Robert E. Anderson (Atlanta: Southern Regional Council, 1971), 69.

27. Joseph P. Blank, "The Lost Years: What Happened to the Children When Prince Edward County, Virginia Closed Its Public Schools," William

Odum Collection, Box 1, "Odum Collection, Washington Post Article," Library, Special Collections, and Archives at Longwood University, Farmville, Virginia.

28. Leeson, "Private Schools Continue to Increase in the South," 25.

29. Timmerman quoted in "South Carolina," *Southern School News*, April 7, 1955.

30. "Byrnes Plans Study Before Commenting on Court Ruling" and "SC Leaders Adopt 'Wait-See' Attitude on Court Decision," *The State*, May 18, 1954, "SC Candidates Accent Separate School Issue," *The State*, May 19, 1954.

31. "Virginia," *Southern School News*, November 4, 1954.

32. Johnston quoted in Suitts, "Segregationists, Libertarians, and the Modern School Choice Movement," *Southern Spaces*, June 4, 2019, https://southern spaces.org/2019/segregationists-libertarians-and-modern-school-choice -movement; Joseph F. Johnston, "Schools, the Supreme Court, and the States' Power to Direct the Removal of Gunpowder," *Alabama Lawyer* 17, no. 3 (1956): 3–10.

33. Suitts, *Overturning Brown*, 12–15; Suitts, "Segregationists, Libertarians, and the Modern 'School Choice' Movement"; *Southern School News*, September 3, 1954, February 3, 1955, February 1961; "Alabama Expecting No Desegregation; 'Free Choice' Amendment Is Adopted," *Southern School News*, undated.

34. Almond quoted in "Massive Resistance Meets Its Match," in Lassiter and Lewis, *The Moderates' Dilemma*, 125–30; Leon Dure, "Virginia's New Freedoms," *Georgia Review* 18, no. 1 (Spring 1964): 3–16; *Southern Spaces*, 41.

35. "Virginia Launches Court Action Under New Laws," *Southern School News*, November 1956.

36. "Bill for Tuition Grants Introduced," *Southern School News*, February 1963.

37. H. Harrison Jenkins, "The Obituaries for Freedom of Choice Are Premature," *Southern Education Report* (January–February 1968).

38. Fritz Hollings, "Freedom of Choice School Desegregation," speech, February 1, 1970, US Senate, Ernest F. Hollings Collection, University of South Carolina, http://digital.tcl.sc.edu/cdm/ref/collection/how/id/33.

39. Hollings, "Freedom of Choice School Desegregation."

40. Patterson, *Brown v. Board of Education*, 136–46; Bolton, *The Hardest Deal of All*, 118–28.

41. "At Least 68 Per Cent of Systems in South Indicate Compliance," *Southern School News*, March 1965; Patterson, *Brown v. Board of Education*, 124–28; Bolton, *The Hardest Deal of All*, 118–28; Patrick J. McGuinn, *No Child Left Behind and the Transformation of Federal Education Policy, 1965–2005* (Lawrence: University Press of Kansas, 2006), 1–50.

42. "School Districts Hasten to Meet Act's Requirements," *Southern School News*, March 1965; "Few Boards Have Received Approval of Compliance Plans," *Southern School News*, April 1965; "Desegregation," *Southern Education Report* (July–August 1965): 31.

43. "Courts Order Seven Systems to Alter Plans," *Southern School News*, July 1964; Tomiko Brown-Nagin, *Courage to Dissent: Atlanta and the Long History of the Civil Rights Movement* (Oxford, UK: Oxford University Press, 2011), 331; Griffin v. School Board, 377 U.S. 218 (1964).

44. Alexander v. Holmes County Bd. of Ed., 396 U.S. 1218 (1969).

45. White, "Managed Compliance," 385–86; Benjamin Muse, "The South's Troubled Year," *Southern Education Report* (June 1969): 14–17; *Southern Education Report* (January–February 1968): 19–21; Michael B. Wise, "School Desegregation: The Court, the Congress, and the President," *School Review* 82, no. 2 (February 1974): 159–60.

46. Jon Hale, *The Freedom Schools: Student Activists in the Mississippi Civil Rights Movement* (New York: Columbia University Press, 2016), 106–7.

47. Bolton, *The Hardest Deal of All*, 171–72; Jerry DeLaughter, "In Crowded Coliseum, Quiet Hotel School Protest Calls Resound," *Memphis Commercial Appeal*, February 9, 1970.

48. Colin Dwyer, "Colson Whitehead, Rep. John Lewis Among National Book Award Winners," National Public Radio, November 16, 2016; Lewis and D'Orso, *Walking with the Wind*, 23–26, 52 (quote), 54–56; Williams, *Self-Taught*.

CHAPTER TWO: MILTON FRIEDMAN AND THE PROBLEMS WITH CHOICE IN CHICAGO

1. Lanny Ebenstein, *Milton Friedman: A Biography* (New York: Palgrave Macmillan, 2007), 5–14.

2. Ebenstein, *Milton Friedman*, 105–10.

3. Ebenstein, *Milton Friedman*, 105–10; Milton and Rose D. Friedman, *Two Lucky People: Memoirs* (Chicago: University of Chicago Press, 1998), 40–41.

4. Friedman and Friedman, *Two Lucky People*, 341.

5. Friedman and Friedman, *Two Lucky People*, x–xi; Ebenstein, *Milton Friedman*, 11.

6. Angela Duckworth et al., "Grit: Perseverance and Passion For Long-Term Goals," *Journal of Personality and Social Psychology* 92, no. 6 (2007): 1087–1101; Angela Duckworth, *Grit: The Power and Passion of Perseverance* (New York: Scribner, 2016); Mohamed Younis, "Most Americans See American Dream as Achievable," Gallup, July 17, 2019, https://news.gallup.com /poll/260741/americans-american-dream-achievable.aspx.

7. "This Year's Economics Prize to an American," Nobel Prize, press release, October 14, 1976, https://www.nobelprize.org/prizes/economic-sciences /1976/press-release.

8. "This Year's Economics Prize to an American."

9. Milton and Rose Friedman, *Free to Choose: A Personal Statement* (New York: Harcourt, 1980); *Free to Choose*, PBS television series, 1980.

10. Milton Friedman, "The Role of Government in Education," in *Economics and the Public Interest*, ed. Robert Solo and Eugene Ewald (New Brunswick, NJ: Rutgers University Press, 1955), 123–44.

11. Friedman, "The Role of Government in Education"; Suitts, *Overturning Brown*, 38–39.

12. Friedman, "The Role of Government in Education," 131.

13. Friedman, "The Role of Government in Education," 131.

14. Friedman, "The Role of Government in Education," 131.

15. Friedman, "The Role of Government in Education"; *Southern Spaces*, 38–39.

16. Milton Friedman, *Capitalism and Freedom*, 40th anniv. ed. (1962; Chicago: University of Chicago Press, 2002), 118.

17. Friedman, *Capitalism and Freedom*, 118.

18. Friedman, "The Role of Government in Education."

19. Friedman, *Capitalism and Freedom*, 117.

20. Steve Suitts, *Overturning Brown: The Segregationist Legacy of the Modern School Choice Movement* (Montgomery, AL: NewSouth Books, 2020), 54–60; Steve Suitts, "Segregationists, Libertarians, and the Modern 'School Choice' Movement," *Southern Spaces* (June 4, 2019), https://southernspaces.org/2019/segregationists-libertarians-and-modern-school-choice-movement; Friedman, *Capitalism and Freedom*, 111–15.

21. Friedman, *Capitalism and Freedom*, 115–17.

22. Nancy MacLean, *Democracy in Chains: The Deep History of the Radical Right's Stealth Plan for America* (New York: Penguin Books, 2017); Andrew Hartman, "The Master Class on the Make: How the White Backlash Found Its Academic Bona Fides," *The Baffler* 37 (December 2017), https://thebaffler.com/salvos/master-class-on-the-make-hartman.

23. Friedman quoted in "Friedman Cautions Against Rights Bill," *Harvard Crimson*, May 5, 1964, https://www.thecrimson.com/article/1964/5/5/friedman-cautions-against-rights-bill-pmilton; Suitts, *Overturning Brown*, 54–60; Suitts, "Segregationists, Libertarians, and the Modern 'School Choice' Movement."

24. Friedman and Friedman, *Two Lucky People*, 368.

25. Milton Friedman, "The Goldwater View of Economics," *New York Times*, October 11, 1964; Friedman and Friedman, *Two Lucky People*, 370; MacLean, *Democracy in Chains*, 88–92.

26. Friedman and Friedman, *Two Lucky People*, 370–71; MacLean, *Democracy in Chains*, 88–92.

27. Ansley Erickson, *Making the Unequal Metropolis: School Desegregation and Its Limits* (Chicago: University of Chicago Press, 2016), 4, 25–27.

28. See Erickson, *Making the Unequal Metropolis*, 4–15.

29. Friedman, *Capitalism and Freedom*, 118.

30. Natalie Y. Moore, *The South Side: A Portrait of Chicago and American Segregation* (New York: Picador, 2016), 40–41; Arnold R. Hirsch, *Making the Second Ghetto: Race and Housing in Chicago, 1940–1960* (Cambridge: Cambridge University Press, 1983), 3; *Urban Renewal and the Negro in Chicago* (Chicago: Chicago Urban League, 1958), 10, Table 1; Isabel Wilkerson, *The Warmth of Other Suns: The Epic Story of America's Great Migration* (New York: Random House, 2010); Nicholas Lemann, *The Promised Land: The Great Black Migration and How It Changed America* (New York: Alfred A. Knopf, 1991). 6.

31. *Urban Renewal and the Negro in Chicago*, 11.

32. On the history of racial covenants, see Jeffrey D. Gonda, *Unjust Deeds: The Restrictive Covenant Cases and the Making of the Civil Rights Movement* (Chapel Hill: University of North Carolina Press, 2015).

33. Moore, *The South Side*, 41–43.

34. Hirsch, *The Making of the Second Ghetto*, 40–42.

35. Wilkerson, *The Warmth of Other Suns*, 372–75; Hirsch, *The Making of the Second Ghetto*, 40–42.

36. Wilkerson, *The Warmth of Other Suns*, 396–98.

37. Moore, *The South Side*, 44–48.

38. *Urban Renewal and the Negro in Chicago*, Table 1 and Table 2; Hirsch, *Making of the Second Ghetto*, 27–29; Worth Kamili Hayes, *Schools of Our Own: Chicago's Golden Age of Black Private Education* (Evanston, IL: Northwestern University Press, 2020), 49–50.

39. Hirsch, *Making of the Second Ghetto*, 31–34.

40. "How Chicago Is Redeveloping Slum Areas," *Chicago Sun-Times*, September 28, 1952; "Preventing Tomorrow's Slums: A Citizens Action Program," Hyde Park Historical Society Collection, Box 78, Folder 17, University of Chicago Library; Hirsch, *Making the Second Ghetto*, 100–107, 122–27; Paul V. Betters, "The United States Housing Act 1949," *Annals of Public and Cooperative Economics* 20, no. 3 (September 1949): 375–78.

41. *Urban Renewal and the Negro in Chicago*, 4; Hayes, *Schools of Our Own*, 27–31.

42. Kimpton quoted in Austin C. Wehrwein, "Chicago U. Spurs Renewal Project," *New York Times*, November 1, 1959; LaDale C. Winling, *Building the Ivory Tower: Universities and Metropolitan Development in the Twentieth Century* (Philadelphia: University of Pennsylvania Press, 2017), 95; Eddie R. Cole, "'We Simply Cannot Operate in Slums': The University and Housing Discrimination," chap. 2 in *The Campus Color Line: College Presidents and the Struggle for Black Freedom* (Princeton, NJ: Princeton University Press, 2020), 51.

43. Cole, "'We Simply Cannot Operate in Slums,'" 41.

44. Cole, "'We Simply Cannot Operate in Slums,'" 50; "The Hyde Park-Kenwood Urban Renewal Survey," Spring–Summer 1956, 171, Hyde Park Historical Society Collection, Box 11, Folder 13 ("Urban Renewal Survey"), University of Chicago Library.

45. *Urban Renewal and the Negro in Chicago*, 13, Table 1.

46. Facts on the Conditions of Hyde Park, February 1957, Hyde Park Historical Society Collection, Box 72, Folder 27, University of Chicago Library; Robert Stevens, "Community Leads Way to Rehabilitation of Cities," *Chicago Tribune*, July 23, 1960.

47. "Director's Report, 1957 Annual Meeting," 3–4, Hyde Park Historical Society Collection, Box 72, Folder 6, "Hyde-Park Kenwood Community Conference, Directors Report, 1957," University of Chicago Library.

48. Robert Stevens, "Community Leads Way to Rehabilitation of Cities," *Chicago Tribune*, July 23, 1960, in Hyde Park Historical Society Collection, Box 78, Folder 13, "Chicago Tribune, 'The Hyde Park Story,'" Special Collections Research Center, University of Chicago.

49. Stevens, "Community Leads Way to Rehabilitation of Cities," *Chicago Tribune*, July 23, 1960.

50. Quoted in Austin C. Wehrwein, "Chicago U. Spurs Renewal Project," *New York Times*, November 1, 1959; Winling, *Building the Ivory Tower*, 95; Margaret Weir, "Urban Poverty and Defensive Localism," *Dissent* 41 (Summer 1994): 337–42; Thomas Sugrue, *The Origins of the Urban Crisis: Race and Inequality in Postwar Detroit* (Princeton, NJ: Princeton University Press, 1996).

51. Wehrwein, "Chicago U. Spurs Renewal Project"; Cole, "'We Simply Cannot Operate in Slums,'" 51; Davarian L. Baldwin, "The '800-Pound Gargoyle': The Long History of Higher Education and Urban Development on Chicago's South Side," *American Quarterly* 67, no. 1 (March 2015): 84–87; Delmont, "Making Philadelphia Safe for 'WFIL-adelphia': Television, Housing, and Defensive Localism in Postwar Philadelphia," *Journal of Urban History* 38, no. 1: 89–113.

52. Hirsch, *The Making of the Second Ghetto*, 42–45, 135–39 ("stable" on 137).

53. Cole, "'We Simply Cannot Operate in Slums,'" 68–73.

54. Hirsch, *Making of the Second Ghetto*, 42–45, 135–39, quote on 137.

55. Cole, "'We Simply Cannot Operate in Slums,'" 49; Wehrwein, "Chicago U. Spurs Renewal Project."

56. Cole, "'We Simply Cannot Operate in Slums,'" 49; Wehrwein, "Chicago U. Spurs Renewal Project"; "Citizens Mass Meeting," in Hyde Park Historical Society Collection, Box 78, Folder 19, University of Chicago Library.

57. Daley quoted in "The Hyde Park Story," 3, in Hyde Park Historical Society Collection, Box 78, Folder "Chicago Tribune, "The Hyde Park Story," University of Chicago Library.

58. Elizabeth Todd-Breeland, *A Political Education: Black Politics and Education Reform in Chicago Since the 1960s* (Chapel Hill: University of North Carolina Press, 2018), 26.

59. See Erickson, *Making the Unequal Metropolis*, 4–15.

60. Dionne Danns, *Desegregating Chicago's Public Schools: Policy Implementation, Politics, and Protest, 1965–1985* (New York: Palgrave MacMillan, 2014), 11–15.

61. Webb v. Board of Education of City of Chicago, 223 F. Supp. 466 (N.D. Ill. 1963).

62. Danns, *Desegregating Chicago's Public Schools*, 13–14.

63. Danns, *Desegregating Chicago's Public Schools*, 4; Nicholas Kryczka, "Building a Constituency for Racial Integration: Chicago's Magnet Schools and the Prehistory of School Choice," *History of Education Quarterly* 59, no. 1 (February 2019): 1–34; Moore, *The South Side*, 113–17.

64. Todd-Breland, *A Political Education*, 27–31; Moore, *The South Side*, 117–18; Danns, *Desegregating Chicago's Public Schools*, 19–20.

65. Danns, *Desegregating Chicago's Public Schools*, 1–3.

66. Danns, *Desegregating Chicago's Public Schools*, 1–3.

67. Todd-Breland, *A Political Education*, 29–31; Danns, *Desegregating Chicago's Public Schools*, 15, 19–21; Moore, *The South Side*, 118–20; on the implications of this history, see Rashad Shabazz, *Spatializing Blackness: Architectures of Confinement and Black Masculinity in Chicago* (Urbana: University of Illinois Press, 2015).

68. Friedman, *Freedom and Capitalism* (Chicago: University of Chicago Press, 1962), 118.

69. Martin Luther King Jr., "Chicago Campaign," chap. 28 in *The Autobiography of Martin Luther King, Jr.*, ed. Clayborne Carson (New York: Time Warner, 1998), in Martin Luther King, Jr. Research and Education Institute,

Stanford, https://kinginstitute.stanford.edu/king-papers/publications
/autobiography-martin-luther-king-jr-contents/chapter-28-chicago
-campaign.

70. Friedman and Friedman, *Two Lucky People*, 341.

71. Friedman quoted in "Friedman Cautions Against Rights Bill"; Suitts,
Overturning Brown, 54–60; Suitts, "Segregationists, Libertarians, and the
Modern 'School Choice' Movement."

CHAPTER THREE: RACISM BY YET ANOTHER NAME

1. Rakes quoted in Celia Wren, "Stars and Strife: A Clash of Cultures at
Boston's City Hall in 1976 Symbolized the City's Years-Long Confrontation
with the Busing of Schoolchildren," *Smithsonian*, April 2006, https://www
.smithsonianmag.com/history/stars-and-strife-113668570.

2. Jack Tager, *Boston Riots: Three Centuries of Social Violence* (Boston: North-
eastern University Press, 2001), 220–21; "Life After Iconic 1976 Photo: The
American Flag's Role in Racial Protest," National Public Radio, September 18,
2016.

3. Wren, "Stars and Strife"; Tager, *Boston Riots*, 221.

4. Millicent Brown, interview by Vanessa Jackson, Atlanta, 2005, Avery
Research Center, Charleston, South Carolina, transcript in possession of the
author; Millicent Brown, interview with the author, February 23, 2020.

5. Lewis and Orso, *Walking with the Wind*, 51–52.

6. Orville Vernon Burton, Beatrice Burton, and Simon Appleford, "'Seeds
in Unlikely Soil': The Briggs v. Elliot School Segregation Case," in *Toward the
Meeting of the Waters: Currents in the Civil Rights Movement of South Carolina
During the Twentieth Century*, ed. Winfred E. Moore and Orville Vernon Burton (Columbia: University of South Carolina Press, 2008), 191.

7. Jonathan Kozol, *Death at an Early Age: The Destruction of the Hearts and
Minds of Negro Children in the Boston Public Schools* (Boston: Houghton Mifflin,
1967); James Bryant Conant, *Slums and Suburbs: A Commentary on Schools in
Metropolitan Areas* (New York: McGraw-Hill, 1961); Holt quoted in Nat Hen-
toff, *Our Children Are Dying* (New York: Viking Press, 1967), ix; *Blackboard
Jungle*, dir. Richard Brooks (1955; Burbank, CA: Warner Home Video, 2005).

8. Matthew F. Delmont, *Why Busing Failed: Race, Media, and the National
Resistance to School Desegregation* (Oakland: University of California Press,
2016), 29–48; Jerald E. Podair, *The Strike That Changed New York: Blacks,
Whites, and the Ocean Hill-Brownsville Crisis* (New Haven, CT: Yale University
Press, 2002), 24–26; Adina Back, "Exposing the 'Whole Segregation Myth':
The Harlem Nine and New York City's School Desegregation Battles," in
Freedom North: Black Freedom Struggles Outside the South, 1940–1980, ed.
Jeanne Theoharis and Komozi Woodard (New York: Palgrave Macmillan,
2003), 69–71.

9. Delmont, *Why Busing Failed*, 38–43; Fred Powledge, "Busing Still an
Issue: Desegregation Disputes Boiling in North," *New York Times*, January 13,
1965.

10. Delmont, *Why Busing Failed*, 23–25; Matthew Delmont, "'Jim Crow
Must Go': Thousands of New York City Students Staged a One-Day Boycott

to Protest Segregation—and It Barely Made the History Books," *Salon*, February 3, 2016, https://www.salon.com/2016/02/03/jim_crow_must_go _thousands_of_new_york_city_students_staged_a_one_day_boycott_to _protest_segregation_and_it_barely_made_the_history_books.

11. Delmont, *Why Busing Failed*, 23–25.

12. Leonard Buder, "275,638 Pupils Stay Home in Integration Boycott," *New York Times*, September 15, 1964; Delmont, *Why Busing Failed*, 48–49.

13. Joseph Lelyveld, "Keating Position on Busing Praised," *New York Times*, September 7, 1964.

14. Camille Walsh, *Racial Taxation: Schools, Segregation, and Taxpayer Citizenship, 1869–1973* (Chapel Hill: University of North Carolina Press, 2018); Delmont, *Why Busing Failed*, 23–25, 74–78.

15. Buder, "275,638 Pupils Stay Home in Integration Boycott"; Delmont, *Why Busing Failed*, 48–49.

16. Fred Graham, "High Court Backs Pairing in Queens," *New York Times*, November 9, 1965.

17. Krasowski quoted in Delmont, *Why Busing Failed*, 70.

18. Frew Powledge, "Poll Shows Whites in City Resent Civil Rights Drive," *New York Times*, September 21, 1964; Delmont, *Why Busing Failed*, 48–49.

19. Buder, "275,638 Pupils Stay Home in Integration Boycott"; Fred Graham, "High Court Backs Pairing in Queens," *New York Times*, November 9, 1965.

20. Todd-Breeland, *A Political Education*, 41–44; Danns, *Desegregating Chicago's Public Schools*, 31–34; Delmont, *Why Busing Failed*, 73–75; "Busing Zealots," *Chicago Tribune*, June 11, 1968; Nicholas Kryczka, "Building a Constituency for Racial Integration: Chicago's Magnet Schools and the Prehistory of School Choice," *History of Education Quarterly* 59, no. 1 (February 2019): 1–34. The U.S. Office of Education was a bureaucratic entity within the larger U.S. Department of the Interior between 1867 and 1972.

21. "Busing Zealots," *Chicago Tribune*, June 11, 1968.

22. Todd-Breeland, *A Political Education*, 42–43; Danns, *Desegregating Chicago's Public Schools*, 32–44.

23. Tager, *Boston Riots*, 192.

24. "Busing Zealots"; Todd-Breeland, *A Political Education*, 42.

25. Danns, *Desegregating Chicago's Public Schools*, 42–43.

26. Jansen quoted in Delmont, *Why Busing Failed*, 30.

27. Delmont, *Why Busing Failed*, 32.

28. Civil Rights Act of 1964, Title VI, 42 U.S.C. § 2000d et seq.

29. Civil Rights Act of 1964, Pub. L. 88–352, 78 Stat. 241 (1964); Joseph Crespino, "The Best Defense Is a Good Offense: The Stennis Amendment and the Fracturing of Liberal School Desegregation Policy, 1964–1972," *Journal of Policy History* 18, no. 3 (2006): 304–25; Delmont, *Why Busing Failed*, 49–53.

30. "Compulsory Busing Opposed by Keating: Keating Announces Opposition to Compulsory Busing of Pupils," *New York Times*, September 6, 1964; R. W. Apple Jr., "Kennedy Says He Opposes Distant Busing of Students," *New York Times*, September 6, 1964.

31. "Text of Senator Goldwater's Address at Madison Sq. Garden in Only Campaign Appearance in City," *New York Times*, October 27, 1964; Goldwater Exhorts 18,000 in Garden 'Victory' Rally," *New York Times*, October 27, 1964; Delmont, *Why Busing Failed*, 93–94.

32. "Nixon Replies," *New Republic*, October 26, 1968, 15; Delmont, *Why Busing Failed*, 118–19; Nixon quoted in James Bolner and Robert Shanley, *Busing: The Political and Judicial Process* (New York: Praeger, 1974), 141.

33. Crespino, "The Best Defense Is a Good Offense," 304–25.

34. Joyce A. Baugh, *The Detroit School Busing Case: Milliken v. Bradley and the Controversy over Desegregation* (Lawrence: University Press of Kansas, 2011), 103–5; Grundy, *Color and Character*, 53–56.

35. Green v. County School Board of New Kent County (no. 695) 391 U.S. 430; Baugh, *The Detroit School Busing Case*, 103.

36. Swann v. Charlotte-Mecklenburg Board of Education 22 Ill. 402 U.S. 1, 91 S. Ct. 1267, 28 L. Ed. 2d 554 (1971).

37. Tager, *Boston Riots*, 171–87; Ronald P. Formisano, *Boston Against Busing: Race, Class, and Ethnicity in the 1960s and 1970s* (Chapel Hill: University of North Carolina Press, 1991), 17, 25.

38. Hale, *The Freedom Schools*, 35; Delmont, *Why Busing Failed*, 85–90; Tager, *Boston Riots*, 192–93; Jeanne Theoharis, "'I'd Rather Go to School in the South': How Boston's School Desegregation Complicates the Civil Rights Paradigm," in Theoharis and Woodard, *Freedom North*, 125–52.

39. Delmont, *Why Busing Failed*, 80–83; Tager, *Boston Riots*, 171–87, 192–93.

40. Delmont, *Why Busing Failed*, 77–80, 84 (Garrity quote), 199–200; Tager, *Boston Riots*, 192–93; Formisano, *Boston Against Busing*, 66–70; Baugh, *The Detroit School Busing Case*, 160.

41. Delmont, *Why Busing Failed*, 77–80; Tager, *Boston Riots*, 191–95; Formisano, *Boston Against Busing*, 53–65.

42. Elizabeth Gillespie McRae, *Mothers of Massive Resistance: White Women and the Politics of White Supremacy* (Oxford: University Press, 2018); 217–40; Theoharis, "'I'd Rather Go to School in the South,'" 140.

43. McRae, *Mothers of Massive Resistance*.

44. Tager, *Boston Riots*, 191–95.

45. Quoted in Tager, *Boston Riots*, 198.

46. Tager, *Boston Riots*, 198–200, 209–14.

47. Gary McMillan, "Alternative Schools Due to Open in 3 Neighborhoods," *Boston Globe*, September 11, 1975; Nick King, "Some Look to Private Schools as Alternative to Busing," *Boston Globe*, May 5, 1975.

48. Robert Jordan, "White Would Discussed [sic] Aid to Private Schools," *Boston Globe*, March 5, 1975.

49. Formisano, *Boston Against Busing*, 140–41; John Kifner, "White Pupils' Rolls Drop a Third in Boston Busing," *New York Times*, December 15, 1975; Jordan, "White Would Discussed [sic] Aid to Private Schools"; Ken Botwright, "Anrig Presses Fahey on Rules for Academies," *Boston Globe*, November 10, 1975.

50. Kifner, "White Pupils' Rolls Drop a Third in Boston Busing."

51. Tager, *Boston Riots*, 222–23; Formisano, *Boston Against Busing*, 2, 211–14; Allan R. Gold, "Boston Ready to Overhaul School Busing Policy," *New York Times*, December 28, 1988.

52. Delmont, *Why Busing Failed*, 12–20, 191–93.

53. Delmont, *Why Busing Failed*, 204–6; Tager, *Boston Riots*, 196–99; Erickson, *Making the Unequal Metropolis*.

54. Todd-Breeland, *A Political Education*, 43–46.

55. Daniel Patrick Moynihan, *The Negro Family: The Case for National Action* (Washington, DC: US Department of Labor, Office of Planning and Research, March 1965).

56. Delmont, *Why Busing Failed*, 206–8.

57. Todd-Breeland, *A Political Education*, 50.

58. Russell Rickford, *We Are an African People: Independent Education, Black Power, and the Radical Imagination* (Oxford: Oxford University Press, 2016), 38.

59. Hale, *The Freedom Schools*, 68; Rickford, *We Are an African People*, 80–82.

60. Hale, *The Freedom Schools*, 179–81; Rickford, *We Are an African People*, 88–97.

61. Moses quoted in Hale, *The Freedom Schools*, 173.

62. Stokely Carmichael, "What We Want," *New York Review of Books* 7 (September 22, 1966): 5–8, available via Civil Rights Movement Archive, https://www.crmvet.org/info/stokely1.pdf.

63. Podair, *The Strike That Changed New York*, 73–76; Clarence Taylor, *Knocking at Our Own Door: Milton A. Galamison and the Struggle to Integrate New York City Schools* (New York: Columbia University Press, 1997), 180–91; Richard D. Kahlenberg, *Tough Liberal: Albert Shanker and the Battles Over Schools, Unions, Race, and Democracy* (New York: Columbia University Press, 2007), 71–72; Heather Lewis, *New York City Public Schools from Brownsville to Bloomberg: Community Control and Its Legacy* (New York: Teachers College Press, 2013), 26–30.

64. Todd-Breeland, *A Political Education*, 69–78.

65. Baugh, *The Detroit School Busing Case*, 71–74; Angela D. Dillard, "Religion and Radicalism: The Reverend Albert B. Cleage, Jr., and the Rise of Black Christian Nationalism in Detroit," in *Freedom North: Black Freedom Struggles Outside the South*, ed. Jeanne Theoharis and Komozi Woodard (New York: Palgrave 2003), 153–76.

66. Quoted in Jeffrey Mirel, *The Rise and Fall of an Urban School System: Detroit, 1907–81* (Ann Arbor: University of Michigan Press, 1993), 331.

67. Mirel, *The Rise and Fall of an Urban School System*, 334–37.

68. Kahlenburg, *Tough Liberal*, 121; Lewis, *New York City Public Schools*, 56–61.

69. Podair, *The Strike That Changed New York*, 75–77; Lewis, *New York City Public Schools*, 52–53.

70. Podair, *The Strike That Changed New York*, 81.

71. Podair, *The Strike That Changed New York*, 87–89; Taylor, *Knocking at Our Own Door*, 191–93.

72. Podair, *The Strike That Changed New York*, 83.

73. Quoted in Mirel, *The Rise and Fall of an Urban School System*, 309.

74. Jeanne Theoharis, *A More Beautiful and Terrible History: The Uses and Misuses of Civil Rights History* (Boston: Beacon Press, 2018), 89.

75. Diana D'Amico, "Teachers' Rights Versus Students' Rights: Race and Professional Authority in the New York City Public Schools, 1960–1986," *American Educational Research Journal* 53, no. 3 (June 2016): 541–72; Podair, *Strike That Changed New York*, 89–92; Kahlenburg, *Tough Liberal*, 71–75.

76. D'Amico, "Teachers' Rights Versus Students' Rights," 546–51; Kahlenburg, *Tough Liberal*, 93–124; Podair, *Strike That Changed New York*, 81–102; Lewis, *New York City Public Schools*, 31–54.

77. Kahlenburg, *Tough Liberal*, 71–72; Brittney Lewer, "Pursuing 'Real Power to Parents': Babette Edwards's Activism from Community Control to Charter Schools," unpublished manuscript, in possession of author.

78. Todd-Breeland, *Political Education*, 50–51; Lewer, "Pursuing 'Real Power to Parents.'"

79. "More Were Killed and Jailed in Watts in '65 Than in Newark," *New York Times*, July 17, 1967. See also Gerald Horne, *Fire This Time: The Watts Uprising and the 1960s* (Charlottesville: University Press of Virginia, 1995); Jerry Cohen and William S. Murphy, *The Lost Angeles Race Riot, August 1965* (New York: E. P. Dutton, 1966); Robert Bauman, *Race and the War on Poverty: From Watts to East L.A.* (Norman: University of Oklahoma Press, 2008), 31–43.

80. Horne, *Fire This Time*, 286–98; Daniel Nabors, "Manic Depression: Lyndon Johnson and the 1965 Watts Riots" (MA thesis, Baylor University, 2009), 58; Bauman, *Race and the War on Poverty*, 43.

81. Gene Roberts, "U.S. Troops Sent Into Detroit; 19 Dead; Johnson Decries Riots," *New York Times*, July 25, 1967; Joe T. Darden and Richard W. Thomas, *Detroit: Race Riots, Racial Conflicts, and Efforts to Bridge the Racial Divide* (East Lansing: Michigan State University Press, 2013), 1–3; Theoharis, *A More Beautiful and Terrible History*, 71–73.

82. Cleage, *Freedom North*; Darden and Thomas, *Detroit*, 2–6; Mirel, *The Rise and Fall of an Urban School System*, 308–10.

83. Clay Risen, *A Nation on Fire: America in the Wake of the King Assassination* (Hoboken, NJ: John Wiley & Sons, 2009); Peter Levy, *The Great Uprising: Race Riots in Urban America During the 1960s* (Cambridge, UK: Cambridge University Press, 2018); J. Samuel Walker, *Most of 14th Street Is Gone: The Washington, DC Riots of 1968* (Oxford, UK: Oxford University Press, 2018).

84. Mirel, *The Rise and Fall of an Urban School System*, 330–33; Dara Walker, "Black Power, Education, and Youth Politics in Detroit, 1966–1973" (PhD diss., Rutgers University, 2018); Dara Walker, "Black Power and the Detroit High School Organizing Tradition," *Black Perspectives*, August 16, 2018, https://www.aaihs.org/Black-power-and-the-detroit-high-school-organizing -tradition-2.

85. Muriel Cohen, "What's Going on at South Boston High School? Overcrowding, Discipline the Major Problems," *Boston Globe*, October 12, 1976.

86. Jon N. Hale, "Future Foot Soldiers or Budding Criminals? The Dynamics of High School Student Activism in the Southern Black Freedom

Struggle," *Journal of Southern History* 84, no. 3 (August 2018): 615–52; Gael Graham, *Young Activists: American High School Students in the Age of Protest* (DeKalb: Northern Illinois University Press, 2006), 5–6; Judith Kafka, "The History of 'Zero Tolerance,'" in *American Public Schooling* (London, UK, 2011), 56–58, 99–103; Judith Kafka, "'Sitting on a Tinderbox': Racial Conflict, Teacher Discretion, and the Centralization of Disciplinary Authority," *American Journal of Education* 114, no. 3 (May 2008): 247–70.

87. ACLU, *Bullies in Blue: The Origins and Consequences of School Policing* (New York: American Civil Liberties Union, 2017), https://www.aclu.org/sites/default/files/field_document/aclu_bullies_in_blue_4_11_17_final.pdf; Hale, "Future Foot Soldiers or Budding Criminals?," 641–51; Kafka, "The History of 'Zero Tolerance,'" 6–7, 92–94; Carl F. Kaestle, *Pillars of the Republic: Common Schools and American Society, 1780–1860* (New York: Macmillan, 1983), 67–69, 160–61; Gerald Grant, *The World We Created at Hamilton High* (Cambridge, MA: Harvard University Press, 1988), 49–53.

88. Breeland, *A Political Education*, 35.

89. Mirel, *The Rise and Fall of an Urban School System*, 220.

90. Mirel, *The Rise and Fall of an Urban School System*, 359.

91. Christine H. Rossell, "Boston's Segregation and White Flight," *Equity and Excellence in Education* 15, no. 1 (1977): 36.

92. Formisano, *Boston Against Busing*, 210–11.

93. Bella English, "12 Years Under Desegregation: She Saw Opportunity as Well as White Flight," *Boston Globe*, April 27, 1986.

94. Todd-Breeland, *A Political Education*, 36.

95. Bonnie V. Winston, "Meanwhile, Many Parents Are Finding Alternatives," *Boston Globe*, April 13, 1986.

96. Formisano, *Boston Against Busing*, 210–11.

97. Mirel, *The Rise and Fall of an Urban School System*, 345–46; Baugh, *The Detroit School Busing Case*, 77–80, 127–30.

98. Delmont, *Why Busing Failed*, 140–41.

99. Wilfred Keyes et al. v. School District no. 1, Denver, Colorado, et al. 413 U.S. 189 (more) 93 S. Ct. 2686; 37 L. Ed. 2d 548; Delmont, *Why Busing Failed*, 128.

100. Potter quoted in Delmont, *Why Busing Failed*, 140.

101. Milliken v. Bradley, 418 U.S. 717 (1974).

102. James E. Ryan, "Brown, School Choice, and the Suburban Veto," 90 *Virginia Law Review* 90, no. 6 (2004): 1635–47; James E. Ryan, *Five Miles Away, a World Apart: One City, Two Schools, and the Story of Educational Opportunity in Modern America* (Oxford: Oxford University Press 2010); Ansley Erickson, "The Rhetoric of Choice: Segregation, Desegregation, and Charter Schools," in *Public Education Under Siege*, ed. Michael Katz and Mike Rose (Philadelphia; University of Pennsylvania Press, 2013), 122–30.

103. Milliken v. Bradley, 418 U.S. 717 (1974).

104. Milliken v. Bradley, 418 U.S. 717 (1974); Baugh, *The Detroit School Busing Case*, 171.

105. Rakes quoted in Wren, "Stars and Strife."

CHAPTER FOUR: FEDERAL SUPPORT OF THE SCHOOL CHOICE MOVEMENT

1. Lyndon B. Johnson, "Johnson's Remarks on Signing the Elementary and Secondary Education Act," April 11, 1965, LBJ Presidential Library, http://www.lbjlibrary.org/lyndon-baines-johnson/timeline/johnsons-remarks-on-signing-the-elementary-and-secondary-education-act.

2. Wayne Urban, *More Than Science and Sputnik: The National Defense Act of 1958* (Tuscaloosa: University of Alabama Press, 2010).

3. Gary Orfield and Susan Eaton, "Back to Segregation," *Nation*, February 13, 2003; Erica Frankenberg, Genevieve Siegel-Hawley, Jongyeon Ee, and Gary Orfield, *Southern Schools More Than a Half-Century After the Civil Rights Revolution* (Civil Rights Project, May 2017), https://www.civilrightsproject.ucla.edu/research/k-12-education/integration-and-diversity/southern-schools-brown-83-report, 8; Erwin Chemerinsky, "The Segregation and Resegregation of American Public Education: The Courts' Role," in *School Resegregation: Must the South Turn Back?*, ed. John Charles Boger and Gary Orfield (Chapel Hill: University of North Carolina Press, 2005), 29.

4. Patterson, *Brown v. Board of Education*, 136–46; Bolton, *The Hardest Deal of All*, 118–28; Danns, *Desegregating Chicago's Public Schools*, 1–3.

5. Delmont, *Why Busing Failed*, 114–29; Joseph Crespino, *Strom Thurmond's America* (New York: Hill and Wang, 2012), 207–10; Frank Brown, "Nixon's 'Southern Strategy' and Forces Against Brown," *Journal of Negro Education* 73, no. 3 (Summer 2004): 201–2.

6. Kevin P. Phillips, *The Emerging Republican Majority* (New Rochelle, NY: Arlington House, 1969), 25.

7. Walter Rugaber, "Wallace off the Critical List; Sweeps Primary in Michigan and Wins Handily in Maryland," *New York Times*, May 17, 1971; Delmont, *Why Busing Failed*, 114–15.

8. Kevin M. Kruse, *White Flight: Atlanta and the Making of Modern Conservatism* (Princeton, NJ: Princeton University Press, 2005), 253–56; Philips, *The Emerging Republican Majority*, 473–74.

9. Crespino, *Strom Thurmond's America*, 211–14; Dean J. Kotlowski, "Nixon's Southern Strategy Revisited," *Journal of Policy History* 10, no. 2 (1998): 208–9, 212–16.

10. "Text of the President's Statement Explaining His Policy on School Desegregation: Nixon Seeks to Raise Education Quality, with Stress on 'Racially Impacted' Areas," *New York Times*, March 25, 1970; Delmont, *Why Busing Failed*, 126–29.

11. "Transcript of Nixon's Statement on School Busing," *New York Times*, March 17, 1972.

12. Emily M. Hodge, "School Desegregation and Federal Inducement: Lessons from the Emergency School Aid Act of 1972," *Educational Policy* 32, no. 1 (March 2016): 1–2, 13; Gary Orfield, *Congressional Power: Congress and Social Change* (New York: Harcourt Brace Jovanovich, 1975), 78–79.

13. Orfield, *Congressional Power*, 173–78; Hodge, "School Desegregation and Federal Inducement," 16.

14. Hodge, "School Desegregation and Federal Inducement," 16.

15. Delmont, *Why Busing Failed*, 114–18; Chemerinsky, "The Segregation and Resegregation of American Public Education," 41–42.

16. Linda Greenhouse, "Warren Burger Is Dead at 87; Was Chief Justice for 17 Years," *New York Times*, June 26, 1995; Rick Perlstein, *Nixonland: The Rise of a President and the Fracturing of America* (New York: Scribner, 2008), 386–91; "Examining the Legacy of Chief Justice Warren Burger," *Constitution Daily*, National Constitution Center, June 9, 2019, https://constitutioncenter. org/blog/examining-the-legacy-of-chief-justice-warren-burger.

17. Baugh, *The Detroit School Busing Case*, 120–21; quotes from Perlstein, *Nixonland*, 386–91, 605; Black, *Schoolhouse Burning*, 179–88.

18. Milliken v. Bradley, 418 U.S. 717 (1974), http://cdn.loc.gov/service/ll /usrep/usrep418/usrep418717/usrep418717.pdf; Delmont, *Why Busing Failed*, 140–41; Gary Orfield, "Segregated Housing and School Resegregation," in *Dismantling Desegregation: The Quiet Reversal of Brown v. Board of Education*, ed. Gary Orfield and Susan Eaton (New York: W. W. Norton, 1996), 296–97.

19. Gary Orfield, "Turning Back to Segregation," in Orfield and Eaton, *Dismantling Desegregation*, 2.

20. Dana Goldstein, *The Teacher Wars: A History of America's Most Embattled Profession* (New York: Penguin Random House, 2014), 166–67.

21. "Reagan on Busing," [1976], Ron Nessen Papers, Box 39, Folder "Reagan—Issues—Busing," Gerald R. Ford Presidential Library, Ann Arbor, Michigan, https://www.fordlibrarymuseum.gov/library/document/0204/1512166.pdf.

22. Joseph Crespino, *In Search of Another Country: Mississippi and the Conservative Counterrevolution* (Princeton, NJ: Princeton University Press, 2007), 1–3.

23. Delmont, *Why Busing Failed*, 211; Orfield, "Turning Back to Segregation," 16.

24. Orfield, "Turning Back to Segregation," 16–19.

25. "1980 Republican Platform," *Patriot Post*, https://patriotpost.us /documents/446; Robert Pear, "Reagan Proposes Vouchers to Give Poor a Choice of Schools," *New York Times*, November 14, 1985.

26. Crespino, *Strom Thurmond's America*, 270–71; Crespino, *In Search of Another Country*, 259–63.

27. Maris Vinovskis, *From a Nation at Risk to No Child Left Behind: National Education Goals and the Creation of Federal Education Policy* (New York: Teachers College Press, 2009), 15–16; Dan Bauman and Brock Read, "A Brief History of GOP Attempts to Kill Education Dept.," *Chronicle of Higher Education*, June 21, 2018, https://www.chronicle.com/article/A-Brief-History-of-GOP/243739; Robert Johnston, "Terrell Bell, Known for Defending Federal Role in Education, Dies," *Education Week*, July 10, 1996, https://www.edweek.org/policy-politics /terrel-bell-known-for-defending-federal-role-in-education-dies/1996/07; "1980 Republican Platform."

28. Vinovskis, *From a Nation at Risk to No Child Left Behind*, 15–16; Noel Epstein and Lee Lescaze, "Terrel Bell Reported Choice to Become Education Secretary," *Washington Post*, January 7, 1981; Bauman and Read, "A Brief History of GOP Attempts to Kill Education Dept."

29. National Commission on Excellence in Education, *A Nation at Risk: The Imperative for Educational Reform* (Washington, DC: US Department of Education, 1983), 5; Ravitch, *Reign of Error: The Hoax of the Privatization Movement and the Danger to America's Public Schools* (New York: Vintage Books, 2013), 10–11.

30. Vinovskis, *From a Nation at Risk to No Child Left Behind*, 18.

31. Vinovskis, *From a Nation at Risk to No Child Left Behind*, 16.

32. National Commission on Excellence in Education, *A Nation at Risk*.

33. National Commission on Excellence in Education, *A Nation at Risk*, 76–77.

34. Goldstein, *Teacher Wars*, 181.

35. Maris Vinovskis, *The Road to Charlottesville: The 1989 Education Summit* (National Education Goals Panel, 1999), https://govinfo.library.unt.edu/negp /reports/negp30.pdf, 6.

36. David C. Berliner and Bruce J. Biddle, *The Manufactured Crisis: Myths, Fraud, and the Attack on America's Public Schools* (Reading, MA: Addison-Wesley, 1995).

37. Vinovskis, "The Road to Charlottesville," 17–18.

38. Vinovskis, "The Road to Charlottesville," 17–18.

39. Vinovskis, *From a Nation at Risk to No Child Left Behind*, 14–15.

40. Clinton quoted in Vinovskis, *From a Nation at Risk to No Child Left Behind*, 25.

41. Vinovskis, *From a Nation at Risk to No Child Left Behind*, 26–27.

42. Vinovskis, *From a Nation at Risk to No Child Left Behind*, 42–51.

43. Vinovskis, "The Road to Charlottesville," 27.

44. President George H. W. Bush, "Address to the Nation on the National Education Strategy," April 18, 1991, American Presidency Project, https:// www.presidency.ucsb.edu/documents/address-the-nation-the-national -education-strategy; Jack Schneider, "George H. W. Bush Laid the Foundation for Education Reform," *The Conversation*, December 3, 2018, https:// theconversation.com/george-h-w-bush-laid-the-foundation-for-education -reform-108018.

45. Vinovskis, *From a Nation at Risk to No Child Left Behind*, 42–51.

46. Carl, *Freedom of Choice*, 100–102.

47. Richard D. Kahlenberg and Halley Potter, "Restoring Shanker's Vision for Charter Schools," *American Educator*, Winter 2014–2015, 9; Joetta L. Sack, "Clinton Turns Spotlight on Performance," *Education Week* 19, no. 35 (May 10, 2000) https://www.edweek.org/leadership/clinton-turns-spotlight-on -performance/2000/05.

48. Vinovskis, *From a Nation at Risk to No Child Left Behind*, 64–65.

49. Vinovskis, *From a Nation at Risk to No Child Left Behind*, 67–75.

50. Michael R. Benezra, "How Policymakers Started the Federal Charter School Movement: A Case Study in Policy Entrepreneurship" (master's thesis, Harvard Extension School, 2016), 10; US Department of Education, "Evaluation of the Public Charter Schools Program, Year One Evaluation Report," 2000, https://www2.ed.gov/rschstat/eval/choice/pcsp-year1/edlite-title.html.

51. H.R. 1804 (103rd): Goals 2000: Educate America Act, https://www .govtrack.us/congress/bills/103/hr1804.

52. "Charter Schools Program State Educational Agencies (SEA) Grant," US Department of Education, https://www2.ed.gov/programs/charter/funding .html.

53. Chemerinsky, "The Segregation and Resegregation of American Public Education," 29.

54. Clinton quoted in Benezra, "How Policymakers Started the Federal Charter School Movement," 53.

55. Sack, "Clinton Turns Spotlight on Performance."

56. Chemerinsky, "The Segregation and Resegregation of American Public Education," 38–41.

57. Grundy, *Color & Character*, 138–56; Sean F. Reardon and John T. Yun, "Integrating Neighborhoods, Segregating Schools: The Retreat from School Desegregation in the South, 1990–2000," in Boger and Orfield, *School Resegregation*, 64–65. On Nashville, see Erickson, *Making the Unequal Metropolis*.

58. US Department of Education, "No Child Left Behind," Executive Summary, January 7, 2002, https://www2.ed.gov/nclb/overview/intro/execsumm .pdf; Erik W. Robelen and Lisa Fine, "Bush Plan: 'No Child Will Be Left Behind,'" *Education Week* 20, no. 20 (January 31, 2001), https://www.edweek.org /policy-politics/no-child-left-behind-an-overview/2015/04; Diane Ravitch, *The Death and Life of the Great American School System: How Testing and Choice are Undermining Education* (New York: Basic Books, 2010), 96–98. H.R.1—No Child Left Behind Act of 2001, https://www.congress.gov/bill/107th-congress; Andrew Rudalevige, "The Politics of No Child Left Behind," *EducationNext* 3, no. 4 (Fall 2003), https://www.educationnext.org/the-politics-of-no-child-left -behind.

59. Robelen and Fine, "Bush Plan"; Ravitch, *The Death and Life of the Great American School System*, 96–98; US Department of Education, "No Child Left Behind."

60. Diane Ravitch, "NCLB: Measure and Punish," chap. 6 in *The Death and Life of the Great American School System*; Linda Darling-Hammond, "Evaluating 'No Child Left Behind,'" *Nation*, May 2, 2007, https://www.thenation.com /article/evaluating-no-child-left-behind; Goldstein, *The Teacher Wars*, 184–88.

61. National Center for Education Statistics, "Educational Institutions," https://nces.ed.gov/fastfacts/display.asp?id=84; Stephanie Stullich et al., *Title I Implementation: Update on Recent Evaluation Findings* (Washington, DC: US Department of Education, 2009), xx, 21; Ravitch, *The Death and Life of the Great American School System*, 104; Darling-Hammond, "Evaluating 'No Child Left Behind.'"

62. Ravitch, *The Death and Life of the Great American School System*, 199–201.

63. Bill and Melinda Gates Foundation, "Investment to Accelerate Creation of Strong Charter Schools," press release, June 7, 2003, https://www .gatesfoundation.org/media-center/press-releases/2003/06/investing-in-high quality-charter-schools.

64. James Forman, Jr. "The Rise and Fall of School Vouchers: A Story of Religion, Race, and Politics," *UCLA Law Review* 54, no. 3 (February 2007): 547–604.

65. "Out-of-State Money Funds 'Local' Pro-Voucher Political Action Groups," "All Children Matter—Organizational File," Box 2, Folder 7, and "Alliance for School Organizational File," Box 2, Folder 8, People for the American Way collection of political ephemera, Bancroft Library, University of California, Berkeley.

66. National Center for Education Statistics, "Number and Enrollment of Public Elementary and Secondary Schools, by School Level, Type, and Charter and Magnet Status: Selected Years, 1990–91 Through 2016–17," https:// nces.ed.gov/programs/digest/d18/tables/dt18_216.20.asp.

67. Shan Carter et al., "On the Issues: Education," *New York Times,* May 23, 2012; David Mark, "2010 Complete Election Coverage: Full Text: Obama Interview," *Politico,* February 12, 2018, https://www.politico.com/news/stories /0208/8457_Page2.html.

68. James Janega and Carlos Sadovi, "Duncan to Join Obama Cabinet," *Chicago Tribune,* December 16, 2008; Arne Duncan, *How Schools Work: An Inside Account of Failure and Success from One of the Nation's Longest Serving Secretaries of Education* (New York: Simon & Schuster, 2018), 57–58; Black, *Schoolhouse Burning,* 35–38.

69. Ana Betriz Cholo, "Businesses Help New Schools; $3.7 Million in Grants for Renaissance 2010," *Chicago Tribune,* February 23, 2005; Don Lubin, "Businesses Back Public School Reform," *Chicago Tribune,* December 6, 2004.

70. Ravitch, *Reign of Error,* 14–16; *Race to the Top Program Executive Summary* (Washington, DC: US Department of Education, 2009), 7, 11, https:// www2.ed.gov/programs/racetothetop/executive-summary.pdf.

71. Stephanie Banchero, "Daley School Plan Fails to Make Grade: Renaissance 2010 Officials Defend Efforts to Upgrade Education over Last 6 Years," *Chicago Tribune,* January 17, 2010.

72. Fabricant and Fine, *Charter Schools and the Corporate Makeover of Public Education,* 65; Joanna Barkan, "Got Dough? How Billionaires Rule Our Schools," *Dissent Magazine,* Winter 2011, https://www.dissentmagazine.org /article/got-dough-how-billionaires-rule-our-schools; Andrew Calkins, William Guenther, Grace Belfiore, and Dave Lash, *The Turnaround Challenge: Why America's Best Opportunity to Dramatically Improve Student Achievement Lies in Our Worst-Performing Schools* (Boston: Mass Insight Education and Research Institute, 2007).

73. Ravitch, *Reign of Error,* 16–17; Duncan, *How Schools Work,* 98–101

74. National Alliance for Public Charter Schools, "Every Student Succeeds Act," https://www.publiccharters.org/our-work/federal-policy/every-student -succeeds-act; "The Every Student Succeeds Act: Explained," *Education Week* 35, no. 14 (December 2015): 17; Dustin Hornbeck, "Federal Role in Education Has a Long History," *The Conversation,* April 26, 2017, https://theconversation .com/federal-role-in-education-has-a-long-history-7480.

75. Kelly P. Kissel, "Why Wal-Mart Family Foundation Is Spending $1 Billion on Charter Schools," *Christian Science Monitor,* January 7, 2016.

76. Dylan Mathews, "Billionaires Are Spending Their Fortunes Reshaping America's Schools. It Isn't Working," *Vox*, October 30, 2018, https://www.vox .com/future-perfect/2018/10/30/17862050/education-policy-charity.

77. "Interview with Betsy Devos, the Reformer," *Philanthropy*, http://www .philanthropyroundtable.org/topic/excellence_in_philanthropy/interview _with_betsy_devos; Erica Green, "To Understand Betsy DeVos's Educational Views, View Her Education" *New York Times*, June 10, 2017.

CHAPTER FIVE: THE SCHOOL CHOICE MENU

1. Kahlenberg, "From All Walks of Life"; Willie, Edwards, and Alves, *Student Diversity, Choice and School Improvement*, 12–14, 21–31; Willie and Alves, *Controlled Choice*.

2. Coit v. Green, 404 U.S. 997 (1971); Bob Jones University v. United States, 461 U.S. 574 (1983); Milton Gaither, *Homeschool: An American History* (New York: Palgrave Macmillan, 2008), 111; Stanley Hanna, "Bob Jones University v. United States: Interpretation and Conclusions," *Journal of Education Finance* 9, no. 2 (Fall 1983): 235–40.

3. Taylor Swaak, "Democrats for Education Reform Release New Poll Suggesting Most Voters Are 'Education Progressives.' Here Are 7 Takeaways," *74*, August 6, 2018, https://www.the74million.org/democrats-for-education -reform-release-new-poll-suggesting-most-voters-are-education-progressives -here-are-7-takeaways.

4. On an extended network of Black school choice reformers, see Keith E. Benson, "To the Black Education Reform Establishment, Be Real with Who You Are and Whose Interest You Represent," https://www.academia.edu/38324301 /To_the_Black_Education_Reform_Establishment_Be_Real_with_Who_You _Are_and_Whose_Interest_You_Represent.pdf?auto=download.

5. Jonathan Kozol, *Death at an Early Age: The Destruction of the Hearts and Minds of Negro Children in the Boston Public Schools* (Boston: Houghton Mifflin, 1967); Jonathan Kozol, *Free Schools* (Boston: Houghton Mifflin, 1972), 14–16.

6. Deborah Meier, "Creating Democratic Schools," *Rethinking Schools* 19, no. 4 (2005), 28–29; Deborah Meier, *The Power of Their Ideas: Lessons for America from a Small School in Harlem* (Boston: Beacon Press, 1995); Lewis, *New York City Public Schools from Brownsville to Bloomberg*, 115–16.

7. Michael Klonsky and Susan Klonsky, *Small Schools: Public School Reform Meets the Ownership Society* (New York: Routledge, 2008); Jack Schneider, "The Right Space: The Small Schools Movement," chap. 3 in *Excellence for All: How a New Breed of Reformers Is Transforming America's Public Schools* (Nashville: Vanderbilt University Press, 2011).

8. Amy Martinelli, "The Powerful Pull of Suncoast High School: How Magnet Schools Turned Desegregation into Choice, 1969–2000" (PhD diss., University of Florida, 2015), 16–18; Lauri Steel and Roger Levine, *Educational Innovations in Multiracial Contexts: The Growth of Magnet Schools in American Education* (Palo Alto, CA: American Institutes for Research in the Behavioral Sciences, 1994), iii, 1–5.

9. Christine H. Rossell, "The Effectiveness of Desegregation Plans," in *School Desegregation in the 21st Century*, ed. Christine H. Rossell, David J.

Armor, and Herbert J. Walberg (Westport, CT: Praeger, 2002), 67–69; Christine H. Rossell, "Magnet Schools: No Longer Famous, but Still Intact," *Education Next* 5, no. 2 (Spring 2005): 44–49.

10. Mira Debs, *Diverse Families, Desirable Schools: Public Montessori in the Era of School Choice* (Cambridge, MA: Harvard Education Press, 2019), 9.

11. Rossell, "Magnet Schools," 44–49.

12. Erica Frankenberg, "Preferences, Proximity, and Controlled Choice: Examining Families' School Choices and Enrollment Decisions in Louisville, Kentucky," *Peabody Journal of Education* 93, no. 4 (2018): 378–94; Cynthia Gersti-Pepin, "Magnet Schools: A Retrospective Case Study of Segregation," *High School Journal* 85, no. 3 (2002): 47–52; Steel and Levine, "Educational Innovations in Multiracial Contexts," ii–iii.

13. Christine H. Rossell, *The Carrot or the Stick for School Desegregation Policy: Magnet Schools or Forced Busing* (Philadelphia: Temple University Press, 1990), 100–108; Baugh, *The Detroit School Busing Case*, 89–91, 120–21.

14. Nicholas Kryczka, "Building a Constituency for Racial Integration: Chicago's Magnet Schools and the Prehistory of School Choice," *History of Education Quarterly* 59, no. 1 (February 2019): 21–22.

15. Debs, *Diverse Families, Desirable Schools*, 1–19.

16. Gary Orfield and Erica Frankenberg, eds., *Educational Delusions? Why Choice Can Deepen Inequality and How to Make Schools Fair* (Berkeley: University of California Press, 2013), 30–32, 255–70.

17. Steve Estes, *Charleston in Black and White: Race and Power in the South after the Civil Rights Movement* (Chapel Hill: University of North Carolina Press, 2015), 85–101.

18. Estes, *Charleston in Black and White*, 100–101.

19. Estes, *Charleston in Black and White*, 100–101.

20. Diette Courrégé, "Board Reviewing Buist Admissions Policy," *Post and Courier* (Charleston, SC), February 18, 2009.

21. Estes, *Charleston in Black and White*, 101–3. On the complexity of race and the intersectionality of race, gender, and sexuality, see Stanley Thangaraj, *Desi Hoop Dreams: Pick-Up Basketball and the Making of Asian American Masculinity* (New York: New York University Press, 2015).

22. Estes, *Charleston in Black and White*, 101–3; Angela Rucker, "Are Schools Breaking Up? Burke, Magnet Problems Erupted After Beating," *Post and Courier*, November 26, 1995.

23. Tony Bartelme, "Battles Await District EXPLOSIVE ISSUES: The Charleston County School Board Will Discuss Removing Racial Quotas and Hiring Private Management for the Alternative School," *Post and Courier*, June 1, 1998; Jennifer Berry Hawes, "Challenges to Diversity: Buist Academy Loses Minorities After Lawsuit Forces Change," *Post and Courier*, May 2, 2004.

24. Courrégé, "Board Reviewing Buist Admissions Policy."

25. Bowers, "Odds of Getting into Buist Academy? On Porter-Gaud, see "Porter-Gaud School Ranking," *Niche*, https://www.niche.com/k12/porter-gaud-school-charleston-sc/rankings.

26. Jennifer Berry Hawes, "Challenges to Diversity: Buist Academy Loses Minorities After Lawsuit Forces Change," *Post and Courier*, May 2, 2004; Erickson, *Making the Unequal Metropolis*, 2–4, 210–43.

27. EdChoice, "What Are School Vouchers?," https://www.edchoice.org /school-choice/types-of-school-choice/what-are-school-vouchers-2.

28. Jim Carl, *Freedom of Choice: Vouchers in American Education* (Santa Barbara: Praeger, 2011), 23–33; "South Carolina," *Southern School News*, April 7, 1955, May 4, 1955; John W. White, "Managed Compliance: White Resistance and Desegregation in South Carolina, 1950–1970" (PhD diss., University of Florida, 2006), 54–58, 389–91; "Byrnes Plans Study Before Commenting on Court Ruling" and "SC Leaders Adopt 'Wait-See' Attitude on Court Decision," *The State*, May 18, 1954); "SC Candidates Accent Separate School Issue," *The State*, May 19, 1954; "Virginia Lawmakers Overwhelmingly Approve Interposition," *Southern School News*, March 1956, 14; "Georgia," *Southern School News*, September 3, 1954, November 4, 1954; Bolton, *The Hardest Deal of All*, 105; Suitts, *Overturning Brown*, 12–17.

29. Carl, *Freedom of Choice*, 61–63.

30. Christopher Jencks, "Private Schools for Black Children," *New York Times* November 3, 1968; Carl, *Freedom of Choice*, 65.

31. Virgil Blum, *Freedom of Choice in Education* (New York: Macmillan, 1958); Carl, *Freedom of Choice*, 88–100.

32. See Gross, *Public vs. Private*.

33. Carl, *Freedom of Choice*, 100–102.

34. Carl, *Freedom of Choice*, 135–52.

35. Zelman v. Simmons-Harris, 536 U.S. 639 (2002).

36. Pierce v. Society of Sisters 268 U.S. 510 (1925); Zelman v. Simmons-Harris, 536 U.S. 639 (2002).

37. Valerie Straus, "Betsy DeVos–Founded Group Lobbies Congress for D.C. Voucher Program Extension," *Washington Post*, May 2, 2017; Christopher Vondracek, "DeVos Backs Federal School Voucher Program," *Washington Times*, January 23, 2019; Andy Kroll and Benjy Hansen-Bundy, "The Family That Gives Together," *Mother Jones*, January 21, 2014, https://www.mother jones.com/politics/2014/01/devos-family-foundations-heritage-americans -prosperity-Blackwater; Emily Deruy, "Betsy DeVos's Misunderstood Alma Mater," *Atlantic*, March 1, 2017, https://www.theatlantic.com/education/archive /2017/03/at-betsy-devoss-alma-mater-a-history-of-fierce-debate/518205; "Amway Reports 2015 Sales of $9.5 Billion USD," Amway, press release, February 3, 2016, https://www.amwayglobal.com/newsroom/amway-reports-2015-sales -9-5-billion-usd.

38. Bill Bennett and Karen Kussle, "Education Freedom Scholarships Will Create Opportunities," Fox News, April 29, 2019, https://www.foxnews.com /opinion/bennett-nussle-education-scholarships; "Sen. Cruz Introduces Education Freedom Scholarships and Opportunity Act," Ted Cruz, press release, February 28, 2019, https://www.cruz.senate.gov/?p=press_release&id=4343.

39. Ray Budde, "The Evolution of the Charter Concept," *Phi Delta Kappan* 78, no. 1 (September 1996): 72–73.

40. Albert Shanker, "National Press Club Speech," March 31, 1988, Walter P. Reuther Library, Wayne State University, http://reuther.wayne.edu/files /64.43.pdf.

41. Richard D. Kahlenberg and Halley Potter, "Restoring Shanker's Vision for Charter Schools," *American Educator* (Winter 2014–2015), https://www.aft .org/ae/winter2014–2015/kahlenberg_potter; Albert Shanker, "Convention Plots New Course: A Charter for Change," *New York Times,* July 10, 1988.

42. Albert Shanker, "National Press Club Speech," March 31, 1988.

43. Kahlenberg and Potter, "Restoring Shanker's Vision for Charter Schools."

44. Albert Shanker, "National Press Club Speech," March 31, 1988; Kahlenberg and Potter, "Restoring Shanker's Vision for Charter Schools," 8–9.

45. *Citizens League, Chartered Schools = Choices for Educators + Quality for All Students* (Minneapolis: Citizens League, 1988), 9–16, https://citizensleague. org/wp-content/uploads/2017/07/PolicyReportEducationNov-1988.pdf.

46. Ted Kolderie, *Beyond Choice to New Public Schools: Withdrawing the Exclusive Franchise in Public Education* (Washington, DC: Progressive Policy Institute, 1990), 1; "Public Charter School Enrollment," National Center for Education Statistics (Washington, DC) https://nces.ed.gov/programs/coe /indicator_cgb.asp.

47. Kahlenberg and Potter, "Restoring Shanker's Vision for Charter Schools," 9.

48. Kahlenberg and Potter, "Restoring Shanker's Vision for Charter Schools," 9.

49. Ted Kolderie, *Beyond Choice to New Public Schools: Withdrawing the Exclusive Franchise in Public Education* (Washington, DC: Progressive Policy Institute, 1990).

50. Budde, "The Evolution of the Charter Concept," 73.

51. Finn quoted in Kahlenberg and Potter, "Restoring Shanker's Vision for Charter Schools," 10; "Unions Consider Charter Schools of Their Own," *New York Times*, September 22, 1996.

52. Arianna Prothero, "Why More Charter Schools Aren't Unionized," *Education Week*, September 18, 2014, http://blogs.edweek.org/edweek/charters choice/2014/09/why_more_charter_schools_arent_unionized.html.

53. Ravitch, *Reign of Error*, 168.

54. Ravitch, *Reign of Error*, 16–18, 170–71; Julie Dunn, "Agassi Hopes Charter School Will Be a Model," *New York Times*, April 21, 2004; Liz Dwyer, "Can Andre Agassi and a Team of Investment Bankers Improve Education (and Turn a Profit)?," *Good*, June 4, 2011, https://www.good.is/articles/can -andre-agassi-and-a-team-of-investment-bankers-improve-education-and -turn-a-profit.

55. Michael Fabricant and Michelle Fine, *Charter Schools and the Corporate Makeover of Public Education* (New York: Teachers College Press, 2012), 69–73.

56. Fabricant and Fine, *Charter Schools and the Corporate Makeover*, 72; Matt Barnum, "Charter Networks KIPP and IDEA Win Big Federal Grants to Fund Ambitious Growth Plans," *Chalkbeat*, April 22, 2019.

57. Derek Black, Bruce Baker, and Preston Green III, "Charter Schools Exploit Lucrative Loophole that Would be Easy to Close," *The Conversation*, February 19, 2019, https://theconversation.com/charter-schools-exploit-lucrative-loophole-that-would-be-easy-to-close-111792; Derek Black, "States Are Favoring School Choice at a Steep Cost to Public Education," April 24, 2018, https://theconversation.com/states-are-favoring-school-choice-at-a-steep-cost-to-public-education-95395; Ravitch, *Reign of Error*, 171.

58. Robin Shulman, "Harlem Program Singled Out as Model: Obama Administration to Replicate Plan in Other Cities to Boost Poor Children," *Washington Post*, August 2, 2009.

59. CREDO (Center for Research on Education Outcomes), *National Charter School Study, 2013* (Stanford, CA: Center for Research on Education Outcomes, 2013), http://credo.stanford.edu/documents/NCSS%202013%20Final%20Draft.pdf.

60. Ravitch, *Reign of Error*, 101–2.

61. James C. Carper and Thomas C. Hunt, "Homeschooling *Redivivus*: Accommodating the Anabaptists of American Education," in *The Dissenting Tradition in American Education* (New York: Peter Lang, 2007), 239–40; Snyder, de Brey, and Dillow, *Digest of Education Statistics, 2017*; Jessica Davis and Kurt Bauman, "School Enrollment in the United States: 2011," US Census Bureau, https://www.census.gov/content/dam/Census/library/publications/2013/demo/p20-571.pdf; Coalition for Responsible Home Education, "Homeschooling by the Numbers," November 2017, https://www.responsiblehomeschooling.org/homeschooling-101/homeschooling-numbers.

62. See Shawn F. Peters, *Homeschooling: The History and Philosophy of a Controversial Practice* (Chicago: University of Chicago Press, 2019); Gaither, *Homeschool*; Carper and Hunt, "Homeschooling *Redivivus*: Accommodating the Anabaptists of American Education," chap. 6 in The Dissenting Tradition in American Education; Gross, *Public vs. Private*.

63. Gaither, *Homeschool*, 110–15.

64. Patrick Farenga, "John Holt and the Origins of Contemporary Homeschooling," *Paths of Learning*, 1999, http://mhla.org/information/resourcesarticles/holtorigins.htm.

65. Holt quoted in Carper and Hunt, "Homeschooling *Redivivus*," 243.

66. John Holt, *Teach Your Own: The John Holt Book of Homeschooling* (New York: Delacorte Press, 1981).

67. Carper and Hunt, "Homeschooling *Redivivus*," 244.

68. See "Our Mission," Home School Legal Defense Association," 2020, https://hslda.org/content/about/mission.asp; National Homeschool Association, https://www.nationalhomeschoolassociation.com; Michael Farris, "Gimme That Old Time Education," *Home School Court Report* (Summer 1988); *Home School Legal Defense Association*, pamphlet, People for the American Way Collection, Box 47, Folder 23, Bancroft Library, University of California, Berkeley.

69. Gaither, *Homeschool*, 196–200.

70. Melinda D. Anderson, "The Radical Self-Reliance of Black Homeschooling," *Atlantic*, May 17, 2018, https://www.theatlantic.com/education/archive/2018/05/Black-homeschooling/560636; Paula Penn-Nabrit, *Morning*

by Morning: How We Home-Schooled Our African-American Sons to the Ivy League (New York: Villard, 2003).

71. Ravitch, *Reign of Error*, 180–83; Rooks, *Cutting School*, 143–47; Benjamin Herold, "Online Classes for K-12 Students: An Overview," *Education Week*, June 23, 2017, https://www.edweek.org/ew/issues/online-classes/index .html; Darren Samuelsohn, "Virtual Schools Are Booming. Who's Paying Attention?" *Politico*, September 23, 2015, https://www.politico.com/agenda/story /2015/09/virtual-schools-education-000227.

72. Trevor Aaronson and John O'Connor, "In K12 Courses, 275 Students to a Single Teacher," *StateImpact*, September 16, 2012, https://stateimpact.npr .org/florida/2012/09/16/in-k12-courses-275-students-to-a-single-teacher; Samuelsohn, "Virtual Schools Are Booming."

73. Katie Ash, "Virtual Education Seen Lacking Accountability," *Education Week*, May 22, 2012, https://www.edweek.org/ew/articles/2012/05/23/32nsba .h31.html; Karen Faucett, "Virtual Schoolteacher," *EducationNext* (Summer 2011), https://www.educationnext.org/virtual-schoolteacher; Susan Dynarski, "Online Courses Are Harming the Students Who Need the Most Help," *New York Times*, January 19, 2018; Nick Pandolfo, "The Teacher You've Never Met: Inside the World of Online Learning," *Hechinger Report*, June 13, 2012, https:// hechingerreport.org/the-teacher-youve-never-met-inside-the-world-of-online -learning; Monica Anderson and Andrew Perrin, "Nearly One-in-Five Teens Can't Always Finish Their Homework Because of the Digital Divide," Pew Research Center, October 26, 2018, https://www.pewresearch.org/fact-tank/2018 /10/26/nearly-one-in-five-teens-cant-always-finish-their-homework-because -of-the-digital-divide; Susan Dynarski, "The School Year Really Ended in March," *New York Times*, May 7, 2020.

74. "K12 Inc. Reports Full Year Fiscal 2018 Revenue Increases 3.3% to $917.7 Million," *Business Wire*, https://www.businesswire.com/news/home /20180807005078/en/K12-Reports-Full-Year-Fiscal-2018-Revenue; Ravitch, *Reign of Error*, 182.

75. Rooks, *Cutting School*, 147–49.

76. Kimberly Hefling, "DeVos Champions Online Charter Schools, but the Results Are Poor," *Politico*, October 8, 2017, https://www.politico.com /story/2017/10/08/education-betsy-devos-online-charter-schools-poor-results -243556; Rooks, *Cutting School*, 139–41.

CHAPTER SIX: RACE AND A CIVIL RIGHTS CLAIM TO SCHOOL CHOICE

1. Howard Fuller, interview with the author, June 26, 2019; Howard Fuller, *No Struggle, No Progress: A Warrior's Life from Black Power to Education Reform* (Milwaukee: Marquette University Press, 2014), 13–46; Jack Dougherty, *More Than One Struggle: The Evolution of Black School Reform in Milwaukee* (Chapel Hill: University of North Carolina Press, 2004), 172–76.

2. Howard Fuller, interview with the author, June 26, 2019; Fuller, *No Struggle, No Progress*, 13–46; Dougherty, *More Than One Struggle*, 172–76.

3. Fuller, *No Struggle, No Progress*, 83–120; Sarah Barber, "Never Stop Working: Examining the Life and Activism of Howard Fuller" (MA thesis, University of Milwaukee, 2012), 20–24; Richard D. Benson II, *Fighting for Our*

Place in the Sun: Malcolm X and the Radicalization of the Black Student Movement, 1960–1973 (New York: Peter Lang, 2015), 85–96.

4. Fuller, *No Struggle, No Progress*, 13–22, 51–59, 99–113, 121–46.

5. Fuller, *No Struggle, No Progress*, 11.

6. Kenneth R. Lamke, "Thompson Backs Inner City District," *Milwaukee Sentinel*, September 2, 1987.

7. Fuller, *No Struggle, No Progress*, 11.

8. Thomas C. Pedroni, *Market Movements: African American Involvement in Voucher Reform* (New York: Routledge, 2007), 51–53; Michael Apple and Thomas Pedroni, "Conservative Alliance Building and African American Support of Vouchers: The End of Brown's Promise or a New Beginning?," *Teachers College Record* 107, no. 9 (September 2005): 2068–105.

9. Charles Barone, Dana Laurens, and Nicholas Munyan-Penney, *A Democratic Guide to Public Charter Schools: Public Opinion*, 2nd ed. (New York: Democrats for Education Reform, 2019), http://dfer.org/wp-content/uploads/2019/05/A-Democratic-Guide-to-Public-Charter-Schools-Public-Opinion.pdf.

10. Tommy Shultz, "National School Choice Poll Shows 67% of Voters Support School Choice," American Federation for Children, January 17, 2019, https://www.federationforchildren.org/national-school-choice-poll-shows-67-of-voters-support-school-choice-2019; Emily Ekins, "Poll: 58% of Americans Favor Vouchers for K–12 Private School," Cato Institute, October 3, 2019, https://www.cato.org/blog/poll-58-americans-favor-vouchers-k-12-private-school.

11. Barone, Laurens, and Munyan-Penney, *Democratic Guide to Public Charter Schools*; Valerie Strauss, "There's a Backlash Against Charter Schools. What's Happening and Why," *Washington Post*, February 11, 2019.

12. Laura Fay, "End of an Era: After 17 Years on Front Lines of School Choice Battles, BAEO Calls It Quits," *74*, October 25, 2017, https://www.the74million.org/end-of-an-era-after-17-years-on-front-lines-of-school-choice-battles-baeo-calls-it-quits.

13. Mary C. Bounds, *A Light Shines in Harlem: New York's First Charter School and the Movement It Led* (Chicago: Lawrence Hill Books, 2014), xii, xiii.

14. Derrick Bell, *Silent Covenants: Brown v. Board of Education and the Unfulfilled Hopes for Racial Reform* (Oxford: Oxford University Press, 2004), 4.

15. Chester E. Finn Jr., *We Must Take Charge: Our Schools and Our Future* (New York: Free Press, 1991), 35.

16. Jonathan Kozol, *Savage Inequalities: Children in America's Schools* (New York: HarperPerennial, 1991), 5.

17. Kozol, *Savage Inequalities*, 83–91.

18. Bounds, *A Light Shines in Harlem*, 2; Anemona Hartocollis, "Charter School Days Dawn in New York," *New York Times*, September 8, 1999.

19. Hartocollis, "Charter School Days Dawn in New York."

20. Bounds, *A Light Shines in Harlem*, 8.

21. Janelle Scott, "School Choice as a Civil Right: The Political Construction of a Claim and Its Implications for School Desegregation," in *Integrating Schools in a Changing Society: New Policies and Legal Options for a Multiracial Generation*, ed. Ericka Frankenberg and Elizabeth Debray (Chapel Hill: University of North Carolina Press, 2011), 39.

22. Barbara Miner, "Distorting the Civil Rights Legacy," *Rethinking Schools* (Spring 2004), http://rethinkingschools.aidcvt.com/special_reports/voucher _report/v_kpsp183.shtml; Scott, "School Choice as a Civil Right," 32–52.

23. Richard J. Herrnstein, Charles Murray, *The Bell Curve: Intelligence and Class Structure in American Life* (New York: Free Press, 1994), 311; Ibram X. Kendi, "Why the Academic Achievement Gap Is a Racist Idea," *Black Perspectives* (October 20, 2016), https://www.aaihs.org/why-the-academic-achievement -gap-is-a-racist-idea.

24. Bolick quoted in Keith Peters, "New Group Pushes for School Choice," *in Family News in Focus*, in "Alliance for School Choice Organizational File," Box 2, Folder 23, People for the American Way collection of political ephemera, Bancroft Library, University of California, Berkeley; "Interview: Clint Bolick," *Frontline*, PBS, https://www.pbs.org/wgbh/pages /frontline/shows/vouchers/interviews/bolick.html; "Hon. Clint Bolick," Federalist Society, https://fedsoc.org/contributors/clint-bolick.

25. "Freedom to Make America's Schools the Best in the World for Our Children," in "The American Alliance for Better Schools Organizational File," Box 2, Folder 8, People for the American Way collection of political ephemera, Bancroft Library, University of California, Berkeley.

26. Citizens for Educational Freedom, "Tuition Tax Credits for Low-Income Families," in "Americans for Educ. Choice Organizational File," Box 8, Folder 22, People for the American Way collection of political ephemera, Bancroft Library, University of California, Berkeley.

27. Benson, "To the Black Education Reform Establishment, Be Real with Who You Are and Whose Interest You Represent"; Rachel Cohen, "Pro-charter School Democrats, Embattled in the Trump Era, Score a Win with Hakeem Jeffries," *The Intercept*, November 30, 2018, https://theintercept .com/2018/11/30/hakeem-jeffries-charter-schools; Beth Hawkins, "'The Movement's Been Hijacked': A Black Lives Matter Leader Quits over Public School Platform," 74, September 7, 2016, https://www.the74million.org/article /the-movements-been-hijacked-a-Black-lives-matter-leader-quits-over-public -school-platform.

28. Williams quoted in Carl, *Freedom of Choice*, 87.

29. Howard Fuller, interview with the author, June 26, 2019.

30. James Forman Jr., "The Secret History of School Choice: How Progressives Got There First," *Georgetown Law Journal* 93 (2005): 1289, https:// digitalcommons.law.yale.edu/cgi/viewcontent.cgi?article=4146&context=fss _papers.

31. Charles T. Clotfelter, *After Brown: The Rise and Retreat of School Desegregation* (Princeton, NJ: Princeton University Press, 2004), 55–56; Gary Orfield, *Schools More Separate: Consequences of a Decade of Resegregation* (Cambridge, MA: Civil Rights Project, Harvard University, 2001), 1–3, https://files.eric.ed .gov/fulltext/ED459217.pdf.

32. Board of Education of Oklahoma City v. Dowell, 498 U.S. 237 (1991); Clotfelter, *After Brown*, 196–98; Orfield, *Schools More Separate*.

33. Parents Involved in Community Schools v. Seattle School Dist. no. 1, 551 U.S. 701 (2007); Ansley Erickson, "The Rhetoric of Choice: Segregation,

Desegregation, and Charter Schools," in *Public Education Under Siege*, ed. Michael Katz and Mike Rose (Philadelphia: University of Pennsylvania Press, 2013), 122–30.

34. Scott, "School Choice as a Civil Right," 44.

35. Erica Frankenberg, Genevieve Siegel-Hawley, Jia Wang, and Gary Orfield, *Choice Without Equity: Charter School Segregation and the Need for Civil Rights Standards* (Los Angeles: Civil Rights Project, 2010), https://escholarship .org/uc/item/4r07q8kg.

36. Ivan Moreno, "US Charter Schools Put Growing Numbers in Racial Isolation," Associated Press, December 3, 2017, https://apnews.com/e9c25534 dfd44851a5e56bd57454b4f5.

37. Nikole Hannah-Jones, interview with Chris Hayes, "Why Is This Happening?" NBC News, July 31, 2018, https://www.nbcnews.com/think /opinion/investigating-school-segregation-2018-nikole-hannah-jones-podcast -transcript-ncna896116.

38. W. E. B. DuBois, "Does the Negro Need Separate Schools?," *Journal of Negro Education* 4, no. 3 (July 1935): 328–29.

39. Moreno, "US Charter Schools Put Growing Numbers in Racial Isolation."

40. Cardell Orrin, interview with the author, November 21, 2019.

41. Fuller, *No Struggle, No Progress*, 100; Barber, "Never Stop Working," 28–34; Benson, *Fighting for Our Place in the Sun*, 85–96.

42. Fuller, *No Struggle, No Progress*, 158–59.

43. Fuller, *No Struggle, No Progress*, 156–59, 165–72; Dougherty, *More Than One Struggle*, 172–76.

44. Fuller, *No Struggle, No Progress*, 173; Barber, "Never Stop Working," 50–61.

45. Fuller, *No Struggle, No Progress*, 156–59, 165–72.

46. Dougherty, *More Than One Struggle*, 176–78.

47. Derrick Bell, "A Model Alternative Desegregation Plan," in *Shades of Brown: New Perspectives on School Desegregation*, ed. Derrick Bell (New York: Teachers College Press, 1980), 124–39; Dougherty, *More Than One Struggle*, 178.

48. Robin D. Barnes, "Black America and School Choice: Charting a New Course," *Yale Law Journal* 106 (1997): 2405, 2409, https://digitalcommons.law .yale.edu/cgi/viewcontent.cgi?article=7768&context=ylj.

49. Fuller, *No Struggle, No Progress*, 173.

50. Derrick Bell, "The Case for a Separate Black School System," *Urban League Review* 11, nos. 1–2 (Summer–Winter 1987–88): 136; Rogers Worthington, "Milwaukee Challenges Black District Plan," *Chicago Tribune*, September 29, 1987; Frederick Hess, *Revolution at the Margins: The Impact of Competition on Urban School Systems* (Washington, DC: Brookings Institution, 2002), 79; Dougherty, *More Than One Struggle*, 189–90; Barbara Miner, *Lessons from the Heartland: A Turbulent Half-Century of Public Education in an Iconic American City* (New York: New Press, 2013), 134–37.

51. Bell, "The Case for a Separate Black School System," 136–45. See also Derrick Bell, "The Case for a Separate Black School System," chap. 13 in *Black*

Education: A Quest for Equity and Excellence, ed. Willy DeMarcell Smith and Eva Wells Chunn (New Brunswick, NJ: Transaction Publishers, 1991).

52. Bell, "The Case for a Separate Black School System," 140

53. Bell, "The Case for a Separate Black School System," 140.

54. "Blacks, Whites Criticize School Resegregation Idea," *Milwaukee Journal*, August 12, 1987; Miner, *Lessons from the Heartland*, 135–37; Kenneth R. Lamke, "Thompson Backs Inner City District," *Milwaukee Sentinel*, September 2, 1987; Chester Sheard, "Langley Says Inner City District Illegal," *Milwaukee Sentinel*, September 28, 1987; Chester Sheard, "NAACP Aide Calls Black School District 'Urban Apartheid,'" *Milwaukee Sentinel*, September 26, 1987.

55. Fuller quoted in Kenneth R. Lamke, "Fuller Defends Plan for Inner City District," *Milwaukee Sentinel*, August 15, 1987; Miner, *Lessons from the Heartland*, 135.

56. Bell, "The Case for a Separate Black School System," 140.

57. Miner, *Lessons from the Heartland*, 135–37; Polly Williams, interview with Jack Dougherty, July 23,1996, "More Than One Struggle Oral History Project," Box 2, Folder 31, Golda Meir Library, University of Wisconsin–Milwaukee.

58. Rogers Worthington, "Milwaukee Challenges Black District Plan" *Chicago Tribune*, September 29, 1987; Frederick Hess, *Revolution at the Margins: The Impact of Competition on Urban School Systems* (Washington, DC: Brookings Institution, 2002), 79; Dougherty, *More Than One Struggle*, 189–90; Miner, *Lessons from the Heartland*, 136–37.

59. Williams quoted in Dougherty, *More Than One Struggle*, 186.

60. Frederick Hess, *Revolution at the Margins: The Impact of Competition on Urban School Systems* (Washington, DC: Brookings Institution, 2002), 72–136; Gary R. George and Walter C. Farrell Jr., "School Choice and African American Students: A Legislative View," *Journal of Negro Education* 59, no. 4 (Autumn 1990): 521–25.

61. Carl, *Freedom of Choice*, 100–102.

62. Polly A. Williams, "Education Is Not Just for the Privileged Few," *Education Week*, February 7, 1996, 41–42; Dougherty, *More Than One Struggle*, 186–90.

63. Fuller quoted in Barber, "Never Stop Working," 76 n268. See also Bill Dahlk, *Against the Wind: African Americans and the Schools in Milwaukee* (Milwaukee: Marquette University Press, 2010), 521.

64. "Just as Bad as Expected," *Commercial Appeal* (Memphis), January 12, 2011; Jane Roberts, "'Huge' Gates Grant—Memphis City Schools One of Four Systems in Nation Chosen for Gates Foundation Funds to Improve Teaching," *Commercial Appeal*, November 19, 2009; Grace Tatter, "As Tennessee Finishes Its Race to the Top, Teachers Caught in the Middle of Competing Changes," *Chalkbeat*, December 15, 2015, https://www.chalkbeat.org/posts/tn/2015/12/15/as-tennessee-finishes-its-race-to-the-top-teachers-caught-in-the-middle-of-competing-changes; Juli Kim, Tim Field, and Elaine Hargrave, *The Achievement School District: Lessons from Tennessee* (Chapel Hill, NC: Public.com/wp-content/uploads/2019/02/Achievement_School_District_Lessons_From_Tennessee-Public_Impact.pdf; Laura Faith Kebede, "NAACP to Put Memphis

in Spotlight in National Debate over Charter Schools," *Chalkbeat*, January 9, 2017, https://www.chalkbeat.org/posts/tn/2017/01/09/naacp-to-put-memphis -in-spotlight-in-national-debate-over-charter-schools.

65. Jane Roberts, "State to Intervene in Running 6 MCS Schools," *Commercial Appeal*, February 28, 2012; *Climbing Out from Under the Rock: Restoring Civil Rights, Economics, and School Justice in Memphis and the Nation*, 4th ed., Hooks Policy Papers (Memphis: University of Memphis, 2018), https://www .memphis.edu/benhooks/pdfs/2018policypapers.pdf.

66. Stephanie Love, interview with the author, November 22, 2019.

67. Jane Roberts, "Charter System Has New Leader" *Commercial Appeal*, May 10, 2011; Jane Roberts, "Charters Lure Outside Interest—Highly Regarded Systems in California Apply for Memphis," *Commercial Appeal*, April 4, 2012.

68. Jane Roberts, "Chartered Course—Underachieving Lest School in Hands of Faith-Based Overseer," *Commercial Appeal*, March 13, 2012.

69. Jane Roberts, "State to Intervene in Running 6 MCS Schools" *Commercial Appeal*, February 28, 2012.

70. Kriner Cash, "Transforming MCS Is a Community Effort," *Commercial Appeal*, April 10, 2010.

71. Zandria F. Robinson, "After Stax: Race, Sound, and Neighborhood Revitalization," in *An Unseen Light: Black Struggles for Freedom in Memphis, Tennessee*, ed. Aram Goudsouzian and Charles McKinney Jr. (Lexington: University Press of Kentucky, 2018), 348–65. For more on Maxine Smith STEAM Academy, see https://www.memphissteamacademy.org; on the Soulsville Foundation and the Soulsville Charter School, see https://soulsvillefoundation.org /our-work.

72. For more on Martin Luther King, Jr. College Preparatory, see http:// fraysercs.org/mlk-prep.

73. Jane Roberts, "Cultural Empowerment," *Commercial Appeal*, April 27, 2014.

74. Shirletta Kinchen, *Black Power in the Bluff City: African American Youth and Student Activism in Memphis, 1965–1975* (Knoxville: University of Tennessee Press, 2016).

75. Robinson, "After Stax," 348–65.

76. Stephanie Love, interview; Jane Roberts, "Schools Need Hands— Involvement Urged from the Community," *Commercial Appeal*, April 13, 2012; "Dr. Bobby White, Founder & CEO," Frayser Community Schools, http:// fraysercs.org/team/bobby-white.

77. Amadou Diallo, "Segregated Schools Are Still the Norm. Howard Fuller Is Fine with That," Hechinger Report, November 16, 2018, https:// hechingerreport.org/segregated-schools-are-still-the-norm-howard-fuller-is -fine-with-that; National Charter Collaborative, http://www.chartercollab .org/nchome.

78. LaTricea Adams, interview with the author, November 22, 2019.

79. Cardell Orrin, interview with the author, November 21, 2019.

80. Roblin Webb, interview with the author, November 27, 2019.

81. NAACP, "Statement Regarding the NAACP's Resolution on a Moratorium on Charter Schools," October 15, 2016, https://www.naacp.org/latest /statement-regarding-naacps-resolution-moratorium-charter-schools.

82. Kimberly Hefling, "NAACP President Tackles Charter School Question," *Politico*, July 12, 2018, https://www.politico.com/story/2018/07/12/naacp -president-charter-schools-derrick-johnson-676432.

83. Matt Barnum, "6 Problems the NAACP Has with Charter Schools— and 5 of Its Ideas for How to Reshape the Sector," *Chalkbeat*, July 27, 2017, https://www.chalkbeat.org/posts/us/2017/07/27/6-problems-the-naacp-has -with-charter-schools-and-5-of-its-ideas-for-how-to-reshape-the-sector.

84. Marc Curnutte, "Local Group Interrupts Ohio NAACP meeting," *Commercial Appeal*, October 16, 2016; Jennifer Pignolet, "Memphis Lift Group Draws Praise—Local NAACP President Cheers Actions at Meeting," *Commercial Appeal*, October 19, 2016; Mark Curnutte, "Memphis Group Interrupts NAACP Meeting in Cincinnati," *Cincinnati Enquirer*, October 15, 2016.

85. Curnutte, "Local Group Interrupts Ohio NAACP Meeting."

86. Pignolet, "Memphis Lift Group Draws Praise."

87. Jennifer Pignolet, "Memphis NAACP Steers Charter Policy—Organization Refines Policy, with Aid from Area Branch," *Commercial Appeal*, July 30, 2017; Laura Faith Kebede, "Five Takeaways from the NAACP's Charter School Hearing in Memphis," *Chalkbeat*, January 9, 2017, https://www.chalkbeat.org /posts/tn/2017/01/11/five-takeaways-from-the-naacps-charter-school-hearing -in-memphis.

88. Pignolet, "Memphis Lift Group Draws Praise"; Jennifer Pignolet, "Memphis NAACP Steers Charter Policy"; Stephanie Love interview.

89. Carpenter quoted in Ira Stoll, "Meet the Memphis Great-Grandmother Who Confronted Elizabeth Warren About School Choice," *EducationNext*, December 5, 2019, https://www.educationnext.org/meet-memphis-great -grandmother-who-confronted-elizabeth-warren-school-choice-sarah -carpenter.

90. Cheyenne Haslett and Sasha Pezenik, "Presidential Candidate Elizabeth Warren Delivers Speech on Black Women Workers' Rights; Interrupted by Pro-Charter School Protesters," ABCNews.com, November 22, 2019, https://abcnews.go.com/Politics/presidential-candidate-elizabeth-warren -deliver-speech-centered-Black/story?id=67178918.

91. Morgan Phillips, "Trump Calls School Choice the Civil Rights Issue of 'All-Time' in This Country," Fox News, June 16, 2020.

92. Lauren Camera, "Cory Booker's School Choice Dilemma," *U.S. News and World Report*, October 24, 2019, https://www.usnews.com/news/elections /articles/2019-10-24/cory-bookers-school-choice-dilemma.

93. Pignolet, "Memphis Lift Group Draws Praise."

94. Stephanie Love interview.

95. Chester E. Finn Jr., *We Must Take Charge: Our Schools and Our Future* (New York: Free Press, 1991), xiv–xv.

96. Finn, *We Must Take Charge*, 245–51.

97. Erickson, "The Rhetoric of Choice."

98. Pamela N. Frazier-Anderson, "Public Schooling in Post-Hurricane Katrina New Orleans: Are Charter Schools the Solution or Part of the Problem?," *Journal of African American History* 93, no. 3 (Summer 2008): 413; Raynard Sanders, David Stovall, and Terrenda White, *Twenty-First-Century Jim Crow Schools: The Impact of Charters on Public Education* (Boston: Beacon Press, 2018), 8–16.

99. Raynard Sanders, "The New Orleans Public Education Experiment: Children Lose—Education Reformers Win," in Sanders, Stovall, and White, *Twenty-First Century Jim Crow Schools*, 8–16; Kim Holmes and Stuart Butler, "From Tragedy to Triumph: Principled Solutions for Rebuilding Lives and Communities," Heritage Foundation, September 12, 2005, https://www .heritage.org/homeland-security/report/tragedy-triumph-principled-solutions -rebuilding-lives-and-communities; Robert P. Stoker and Michael J. Rich, *Lessons and Limits: Tax Incentives and Rebuilding the Gulf Coast after Katrina* (Washington, DC: Brookings Institution, 2006), https://www.brookings.edu/wp -content/uploads/2016/06/20060808_GOZones.pdf.

100. Sanders, "The New Orleans Public Education Experiment," 8–16; Douglas N. Harris, *Charter School City: What the End of Traditional Public Schools in New Orleans Means for American Education* (Chicago: University of Chicago Press, 2020).

101. Mary Moran, "Howard Fuller Explains What's Happening in New Orleans," *Education Post*, August 7, 2015, https://educationpost.org/howard -fuller-explains-whats-happening-in-new-orleans; Thomas C. Pedroni, *Market Movements: African American Involvement in Voucher Reform* (New York: Routledge, 2007), 4, 51–69.

102. Howard Fuller, interview with the author, November 25, 2019; Fuller, *No Struggle, No Progress*, 273. See also Black Education for New Orleans, https://Blackedunola.org/howard-fuller.

103. Sanders, "The New Orleans Public Education Experiment," 3; Harris, *Charter School City.*

104. Howard Fuller, interview with the author, November 25, 2019.

105. Howard Fuller, "74 Interview: Howard Fuller on Schooling Elizabeth Warren About Charters, African-American Families, School Choice and Her Education Plan," 74, December 5, 2019, https://www.the74million.org/article /74-interview-howard-fuller-on-schooling-elizabeth-warren-about-charters -african-american-families-school-choice-her-education-plan.

106. Howard Fuller, interview with the author, June 26, 2019.

CHAPTER SEVEN: THE SINKING SHIP OF PUBLIC EDUCATION AND THE FAILURE OF CHOICE

1. Friedman and Friedman, *Two Lucky People*, 350.

2. Cal Thomas, "Friedman's Greatest Legacy: School Choice?," *Real Clear Politics*, November 22, 2006, https://www.realclearpolitics.com/articles/2006 /11/the_other_milton_friedman.html.

3. James Anderson, *Education of Blacks in the South, 1860–1935* (Chapel Hill: University of North Carolina Press, 1988); Williams, *Self-Taught;*

Christopher Span, *From Cotton Field to Schoolhouse: African American Education in Mississippi, 1862–1875* (Chapel Hill: University of North Carolina Press, 2009).

4. W. E. Burghardt Du Bois, "Does the Negro Need Separate Schools?," *Journal of Negro Education* 4, no. 3 (July 1935): 328–29.

5. Gary Orfield and Jongyeon Ee, "Our Segregated Capital: An Increasingly Diverse City with Racially Polarized Schools," Civil Rights Project, February 9, 2017, https://www.civilrightsproject.ucla.edu/; Myron Orfield and Thomas Luce, "Charter Schools in Chicago: No Model for Education Reform," Institute on Metropolitan Opportunity, University of Minnesota Law School Scholarship Repository, 2016, https://scholarship.law.umn.edu/; "Study: Charter Schools Have Worsened School Segregation" *Chicago Sun-Times,* October 13, 2014; Suchi Saxena, "New York City Public Schools: Small Steps in the Biggest District," Century Foundation, October 14, 2016, https://tcf.org/content/report/new-york-city-public-schools; New York City Charter School Center, "NYC Charter School Facts," https://www.nyccharterschools.org/sites/default/files/resources/NYC-Charter-Facts.pdf.

6. "Choice Without Equity: Charter School Segregation and the Need for Civil Rights Standards," Civil Rights Project, https://www.civilrightsproject.ucla.edu. For a larger historical context, see Gary Orfield, *Schools More Separate: Consequences of a Decade of Resegregation* (Cambridge, MA: Harvard Civil Rights Project, 2001), 5–6, https://files.eric.ed.gov/fulltext/ED459217.pdf.

7. Pamela Grundy, *Color and Character: West Charlotte High and the American Struggle over Educational Equality* (Chapel Hill: University of North Carolina Press, 2017); Helen F. Ladd, Charles T. Clotfelter, and John B. Holbein, "The Growing Segmentation of the Charter School Sector in North Carolina," *Education Finance and Policy* 12, no. 4 (Fall 2017): 24; Kris Nordstrom, *Stymied by Segregation: How Integration Can Transform North Carolina Schools and the Lives of Its Students* (Raleigh: North Carolina Justice Center, 2018), https://media2.newsobserver.com/content/media/2018/3/15/STYMIED%20BY%20SEGREGATION%20-%20Integration%20can%20Transform%20NC--FINAL.PDF.

8. Matthew Gonzales, "The IPS Magnet School Conundrum," *Indianapolis Monthly,* February 8, 2018, https://www.indianapolismonthly.com/news-and-opinion/news/the-ips-magnet-school-conundrum.

9. Nikole Hannah-Jones with Dianna Douglass, "Are Private Schools Immoral? A Conversation with Nikole Hannah-Jones about Race, Education, and Hypocrisy," *Atlantic,* December 14, 2017, https://www.theatlantic.com/education/archive/2017/12/progressives-are-undermining-public-schools/548084.

10. Caroline Bauman, "Memphis-Shelby County Spotlighted in National Report on School District Secession," *Chalkbeat,* June 21, 2017, https://www.chalkbeat.org/posts/tn/2017/06/21/memphis-shelby-county-spotlighted-in-national-report-on-school-district-secession; EdBuild, "Fractured: The Accelerating Breakdown of America's School Districts," 2019, https://edbuild.org/content/fractured.

11. Caroline Bauman, "Memphis-Shelby County Spotlighted in National Report on School District Secession," *Chalkbeat,* June 21, 2017, https://www

.chalkbeat.org/posts/tn/2017/06/21/memphis-shelby-county-spotlighted-in
-national-report-on-school-district-secession; Laura Faith Kebede, "Budget
Cuts Loom for Shelby County Schools, Again—Here's What We Know,"
Chalkbeat, April 5, 2016, https://www.chalkbeat.org/posts/tn/2016/04/05
/budget-cuts-loom-for-shelby-county-schools-again-heres-what-we-know;
Caroline Bauman, "Low Enrollment a Telltale for Closing Memphis Schools.
Here's What the Numbers Show," *Chalkbeat*, November 2, 2016, https://www
.chalkbeat.org/posts/tn/2016/11E/02/low-enrollment-a-telltale-for-closing
-memphis-schools-heres-what-the-numbers-show; Micaela Watts, "For a
Second Year, Layoffs Impact About 500 Shelby County Educators," *Chalkbeat*,
May 27, 2016, https://www.chalkbeat.org/posts/tn/2016/05/27/for-a-second
-year-layoffs-impact-about-500-shelby-county-educators; EdBuild, "Fractured."

12. Julie Underwood, "Under the Law: Segregation and Secession," *Phi
Delta Kappan* 100, no. 5 (2019), 74–75; Nikole Hannah-Jones, "The Resegregation of Jefferson County," *New York Times Magazine*, September 6, 2017.

13. Hannah-Jones, "The Resegregation of Jefferson County"; Robert
Carter, "Group Lays out Plan for Gardendale Schools to Split from County,"
North Jefferson News (Gardendale, AL), April 23, 2013; EdBuild, "Fractured."

14. Underwood, "Under the Law," 74–75; Alex Johnson, "Court Overturns Alabama Town's Plan to Secede from Local School System," NBC
News, February 13, 2018, https://www.nbcnews.com/news/us-news/court
-overturns-alabama-town-s-plan-secede-local-school-system-n847796; Ed-
Build, "Fractured."

15. EdBuild, "Fractured."

16. James E. Ryan, "Brown, School Choice, and the Suburban Veto," *Virginia Law Review* 90, no. 6 (2004): 1635–47.

17. Christopher M. Span and Ishwanzya D. Rivers, "An Intergenerational
Comparison of African American Student Achievement Before and After
Compensatory Education and the Elementary and Secondary Education
Act," *Teachers College Record* 114, no. 6 (2012): 1–17; Nikole Hannah-Jones,
"The Problem We All Live With: Part One," *This American Life*, National
Public Radio, July 31, 2015, https://www.thisamericanlife.org/562/the
-problem-we-all-live-with-part-one; Rucker C. Johnson and Alexander
Nazaryan, *Children of the Dream: Why School Integration Works* (New York:
Basic Books, 2019).

18. General estimate compiled by Fabricant and Fine, *Charter Schools
and the Corporate Makeover of Public Education*, 28–30; Walton Family Foundation, "Walton Family Foundation Announces Major Investments to Fuel
High-Quality School Growth Nationwide," press release, June 19, 2018,
https://www.waltonfamilyfoundation.org/about-us/newsroom/major
-investments-to-fuel-high-quality-school-growth-nationwide; Walton Family Foundation, "Building Equity Initiative Overview," press release, April 4,
2018, https://www.waltonfamilyfoundation.org/about-us/newsroom/building
-equity-initiative-overview; Howard Blume, "Backers Want Half of LAUSD
Students in Charter Schools in Eight Years, Report Says," *Los Angeles Times*,
September 21, 2015; Arianna Prothero and Francisco Vara-Orta, "As Eli Broad
Steps Down, Will His Influence on K–12 Education Last?," *Education Week*,

October 16, 2017, https://www.edweek.org/policy-politics/as-eli-broad-steps
-down-will-his-influence-on-k-12-education-last/2017/10; Carolyn Phenicie,
"Gates Foundation Announces $92 Million Going to School Networks Work-
ing to Boost High School Graduation, College Enrollment," 74, August 28,
2018, https://www.the74million.org/article/gates-foundation-announces-92
-million-going-to-school-networks-working-to-boost-high-school-graduation
-college-enrollment; and Schneider and Berkshire, *Wolf at the Schoolhouse
Door.*

19. Moriah Balingit, "Billionaire Bill Gates Announces a $1.7 Billion
Investment in U.S. Schools," *Washington Post*, October 19, 2017; David M.
Herszenhorn, "Billionaires Start $60 Million Schools Effort," *New York Times*,
April 25, 2017.

20. Mercedes K. Schneider, *School Choice: The End of Public Education* (New
York: Teachers College Press, 2016), 75–78; Abby Jackson, "The Walmart
Family Is Teaching Hedge Funds How to Profit from Publicly Funded
Schools," *Business Insider*, March 17, 2015, https://www.businessinsider.com
/walmart-is-helping-hedge-funds-make-money-off-of-charter-schools-2015–3.

21. Fabricant and Fine, *Charter Schools and the Corporate Makeover of Public
Education*, 66.

22. Robert L. Rose, "Johnson Controls to Buy Prince Automotive Unit,"
Wall Street Journal, July 19, 1996; "Amway Reports 2015 Sales of $9.5 Billion
USD," February 3, 2016, https https://www.amwayglobal.com/newsroom
/amway-reports-2015-sales-9-5-billion-usd; "Interview with Betsy Devos, the
Reformer," *Philanthropy*, http://www.philanthropyroundtable.org/topic
/excellence_in_philanthropy/interview_with_betsy_devos; Erica Green, "To
Understand Betsy DeVos's Educational Views, View Her Education" *New York
Times*, June 10, 2017, https://www.nytimes.com/2017/06/10/us/politics/betsy
-devos-private-schools-choice.html.

23. American Civil Liberties Union, "Background on Betsy DeVos from
the ACLU of Michigan," https://www.aclu.org/other/background-betsy-devos
-aclu-michigan; Corinne Cathart, "Betsy DeVos: Everything You Need to
Know," ABC News, November 23, 2016, https://abcnews.go.com/Politics
/betsy-devos/story?id=43745520.

24. National Center for Education Statistics, "Public Charter School
Enrollment," https://nces.ed.gov/programs/coe/indicator_cgb.asp; "Just the
FAQs—School Choice," Center for Education Reform, https://edreform.com
/2011/11/just-the-faqs-school-choice; National Center for Education Statistics,
"Private School Enrollment," https://nces.ed.gov/programs/coe/indicator_cgc
.asp; Council for American Private Education, "Facts and Studies," https://
www.capenet.org/facts.html; Brian D. Raty, "Research Facts on Home
schooling," National Home Education Research Institute, March 23, 2020,
https://www.nheri.org/research-facts-on-homeschooling; National Home
Education Research Institute, "Number and Enrollment of Public Elementary
and Secondary Schools," https://nces.ed.gov/programs/digest/d18/tables/dt18
_216.20.asp?current=yes; Gary Miron, Christopher Shank, and Caryn David-
son, *Full-Time Virtual and Blended Schools: Enrollment, Student Characteristics,
and Performance* (Boulder, CO: National Education Policy Center, 2018),

https://nepc.info/sites/default/files/publications/RB%20Miron%20Virtual %20Schools%202018_0.pdf; US Census Bureau, "U.S. School Spending per Pupil Increased for Fifth Consecutive Year, U.S. Census Bureau Reports," press release, May 21, 2019, https://www.census.gov/newsroom/press-releases /2019/school-spending.html.

25. Gordon Lafer, *Breaking Point: The Cost of Charter Schools for Public School Districts* (Oakland, CA: In the Public Interest, 2018), https://www.inthepublic interest.org/wp-content/uploads/ITPI_Breaking_Point_May2018FINAL.pdf; Brian Washington, "How to Prevent Charter Schools from Draining away Public School Funding in Your Community," Education Votes, National Education Association, May 27, 2018, https://educationvotes.nea.org/2018/05/27 /how-to-prevent-charter-schools-from-draining-away-public-school-funding -in-your-community; "Public Elementary and Secondary Charter Schools and Enrollment, by State," National Center for Education Statistics, https://nces .ed.gov/programs/digest/d17/tables/dt17_216.90.asp.

26. Derek Black, Bruce Baker, and Preston Green III, "Charter Schools Exploit Lucrative Loophole That Would Be Easy to Close," Conversation, February 19, 2019, https://theconversation.com/charter-schools-exploit-lucrative -loophole-that-would-be-easy-to-close-111792.

27. Dave Yost, *State of Ohio, Franklin County, Public Interest Report, Community School Facility Procurement* (Columbus: Office of the Auditor of the State, 2019), https://ohioauditor.gov/auditsearch/Reports/2019/Community_School _Facility_Procurement_Public_Interest_Report.pdf; Black, Baker, and Green, "Charter Schools Exploit Lucrative Loophole."

28. Keith Benson, "Renaissance Schools Don't Make Camden Public Schools Better for Our Kids," *Philadelphia Inquirer*, January 1, 2018.

29. Center for Public Democracy and Integrity for Education, *Charter School Vulnerabilities to Waste, Fraud, and Abuse* (May 2014), https://popular democracy.org/news/charter-school-vulnerabilities-waste-fraud-and-abuse; Noliwe Rooks, *Cutting School: Privatization, Segregation, and the End of Public Education* (New York: New Press, 2017), 161–63. For more on the Center for Public Democracy and Integrity for Education, see https://populardemocracy .org/about-us.

30. John Oliver, quoted in Valerie Straus, "John Oliver Hysterically Savages Charter Schools—and Charter Supporters Aren't Happy," *Washington Post*, August 22, 2016.

31. Rooks, *Cutting School*, 2, 49–78; Anderson, *Education of Blacks in the South.*

32. Bruce Fuller, Richard Elmore, and Gary Orfield, *Who Chooses? Who Loses? Culture, Institutions, and the Unequal Effects of School Choice* (New York: Teachers College Press, 1996); Erica Frankenberg, Genevieve Siegel-Hawley, and Jia Wang, "Choice Without Equity: Charter School Segregation," *Educational Policy Analysis Archives* 19, no. 1 (January 10, 2011), http://epaa.asu.edu /ojs/article/view/779; Julian Vasquez Heilig, Amy Williams, Linda McSpadden McNeil, and Christopher Lee, "Is Choice a Panacea? An Analysis of Black Secondary Student Attrition from KIPP, Other Privately Operated Charters, and Urban Districts," *Berkeley Review of Education* 2 no. 2 (2011): 153–78; Valerie Straus, "Do Self-Selection and Attrition Matter in KIPP Schools?," *Washington*

Post, June 14, 2011; New York City Independent Budget Office, "Staying or Going? Comparing Student Attrition Rates at Charter Schools with Nearby Traditional Public Schools," *Schools Brief* (January 2014), https://ibo.nyc.ny.us /iboreports/2014attritioncharterpublic.pdf; Robert Bifulco and Helen F. Ladd, "The Impact of Charter Schools on Student Achievement: Evidence from North Carolina," *Education Finance and Policy* 1, no. 1 (Winter 2006): 673–82; Ira Nichols-Barrer, Brian P. Gill, Philip Gleason, and Christina Clark Tuttle, "Does Student Attrition Explain KIPP's Success?," *Education Next* 14, no. 4 (September 2014), https://www.educationnext.org/student-attrition-explain -kipps-success.

33. Frankenberg, Siegel-Hawley, and Wang, "Choice Without Equity"; Courtney A. Bell, "All Choices Created Equal? The Role of Choice Sets in the Selection of Schools," *Peabody Journal of Education: Issues of Leadership, Policy, and Organizations* 84, no. 2 (2009): 191–208.

34. Aiko Kojima, interview with the author, August 21, 2020.

35. Stephanie Love, interview with the author, November 22, 2019 (minutes 32:00 and 11:12).

36. Rooks, *Cutting School,* 4.

37. David Stovall, "Charter Schools and the Event of Educational Sharecropping," in Sanders, Stovall, and White, *Twenty-First-Century Jim Crow Schools,* 41.

38. Deborah Meier, "Choice Can Save Public Education," *Nation,* March 4, 1991, 252–53, 266–68, 270–71.

39. CREDO (Center for Research on Education Outcomes), *National Charter School Study Executive Summary 2013* (Stanford, CA: Center for Research on Education Outcomes, Stanford University, 2015), https://credo.stanford.edu /sites/g/files/sbiybj6481/f/ncss_2013_executive_summary.pdf; CREDO (Center for Research on Education Outcomes), "Urban Charter School Study Report on 41 Regions" (Stanford, CA: Center for Research on Education Outcomes, Stanford University, 2015), 26–31, https://urbancharters.stanford.edu /download/Urban%20Charter%20School%20Study%20Report%20on%2041 %20Regions.pdf.

40. Bill and Melinda Gates Foundation, "CREDO Study: Urban Charter Schools Making Significant Positive Impact," https://k12education.gates foundation.org/blog/credo-study-urban-charter-schools-making-significant -positive-impact.

41. CREDO, "Urban Charter School Study Report on 41 Regions."

42. Frankenberg, Siegel-Hawley, and Wang, "Choice Without Equity."

43. Mark Binelli, "Michigan Gambled on Charter Schools. Its Children Lost," *New York Times Magazine,* September 5, 2017.

44. Julian Vasquez Heilig, "Policy Brief: Should Louisiana and the Recovery School District Receive Accolades for Being Last and Nearly Last?," Network for Public Education, August 28, 2015, https://networkforpubliceducation .org/policy_brief_louisiana.

45. Alexandra Usher and Nancy Kober, "Keeping Informed About School Vouchers: A Review of Major Developments and Research," Schott Foundation for Public Education, July 2011, http://schottfoundation.org/resources/keeping

-informed-about-school-vouchers-review-major-developments-and-research; Martin Carnoy, "School Vouchers Are Not a Proven Strategy for Improving Student Achievement," Economic Policy Institute, February 28, 2017, https:// www.epi.org/publication/school-vouchers-are-not-a-proven-strategy-for -improving-student-achievement.

46. American Civil Liberties Union, "Background on Betsy DeVos from the ACLU of Michigan."

47. Andrew Ujifusa, "See Betsy DeVos' Donations to Senators Who Will Oversee Her Confirmation," *Education Week*, December 1, 2016, https://www .edweek.org/policy-politics/see-betsy-devos-donations-to-senators-who-will -oversee-her-confirmation/2016/12.

48. Andrew Ujifusa, "Betsy DeVos-Led Group Should Pay $5.3 Million Campaign Fine, Dem. Senators Say," *Education Week*, December 14, 2016, https://www.edweek.org/policy-politics/betsy-devos-led-group-should-pay-5 -3-million-campaign-fine-dem-senators-say/2016/12; Randy Ludlow, "Group Once Led by Trump Education Secretary Nominee Owes $5.3 Million to Ohio," *Columbus Dispatch*, November 23, 2016.

49. Paul Bowers, "Frustrated with School Board, Charleston Power Players Aim to Shake up November Election," *Post and Courier*, June 7, 2018; Paul Bowers, "In Charleston School Board Race, One Dark-Money Group Spent Big and Won," *Post and Courier*, March 2, 2019; Annie Waldman, "How Teach for America Evolved into an Arm of the Charter School Movement," ProPublica, June 18, 2019, https://www.propublica.org/article/how-teach-for-america-evolved-into -an-arm-of-the-charter-school-movement; Valerie Straus, "From South Carolina to California, Charter School–Loving Billionaires Are Plowing Money into Midterm Local and Education Races," *Washington Post*, November 5, 2018; "Teach for America–South Carolina Receives $5,000 Grant for STEM Educators," Teach for America, press release, December 2, 2016.

50. Eric Brunner, Joshua Hyman, and Andrew Ju, "School Finance Reforms, Teachers' Unions, and the Allocation of School Resources," *Review of Economics and Statistics*, July 2, 2020, 473–89; Matt Barnum, "Are Teachers Unions Helping or Hurting Schools? Here's What the Newest Research Tells Us," *Chalkbeat*, April 15, 2019, https://www.chalkbeat.org/posts/us/2019/04/15 /teachers-unions-schools-wisconsin-funding-research.

51. Friedman and Friedman, *Two Lucky People*, 349.

52. Dave Umhoefer, "For Unions in Wisconsin, a Fast and Hard Fall Since Act 10," *Milwaukee Journal Sentinel*, November 27, 2016; Sabrina Tavernise, "Ohio Public Worker Bill Keeps Bargaining but Bars Strikes," *New York Times*, March 1, 2011; Jim Leckrone, "Ohio Governor Signs Anti-Union Bill," Reuters, March 21, 2011.

53. Amanda Ripley, "Rhee Tackles Classroom Challenge," *Time*, November 26, 2008, http://content.time.com/time/subscriber/article/0,33009 ,1862444,00.html; "The Education of Michelle Rhee," *Frontline*, PBS, January 8, 2013, https://www.pbs.org/wgbh/frontline/film/education-of-michelle-rhee /transcript.

54. "D.C. Deal with Teachers Union a Model for U.S.?," *All Things Considered*, NPR, April 7, 2010; Valerie Straus, "Michelle Rhee's Empty Claims

About Her D.C. Schools Record," *Washington Post*, January 31, 2012; Sam Dillon, "A School Chief Takes on Tenure, Stirring a Fight," *New York Times*, November 12, 2008.

55. Diane Ravitch, "The Mystery of Michelle Rhee," in *Reign of Error*, 145–55; Waldman, "How Teach for America Evolved."

56. Raynard Sanders," The New Orleans Public Education Experiment," in Sanders, Stovall, and White, *Twenty-First-Century Jim Crow Schools*, 15–16; Campbell Robinson, "Louisiana Illegally Fired 7,500 Teachers, Judge Rules," *New York Times*, June 21, 2012.

57. Anna M. Phillips, "California's Broken Charter School Law Has Defied Reform. Can Newsom Break the Gridlock?," *Los Angeles Times*, March 29, 2019.

58. Jason McGahan, "How Wealthy Charter-School Advocates Have Shaped the Race for California Governor," *Los Angeles Magazine*, June 4, 2018, https://www.lamag.com/citythinkblog/governors-race-2018; Ryan Menezes and Maloy Moore, "Track the Millions Flowing into California's Race for Governor," *Los Angeles Times*, November 5, 2018.

59. Seema Mehta and Ryan Menezes, "A Few Rich Charter School Supporters Are Spending Millions to Elect Antonio Villaraigosa Governor," *Los Angeles Times*, May 14, 2018; McGahan, "How Wealthy Charter-School Advocates Have Shaped the Race for California Governor"; Anna M. Phillips, "California's Broken Charter School Law Has Defied Reform. Can Newsom Break the Gridlock?," *Los Angeles Times*, March 29, 2019.

60. David Zahniser, Anna Phillips, and Howard Blume, "Why Didn't School Board President Ref Rodriguez Just Write Himself a Big Check?," *Los Angeles Times*, September 17, 2017; Howard Blue, Sonali Kohli, and Joy Resmovits, "Ref Rodriguez, Facing Criminal Charges, Resigns as L.A. School Board President," *Los Angeles Times*, September 19, 2017.

61. Kyles Stokes, "Complaints Piling up Against LAUSD Board Member Ref Rodriguez," KPCC ("The Voice of Southern California"), October 18, 2017, https://www.scpr.org/news/2017/10/18/76774/complaints-piling-up-against-lausd-board-member-re.

62. Mary Bailey Estes, "Charter Schools and Students with Special Needs: How Well Do They Mix?," *Education and Treatment of Children* 23, no. 3 (August 2000): 369–80; Joseph R. McKinney, "Charter Schools: A New Barrier for Children with Disabilities," *Educational Leadership* 54, no. 2 (October 1996), 22–25; Gary Miron, "Charters Should Be Expected to Serve All Kinds of Students," *Education Next* 14, no. 4 (Fall 2014), https://www.educationnext.org/charters-expected-serve-kinds-students; *State of Denial: California Charter Schools and Special Education Students* (California Teachers Association and United Teachers Los Angeles, 2019), https://www.utla.net/sites/default/files/report_-_final.pdf.

63. Paul Tough, "What It Takes to Make a Student," *New York Times Magazine*, November 26, 2006; Sam Dillon, "2 Entrepreneurs in World of Education Are Leading the Way on Change," *New York Times*, June 19, 2008.

64. Daniel J. Losen, Michael A. Keith II, Cheri L. Hodson, and Tia E. Martinez, "Charter Schools, Civil Rights and School Discipline: A Compre-

hensive Review," Civil Rights Project, March 15, 2016, https://civilrights
project.ucla.edu/resources/projects/center-for-civil-rights-remedies/school
-to-prison-folder/federal-reports/charter-schools-civil-rights-and-school
-discipline-a-comprehensive-review.

65. Peter Bergman and Isaac McFarlin Jr., "Education for All? A Nationwide Audit Study of Schools of Choice," December 2018, 3, https://web.archive
.org/web/20190126191458/http://www.columbia.edu/~psb2101/Bergman
McFarlin_school_choice.pdf.

66. Julian Vasquez Heilig, Amy Williams, Linda McSpadden McNeil, and
Christopher Lee, "Is Choice a Panacea? An Analysis of Black Secondary Student Attrition from KIPP, Other Privately Operated Charters, and Urban Dis-
tricts," *Berkeley Review of Education* 2 no. 2 (2011): 153–78; Valerie Straus, "Do
Self-Selection and Attrition Matter in KIPP Schools?," *Washington Post*, June
14, 2011; "Staying or Going? Comparing Student Attrition Rates at Charter
Schools with Nearby Traditional Public Schools," *Schools Brief* (New York City
Independent Budget Office), January 2014, https://ibo.nyc.ny.us/iboreports
/2014attritioncharterpublic.pdf; Bifulco and Ladd, "The Impact of Charter
Schools on Student Achievement"; Nichols-Barrer, Gill, Gleason, and Tuttle,
"Does Student Attrition Explain KIPP's Success?"

CHAPTER EIGHT: RESISTING SCHOOL CHOICE THROUGH COUNTERNARRATIVES AND COALITIONS

1. Ronsha Dickerson, interview with the author, August 5 and 13, 2020.

2. Ronsha Dickerson, interview with the author, August 5, 2020; "N.J.A.C.
6A:31, Renaissance Schools," New Jersey Department of Education, https://
www.state.nj.us/education/code/current/title6a/chap31.pdf; John Mooney,
"Explainer: Getting Inside the Urban Hope Act—and 'Renaissance Schools,'"
NJ Spotlight News, September 30, 2014, https://www.njspotlight.com/2014/09
/14-09-29-explainer-getting-inside-the-urban-hope-act-and-renaissance
-schools; Phil Dunn, "N.J. Governor Announces Takeover of Camden
School," *USA Today*, March 25, 2013.

3. Keith Benson, interview with the author, March 27 and August 19,
2020; Eliza Shapiro, "How an Unknown Reformer Rescued One of America's
Most Troubled School Districts," *Politico*, June 30, 2018, https://www.politico
.com/magazine/story/2018/06/30/camden-superintendent-education-reform
-paymon-rouhanifard-218940; Phaedra Trethan, "Camden Schools Superintendent Submits Resignation," *Courier-Post* (Cherry Hill, NJ), April 11, 2018;
Rebecca Everett, "Under Proposal, Historic Camden High School to Be Replaced by 4 Small 'Academies,'" NJ.com, October 4, 2016, https://www.nj
.com/camden/2016/10/under_proposal_camden_high_school_to_be_replaced
_b.html; Mark Weber, Bruce Baker, and Joseph Oluwole, *"One Newark's" Ra-
cially Disparate Impact on Teachers* (New Jersey Education Policy Forum, 2014),
https://njedpolicy.files.wordpress.com/2014/03/weber-baker-oluwole-staffing
-report_3_10_2014_final2.pdf.

4. James Cersonsky and Student Nation, "What You Should Know About
the Philly Student Walkout," *Nation*, May 17, 2013, https://www.thenation
.com/article/archive/what-you-should-know-about-philly-student-walkout;

"Philly Students Walkout, Teachers Protest Severe Budget Cuts," NBC Philadelphia, May 17, 2013, https://www.nbcphiladelphia.com/news/local/philly-teachers-protest-budget-cuts-student-walkouts/2144731; Ronsha Dickerson, interview with the author, August 5, 2020.

5. Ronsha Dickerson, interview with the author, August 5 and 13, 2020; Phil Dunn, "Camden Student Protest Draws Praise, Attention," *Courier-Post*, May 14, 2014; Jason Laday, "Camden High School Students Walk Out of Class to Protest Teacher Layoffs," NJ.com, May 14, 2014, https://www.nj.com/camden/2014/05/camden_high_school_students_walk_out_of_class_to_protest.html.

6. LaRaviere quoted in Noreen S. Ahmed-Ullah and Bill Ruthhart, "Principal Says Emanuel Administration Stifles Dissent," *Chicago Tribune*, May 14, 2014.

7. Troy LaRaviere, "Under Emanuel, Principals Have No Voice," *Chicago Sun-Times*, May 10, 2014; Diane Ravitch, "Troy A. LaRaviere: How Chicago Neighborhood Schools Outperformed Charter Schools," *Diane Ravitch's Blog*, September 4, 2014, https://dianeravitch.net/2014/09/04/troy-a-lariviere-how-chicago-neighborhood-schools-outperformed-charter-schools.

8. Eve L. Ewing, *Ghosts in the Schoolyard: Racism and School Closing on Chicago's South Side* (Chicago: University of Chicago Press, 2018); Noreen S. Ahmed-Ullah, John Chase, and Bob Secter, "CPS Approves Largest School Closure in Chicago's History," *Chicago Tribune*, May 23, 2013.

9. Troy LaRaviere, interview with the author, January 9, 2019; Ravitch, "Troy A. LaRaviere"; Noreen S. Ahmed-Ullah, "Chicago's Noble Charter School Network Has Tough Discipline Policy," *Chicago Tribune*, April 7, 2014; Stovall, "Charter Schools and the Event of Educational Sharecropping," 62–64.

10. Keith Benson and Ronsha Dickerson, "Commentary: How an Undeserving Leader Is Destroying Education in Camden," *Courier-Post*, May 25, 2017.

11. Arthur Barclay and Felisha Reyes Morton, "Commentary: Progress Made Possible in Camden's Schools," *Courier-Post*, May 30, 2017.

12. David Omotoso Stovall, *Born Out of Struggle: Critical Race Theory, School Creation, and the Politics of Interruption* (Albany: State University of New York Press, 2016), 4; Daniel G. Solórzano and Tara J. Yosso, "Critical Race Methodology: Counter-Storytelling as an Analytical Framework for Education Research," *Qualitative Inquiry* 8, no. 1 (2002): 23–44.

13. Stovall, "Charter Schools and the Event of Educational Sharecropping," 67.

14. Ronsha Dickerson, interview with the author, August 13, 2020.

15. Ronsha Dickerson, interview with the author, August 5 and 13, 2020; Everett, "Under Proposal, Historic Camden High School to Be Replaced by 4 Small 'Academies'"; Phaedra Trethan, "Christie, at School Dedication in Camden, Looks Back on Changes in City," *Courier-Post*, May 7, 2018.

16. Save Camden Public Schools Unity Community Center of South Jersey, Inc. v. Camden City Board of Education (April 24, 2018) DOCKET NO. A-0133–16T2, https://law.justia.com/cases/new-jersey/appellate-division-published/2018/a0133-16.html; Jim Walsh, "Court Rules for Camden Voters

in School Fight," *Courier-Post*, April 24, 2018; George Woolston, "This November, Camden Residents Will Vote to Determine School Board Type," *TAP into Camden*, October 4, 2018, https://www.tapinto.net/towns/camden /sections/education/articles/this-november-camden-residents-will-vote-to -determine-school-board-type.

17. Troy LaRaviere interview; LaRaviere, "Under Emanuel, Principals Have No Voice."

18. LaRaviere, "Under Emanuel, Principals Have No Voice."

19. Troy LaRaviere interview.

20. Troy LaRaviere, interview.

21. Juan Perez Jr., "Alderman Blasts Principal's Ouster," *Chicago Tribune*, April 23, 2016.

22. Juan Perez Jr., "Troy LaRaviere Blasts CPS, Details Reasons He Was Ousted as Blaine Principal," *Chicago Tribune*, May 13, 2016.

23. Juan Perez Jr., "Alderman Blasts Principal's Ouster," *Chicago Tribune*, April 23, 2016; Juan Perez Jr., "LaRaviere to Discuss His CPS Ouster Case Thursday," *Chicago Tribune*, May 12, 2016.

24. Amanda Kerr, "Marching Burke Students, Supporters Fight for School, Protest Charter Idea," *Post and Courier*, May 25, 2015.

25. Quality Education Project, "Charter School Resolution," June 7, 2015, Quality Education Files, Avery Research Center, College of Charleston, and in possession of author; Amanda Kerr, "Marching Burke Students, Supporters Fight for School, Protest Charter Idea," *Post and Courier*, May 25, 2015.

26. Molly Smith, "Raleigh Egypt Parents Call Charter School Transition a 'Hostile Takeover,'" WREG Memphis, October 27, 2014, https://wreg.com /2014/10/27/raleigh-egypt-parents-call-charter-school-transition-a-hostile -takeover; Daarel Burnette II, "Exclusive: Green Dot Public Schools Pulls Out of Raleigh-Egypt ASD Takeover," *Chalkbeat*, November 20, 2014; https:// tn.chalkbeat.org/2014/11/20/21092121/exclusive-green-dot-public-schools -pulls-out-of-raleigh-egypt-asd-takeover; Stephanie Love, correspondence with the author, February 9, 2020.

27. Arianna Prothero, "Charter Operators Pull back from Memphis Turnaround Effort," *Education Week*, April 21, 2015, https://www.edweek.org/ew /articles/2015/04/22/charter-operators-pull-back-from-memphis-turnaround .html; Bill Dries, "Frayser Battleground for Achievement Schools" *Daily News* (Memphis), October 31, 2014.

28. Elisabeth Greer, interview with the author, August 20, 2020; Aiko Kojima, interview with the author, August 21, 2020; Juan Perez Jr., "'We've Finally Won One,' National Teachers Academy Supporters Say After CPS Drops Plans for High School," *Chicago Tribune*, December 4, 2018; "We Are NTA," http://wearenta.weebly.com.

29. Norman Stockwell, "'Education Must Be Available to Every Child': An Interview with Jitu Brown," *Progressive*, December 1, 2017, https://progressive .org/magazine/education-must-be-available-to-every-child-an-interview-wi; Sanders, Stovall, and White, *Twenty-First-Century Jim Crow Schools*, 108; Journey for Justice Alliance, "History," https://j4jalliance.com/history-2-2; Yolanda Perdomo, "Dyett High School Hunger Strike Ends After 34 Days,"

WBEZ, September 20, 2015, https://www.wbez.org/stories/dyett-high-school
-hunger-strike-ends-after-34-days/fcb33f6e-2e76-4d19-adea-ad7887e5a008;
"The Dyett Hunger Strike, One Year On," Schott Foundation for Public Education, August 30, 2016, http://schottfoundation.org/blog/2016/08/30/dyett
-hunger-strike-one-year; "Dyett High School Hunger Strike Ends" *Chicago
Tribune*, September 20, 2015.

30. Journey for Justice Alliance, "A Moratorium on School Privatization,"
https://j4jalliance.com/project-details-2.

31. Jitu Brown, "#FightForDyett: Fighting Back Against School Closings
and the Journey for Justice," in *Lift Us Up, Don't Push Us Out! Voices from the
Front Lines of the Educational Justice Movement*, ed. Mark R. Warren and David
Goodman (Boston: Beacon Press, 2018), 52–53.

32. Ronsha Dickerson, interview with the author, August 5, 2020, August
13, 2020, and September 15, 2020; Vincent DeBlasio, "Camden Residents Offer Support of Gov. Murphy," *TAP into Camden*, May 21, 2019, https://www
.tapinto.net/towns/camden/sections/government/articles/camden-residents
-offer-support-of-gov-murphy; Catherine Dunn, "As Tax-Credit Controversy
Rages on, Gov. Murphy Tours Camden Businesses," *Philadelphia Inquirer*, July
4, 2019; Phaedra Trethan, "For New EDA Chief, a Bus Tour of the 'Real'
Camden," *Courier-Post* (Cherry Hill, NJ), June 6, 2019.

33. Keith Benson, interview with the author, March 27, 2020.

34. Ronsha Dickerson, interview with the author, August 5 and 13, 2020.

35. Jennie Biggs, correspondence with the author, August 3, 2020; Natasha
Irskine, interview with the author, August 24, 2020; Elizabeth Greer, inter-
view with the author, August 20 and 27, 2020; "About," Raise Your Hand for
Illinois Public Education, https://www.ilraiseyourhand.org/about.

36. Carol Burris and Jeff Bryant, *Asleep at the Wheel: How the Federal Charter Schools Program Recklessly Takes Taxpayers and Students for a Ride* (Network
for Public Education, 2019, https://networkforpubliceducation.org/asleep
atthewheel.

37. Marla Kilfoyle, interview with the author, February 12, 2020.

38. William J. Barber II, "America's Moral Malady," *Atlantic*, February
2018, https://www.theatlantic.com/magazine/archive/2018/02/a-new-poor
-peoples-campaign/552503.

39. Brown, "#FightForDyett," 53; Stockwell, "Education Must Be Available to Every Child."

40. Benson, "To the Black Education Reform Establishment, Be Real with
Who You Are and Whose Interest You Represent."

41. Stovall, *Born Out of Struggle*, ix–xvi, 3; Ana Beatriz Cholo, "Little Village High Tab: $60 Million," *Chicago Tribune*, September 25, 2003; Ana Beatriz
Cholo, "Little Village Getting School It Hungered For," *Chicago Tribune*, February 27, 2005.

42. Hale, *The Freedom Schools*, 222–23; Lisa Deer Brown and the McComb
Young People's Project, conversations with the author, July 2, 2012; Umar Fa-
rooq, "Baltimore Algebra Project Stops Juvenile Detention Center," *Nation*, January 24, 2012, https://www.thenation.com/article/archive/baltimore-algebra
-project-stops-juvenile-detention-center/; Hale, *The Freedom Schools*, 222–23.

43. Charles Payne, "Miss Baker's Grandchildren: An Interview with the Baltimore Algebra Project," in *Quality Education as a Constitutional Right: Creating a Grassroots Movement to Transform Public Schools*, ed. Theresa Perry et al. (Boston: Beacon Press, 2010), 4.

44. Theresa Moran, "Chicago Teachers Say They'll Strike for the Kids," *Labor Notes*, August 28, 2012, https://labornotes.org/2012/08/chicago-teachers-say-theyll-strike-kids; Diane Rado, "Chicago Teacher Strike: Issues at the Center of Contract Negotiations, *Chicago Tribune*, September 17, 2012; Monica Davey and Steven Greenhouse, "School Days Resume in Chicago as the Lessons from a Strike Are Assessed," *New York Times*, September 19, 2012; Greg McCune, "Chicago Teachers Union Ratifies Deal That Ended Strike," *Chicago Tribune*, October 4, 2012.

45. Cantor quoted in Amy Goodman, "Striking Teachers, Parents Join Forces to Oppose 'Corporate' Education Model in Chicago," *Democracy Now*, September 10, 2012, https://www.democracynow.org/2012/9/10/striking_teachers_parents_join_forces_to.

46. Juan Perez Jr., "Little Progress in New Strike," *Chicago Tribune*, December 5, 2018.

47. Stan Karp and Adam Sanchez, "The 2018 Wave of Teacher Strikes: A Turning Point for Our Schools?," *Rethinking Schools* 32, no. 4 (Summer 2018); Jasmine Kerrisey, "Teacher Strike Wave: By the Numbers," *Labor Notes*, October 4, 2018, http://www.labornotes.org/blogs/2018/10/teacher-strike-wave-numbers; Dylan Scott, "The Strike That Brought Teachers Unions Back from the Dead," *Vox*, July 5, 2019, https://www.vox.com/the-highlight/2019/6/28/18662706/chicago-teachers-unions-strike-labor-movement.

48. See Derek W. Black, "The Current Crisis," chap. 1 in *Schoolhouse Burning: Public Education and the Assault on American Democracy* (New York: Public Affairs, 2020).

49. Keith Benson, interview with the author, August 19, 2020.

50. Katara Patton, "Interview with Mayoral Candidate Troy LaRaviere," *Chicago Defender*, October 24, 2018; Troy LaRaviere interview.

51. Bill Ruthhart, "LaRaviere Campaign Site Takes Shots at Emanuel," *Chicago Tribune*, January 17, 2018; Bill Ruthhart, "LaRaviere Ad Tells Emanuel: 'Get the Hell Out,'" *Chicago Tribune*, August 5, 2018; Troy LaRaviere interview.

52. Mike Vilensky, "Democrat Todd Kaminsky Leads N.Y. State Senate Race," *Wall Street Journal*, April 20, 2016; Marla Kilfoyle, interview with the author, February 12, 2020.

53. Miguel A. Gonzales, "With Nearly 1,800 Educators on the Ballot, a #RedForEd Wave is Poised to Make a Big Splash in November," National Education Association, press release, November 2, 2018, http://www.nea.org/home/73989.htm; "Over 170 Teachers Ran for State Office in 2018," *Education Week*, July 17, 2018, https://www.edweek.org/policy-politics/over-170-teachers-ran-for-state-office-in-2018-heres-what-we-know-about-them; Madeline Will and Sarah Schwartz, "Dozens of Teachers Were Elected to State Office. Many More Fell Short," *Education Week*, November 6, 2018, https://www.edweek.org/ew/articles/2018/11/08/dozens-of-teachers-were-elected-to-state.html; Katie

Reilly, "Most Teachers Running for Office Lost on Tuesday. Here's Why Educators Are Celebrating the 2018 Midterms Anyway," *Time*, November 9, 2018, https://time.com/5447995/teacher-education-2018-midterm-elections.

54. Katie Reilly, "'Our Voices Were Heard': Dozens of Teachers Advance in Oklahoma Primaries After Walkouts," *Time*, June 27, 2018, https://time.com /5323467/oklahoma-primaries-teachers-running-for-office; Reilly, "Most Teachers Running for Office Lost on Tuesday"; David Williams, "16 Oklahoma Educators Elected to Office on Tuesday," CNN.com, November 7, 2018.

55. Waldran quoted in Kyle Hinchey, "Teachers Share Disappointment with Election Results, Excitement for the Future," *Tulsa World*, November 11, 2018.

56. Black, *Schoolhouse Burning*, 43–44.

57. Don Kaufman, "Why Education May Be the Issue That Breaks Republicans' Decade-Long Grip on Wisconsin," *New Yorker*, August 15, 2018, https://www.newyorker.com/news/dispatch/why-education-may-be-the-issue -that-breaks-republicans-decade-long-grip-on-wisconsin; "Tony Evers," *Chippewa Herald* (Chippewa Falls, WI), March 30, 2013; Patrick Coolican, "Tim Walz Defeats Jeff Johnson in High-Stakes Election for Minnesota Governor," *Star Tribune*, November 7, 2018; Miguel A. Gonzales, "With Nearly 1,800 Educators on the Ballot, a #RedForEd Wave Is Poised to Make a Big Splash in November," National Education Association, press release, November 2, 2018.

58. Jason McGahan, "How Wealthy Charter-School Advocates Have Shaped the Race for California Governor," *Los Angeles Magazine*, June 4, 2018, https://www.lamag.com/citythinkblog/governors-race-2018; "California's Students Win, Futures Brighter with Election Victory of Gavin Newsom for Governor—State Superintendent Race Too Close to Call," California Teachers Association, press release, November 7, 2018, https://www.cta.org/en /About-CTA/News-Room/Press-Releases/2018/11/20181107.aspx.

59. "About," Public Funds Public Schools, https://pfps.org/about.html; "Judge Overturns Expanded Wis. Voucher Plan," *Education Week*, January 22, 1997, https://www.edweek.org/policy-politics/judge-overturns-expanded -wis-voucher-plan/1997/01; Mark Walsh, "Ohio Court Clears Cleveland's Voucher Pilot" Education Week, August 7, 1996, https://www.edweek.org /education/ohio-court-clears-clevelands-voucher-pilot/1996/08; Derek Black, conversation with the author, February 18, 2019.

60. Erin Golden, Twin Cities School Segregation Case Proceeds After Ruling on Charter Schools," *Star Tribune*, June 12, 2019; Herbert White, "NC Lawsuit Challenges Mecklenburg Town Charter Schools Legislation," *Charlotte Post*, May 1, 2020.

61. "About," Litigation, Public Funds Public Schools.

62. Cain v. Horne, 202 P.3d 1178 (Ariz. 2009); Schwartz v. Lopez 382 P.3d 886 (2016); Louisiana Fed'n of Teachers v. State of Louisiana, 118 So.3d 1033 (La. 2013); "About," Public Funds Public Schools.

63. "In re Renewal Application of TEAM Academy Charter School," Education Law Center, https://edlawcenter.org/litigation/in-re-renewal-application -of-team-academy-charter-school.

64. Carley Lanich, "Hammond, Lake Ridge Schools Join Lawsuit Challenging State's $1 Charter Law," *Times of Northwest Indiana*, November 23,

2019; Dave Bangert, "West Lafayette Taxpayers Look to Join Lawsuit Against Indiana's $1 Charter School Law," *Journal and Courier* (Lafayette, IN), December 5, 2019.

65. Derek W. Black, "Preferencing Educational Choice: The Constitutional Limits," *Cornell Law Review* 103, no. 6 (2018): 1359–1430, https://scholarship .law.cornell.edu/clr/vol103/iss6/5; Derek Black, conversation with the author, February 18, 2019.

66. "About," Public Funds Public Schools; Associated Press, "Arizona Proposition 305 Fails, Blocking Expansion of School Vouchers for Families," ABC 15 Arizona, November 6, 2018, https://www.abc15.com/news/state/arizona -proposition-305-fails-reducing-school-vouchers-available-to-families.

67. "About," Public Funds Public Schools.

68. See Black, *Schoolhouse Burning*; Richard Kluger, *Simple Justice: The History of* Brown v. Board of Education *and Black Americans' Struggle for Equality* (New York: Vintage Books, 2004).

69. Gary R. George and Walter C. Farrell Jr., "School Choice and African American Students: A Legislative View," *Journal of Negro Education* 59, no. 4 (Autumn 1990): 521–25.

70. Terrenda White, "From Community Schools to Charter Chains," in Sanders, Stovall, and White, *Twenty-First Century Jim Crow Schools*, 104.

71. Rucker C. Johnson and Alexander Nazaryan, *Children of the Dream: Why School Integration Works* (New York: Basic Books, 2019), 45, 57–66; John Charles Boger and Gary Orfield eds., *School Resegregation: Must the South Turn Back?* (Chapel Hill: University of North Carolina Press, 2005), 7–9; David Grissmer, Ann Flanagan, and Stephanie Williamson, "Why Did the Black-White Score Gap Narrow in the 1970s and 1980s," in *The Black-White Test Score Gap*, ed. Christopher Jencks and Meredith Phillips (Washington, DC: Brookings Institution, 1998), 185–87; David W. Grissmer, Stephanie Williamson, Sheila Nataraj Kirby, and Mark Berends, "Exploring the Rapid Rise in Black Achievement Scores in the United States (1970–1990)," in *The Rising Curve: Long-Term Gains in IQ and Related Measures*, ed. Ulric Neisser (Washington, DC: American Psychological Association, 1998), 251–85. On the early history of the National Assessment of Educational Progress (NAEP), see Richard Rothstein, Tamara Wilder, and Rebecca Jacobson, "Early NAEP," chap. 6 in *Grading Education: Getting Accountability Right* (New York: Teachers College Press, 2008); Erica Frankenberg, "School Integration—The Time Is Now," introduction to *Lessons in Integration: Realizing the Promise of Racial Diversity in American Schools*, ed. Erica Frankenberg and Gary Orfield (Charlottesville: University of Virginia Press, 2007); Michelle Burris, "The Benefits of Socioeconomically and Racially Integrated Schools and Classrooms," Century Foundation, April 26, 2019, https://tcf.org/content/facts/the-benefits-of -socioeconomically-and-racially-integrated-schools-and-classrooms.

72. Christopher M. Span and Ishwanzya D. Rivers, "Reassessing the Achievement Gap: An Intergenerational Comparison of African American Student Achievement before and after Compensatory Education and the Elementary and Secondary Education Act," *Teachers College Record* 114, no. 6 (June 2012): 1–17; Richard Rothstein, "For Public Schools, Segregation Then,

Segregation Since: Education and the Unfinished March," *Economic Policy Institute*, August 27, 2013, https://www.epi.org/publication/unfinished-march -public-school-segregation; Johnson and Nazaryan, *Children of the Dream*; Erica Frankenberg and Gary Orfield, *Lessons in Integration: Realizing the Promise of Racial Diversity in American Schools* (Charlottesville: University of Virginia Press, 2007).

73. Rothstein, "For Public Schools, Segregation Then, Segregation Since."

74. Johnson and Nazaryan, *Children of the Dream*, 63–65; Valerie Straus and Rucker C. Johnson, "Why School Integration Works," *Washington Post*, May 16, 2019; Nikole Hannah-Jones, "It Was Never About Busing," *New York Times*, July 14, 2019).

75. Johnson and Nazaryan, *Children of the Dream*, 65.

76. Troy LaRaviere interview.

77. Nikole Hannah-Jones, "Choosing a School for My Daughter in a Segregated City," *New York Times Magazine*, June 9, 2016.

INDEX

Notes are indicated by "n" following the page number.

Academic Magnet High School (Charleston, South Carolina), 121–23
accountability movement, 99, 101–2, 103, 105, 107–8
achievement gap, 144, 169, 211–12
Achievement School District (Memphis), 154, 158, 167
Adams, LaTricea, 156
Agassi, Andre, 131
Alabama: *Brown v. Board of Education*, response to, 23; Citizens' Councils in, 24; racism in, 168; White rights, defense of, 28–29
Alexander, Lamar, 101, 102, 104
Alexander v. Holmes County Board of Education, 26, 34, 35
All Children Matter (PAC), 110–11, 182
Alliance for School Choice, 111, 127, 145
Almond, J. Lindsay, 24, 30
alternative school movement, 118–19
American Alliance for Better Schools, 145
American Dream, 39, 41–42
American Federation for Children, 141
American Housing Act (1949), 53

America 2000 education goals, 102
Anderson, Melinda, 135
Arizona: *Cain v. Horne*, 209; school performance in, 181; special needs students in, 186; voucher program, defeat of, 209–10
Asleep at the Wheel (NPE), 200
Atkins, Thomas, 75

Baker, Ella, 66, 203
Baltimore, Algebra Project, 203
Banks, Valerie, 144
Barber, William J., II, 201
Barbic, Chris, 154–55, 156, 158
Barclay, Arthur, 194
Barnes, Robin D., 151
Beals, Melba Pattillo, 20
Bell, Derrick, 143, 150–51, 152, 153
Bell, Terrell, 97
Benson, Keith: activism of, 205, 206; on coalition building, 200; on hybrid schools, 191; NAACP and, 195; on profiteering by charter operators, 174; on resistance to school choice, 202; school choice, critiques of, 193–94
Bill and Melinda Gates Foundation: on CREDO report, 180, 181; expenditures by, 110, 113, 114, 154, 186; influence of, 171
Birmingham movement, 142
Black, Derek, 132

Black, Indigenous, and People of
Color (BIPOC) individuals: in
Camden, grassroots organizing of,
195; digital divide and, 137; free
school movement and, 118; sup-
port for school choice, 12. *See also*
people of color
Black Alliance for Educational
Options (BAEO), 141, 142
blackboard jungles, 31, 54, 66
Black Education for New Orleans, 161
Black Lives Matter movement, 14, 146
Black Panther Party, 78
Bloomberg, Michael, 185
Blum, Richard, 125
*Board of Education of Oklahoma City
Public Schools v. Dowell*, 106, 147
Bob Jones University, 97
Bob Jones University v. United States,
97, 117
Bolick, Clint, 145
Booker, Cory, 159
Boston: busing in, 62–64, 73–75;
school privatization in, 75–76;
White flight from, 85–86
Broad, Eli, 110, 185
Brown, Doris, 86
Brown, Jitu, 199, 201
Brown, Millicent, 63, 65, 89
Brown v. Board of Education: cases
comprising, 64; evidence used in,
67; failures of, 143; Friedman and,
44; Lewis and, 17–18; NAACP
and, 7; as precedent, 70; on race
and education, 169
Bryan, Hazel, 20, 88
Buchanan, James, 47
Buchanan v. Warley, 50
Budde, Ray, 128, 129, 131, 133
Buist Academy (Charleston, South
Carolina), 8, 121–23
Burger, Warren, 94
Burke High School (Charleston,
South Carolina), 1–3, 5–6, 122, 197
Bush, George H. W., 102, 103
Bush, George W., 101, 102–3, 107,
127, 140–41, 187

busing: Black attitudes toward, 77; in
Boston, 62–64, 73–75; buses, symbolism of, 64; in Chicago, 69–71;
controversy over, media portrayals
of, 76–8; New York City school
desegregation and, 67–68; Nixon's attitudes toward, 93; North's
response to, 91; perceptions
of, as violent, 76–77; political
opposition to, 71–72; Reagan on,
96; suburbs and, 86–88. *See also*
racism and foundations of school
choice model
Byrd, Harry F., Sr., 19
Byrnes, James "Jimmy," 22, 25

Cain v. Horne, 209
California: charter schools in, 129,
184–85; governor's race (2018),
208; school funding in, 173; special
needs students in, 186. *See also* Los
Angeles
Camden, New Jersey: resistance to
school choice in, 193–94; state
takeover of schools in, 190–92
Canada, Geoffrey, 12–13, 132
Cantor, Phil, 204
Carmichael, Stokely, 79, 140
Carpenter, Sarah, 158–59, 175
Carter, Jimmy, 95
Cash, Kriner, 155
Catholic schools, 125
Center for Public Democracy, 174
Center for Research on Education
Outcomes (CREDO, Stanford
University), 170, 180–81
Center on Education Policy, 181
Chamber of Commerce, on Tennes-
see public schools, 154
Chaney, James, 96
Charleston, South Carolina: Buist
Academy, 8, 121–23; Burke High
School, 1–3, 5–6, 122, 197; magnet
schools in, 121–23; pro-school
choice lobbying in, 182; racial
makeup of, 2; resistance to school
choice in, 189, 197

Charlotte and Mecklenburg County, North Carolina, desegregation efforts in, 106–7

Charlottesville Education Summit, 102, 104

Charter School Expansion Act (1998), 105

charter schools: Charter Schools Program, 114; under Clinton, 105, 106; corporatization of, 179; discussion of, 128–33; expenditures on, 219n12; for-profit charter schools, 13, 130–31, 179; growth of, 9, 111; in Memphis, 154–56, 179; under NCLB Act, 109; Obama on, 111; profit motive and, 173–74; under Race to the Top Program, 113; segregation in, 147–49; single-site schools, 156–57; student suspensions, 187; teachers' strikes, 204

Chicago: Chicago Land Clearance Commission, 53; Chicago Urban League, 49–50, 53, 54; community control movement in, 80; direct action in, 203–4; educational justice movement, 189; Redmond Plan, 69, 120; Renaissance 2010 plan, 112, 113, 196, 202; resistance to busing in, 69–70; resistance to school choice in, 192–93, 194, 198, 200, 202; segregation in, 39, 42–43, 49–54; South East Chicago Commission, 56; as stage for school choice, 38–39; White flight from, 52, 85, 86

Chicago, Friedman and school choice in, 38–61; Friedman, rise of, 38–49; segregated public schools in Chicago, 57–61; segregation in Chicago, 39, 42–43, 49–54; University of Chicago and, 54–57

Chico, Gary, 202

Christie, Chris, 190, 193

Cicero, Illinois, racism in, 50

Citizens' Councils, 24, 26

Citizens for Educational Freedom, 145

Citizens League (Minnesota), 129

civil rights: civil rights activism and freedom of choice, 33–36; civil rights perspective on resistance to school choice, 210–11. *See also* civil rights claim to school choice, racism and

Civil Rights Act (1964): Friedman's opposition to, 47, 61; Johnson and, 90; school desegregation, definition of, 71; Title IV, 71; Title VI, 59

civil rights claim to school choice, racism and, 139–63; charter schools and, 147–49; Fuller and, 139–42, 149–54, 162–63; Memphis, school reform in, 154–57; Milwaukee, school reform in, 150–54; NAACP and, 157–59; New Orleans after Hurricane Katrina, 160–61; resegregation and, 147; school choice, bipartisan support for, 104, 111, 159–60; school choice, Black support for, 145–46, 162–63; Wyatt Tee Walker and, 142–45

Civil Rights Project (UCLA), 147, 166–67, 187

Clark, Harvey, 50

Clark, Kenneth and Mamie, 67

class (social), 8–9, 178

Cleage, Albert, 80

Cleveland, voucher system in, 125–26

Clinton, Bill, 14, 101, 102, 104–6

Clinton, Hillary, 172

Coalition for Kids, 182–83

coalitions, importance of building, 198–203. *See also* resisting school choice through counternarratives and coalitions

Cobb, Charlie, 78

Cody, Anthony, 200

Cody, John, 70

Coggs, G. Spencer, 153

Coggs, Marcia, 152

Cohen, Muriel, 84

Coit v. Green, 117

College of Charleston (South Carolina), 25
color-blind rhetoric and ideology, 82,
95, 122, 169–70, 175
Committee for Economic Development (public policy organization),
100
community control movement,
78–83, 124
community empowerment, 176,
178–80
Conant, James, 66
Congress, creation of Opportunity
Zones, 160. *See also* federal support
of school choice movement
Congress of Racial Equality (CORE),
64, 139
Connor, Bull, 144
Constitution, supposed
color-blindness of, 169
controlled choice, 5, 116–17
Coordinating Council of Community
Organizations (CCCO), 58–59
corporate interests, 170–71
corruption in school choice networks,
182–83
counternarratives. *See* resisting
school choice through counternar-
ratives and coalitions
Counts, Dorothy, 20
COVID-19 pandemic, 136, 137–38
Cox, John, 185, 208
CREDO (Center for Research on
Education Outcomes, Stanford
University), 170, 180–81
Crespino, Joseph, 73, 96
cyber schools (virtual schooling,
online education), 135–38

Daley, Richard: anti-desegregation
efforts, 69; Civil Rights Act and,
59; Duncan and, 112; on Hyde
Park–Kenwood renewal, 56; Johnson and, 91; Little Village school
and, 202; Renaissance 2010 plan,
112, 113, 196, 202
D.C. Parents for School Choice, 144

Deadrich, Katie, 90
Debs, Mira, 119
Defenders of State Sovereignty and
Individual Liberties (Virginia), 28
defensive localism, 55
DeLaine, Joseph, 64
Delmont, Matthew, 55, 70, 76
Democratic Party, 15, 104
Democrats for Education Reform,
141
Dennis, Dave, 165, 210
Department of Education: creation
of, 95; Duncan at, 14, 112–13; Reagan and, 97; reduced funding for,
101; school choice, reliance on, 14,
111; on school choice under NCLB
Act, 109
Department of Health, Education,
and Welfare (HEW), 33, 59, 69, 94
Department of Justice, 94, 97, 121–22
desegregation: benefits of, 211–12;
under Clinton, 105; desegregation
assistance centers, 97; failure of,
146; as goal of magnet schools,
120; impact on Whites, 212–13;
Johnson's support for, 90–91;
New York City efforts on, 66–69;
northern views of, 64–66, 70–71;
under Reagan, 97–102; school
choice and, 4–6, 19; Whites' attitudes toward, 77, 88–89. *See also*
integration; racism and foundations of school choice model
Detroit: community control movement in, 80, 82; inner city violence
in, 83; school performance in,
181; suburban busing and, 86–87;
White flight from, 85
DeVos, Betsy: All Children Matter
and, 182; California gubernatorial
race and, 185; Fuller and, 141; as
K12 Inc. financial backer, 138;
school choice, support for, 14, 110,
127, 159, 171–73; on school choice,
12, 163; school privatization
agenda, 162; as secretary of education, appointment of, 114–15

Dickerson, Ronsha, 190–92, 193–94, 195, 199–200, 205
disabled/special needs students, 186–88
District Court for the Southern District of Mississippi, *Evers v. Jackson Municipal Separate School District*, 34
Dougherty, Jack, 150
Douglass, Frederick, 7
Du Bois, W. E. B., 148–49, 163, 165–66, 168
Duckworth, Angela, 41
Duncan, Arne: Chicago and, 192–93; educational policies of, 14, 112–13, 204; mentioned, 206; Renaissance 2010 plan, 112, 113, 196, 202; Tennessee public schools and, 154
Dure, Leon, 30

Eckford, Elizabeth, 20
economy and economics: economic argument for choice, 166; economic impact of choice, 172; segrenomics, 174–75. *See also* Friedman, Milton
EdChoice (Milton and Rose D. Friedman Foundation), 9, 114, 123, 164
education: as civil right, 17–18, 19; educational justice movement, 189; educators as political actors, 205–8; equalization plans, 22–23; Friedman's views on, 44–45; politicization of, 7; profit motive in, 13; public opinion of, 11. *See also* freedom of choice in education; public education (public schools)
Eisenhower, Dwight D., 20
Elementary and Secondary Education Act (1965), 32, 41, 90, 104, 112, 113, 119
Eli and Edythe Broad Foundation, 171
Emanuel, Rahm, 192–93, 196, 205, 206
Emanuel AME Church (Charleston, South Carolina), killings at, 8

Emergency School Aid Act (1972), 94, 97, 119
Equal Education Opportunity Act (1974), 71
equalization plans, 22–23
Erickson, Ansley, 48–49, 57
Evers, Tony, 207–8
Evers v. Jackson Municipal Separate School District, 34
Every Student Succeeds Act (2015), 113–14

Fabricant, Michael, 171
failure of school choice, deterioration of public education and, 164–88; budget shortfalls from school choice, 173–76; choice programs, failures of, 180–82; community empowerment and, 176, 178–80; corporate interests and, 170–71; corruption in school choice networks, 182–83; DeVos and, 171–73; disabled/special needs students and, 186–88; Friedman and, 164–65; in Los Angeles, 184–86; racism's impact on, 165–70; social and economic capital and, 176–78; teachers' unions and, 183–84
Farrell, Walter, 152
Faubus, Orval, 20, 23–24
Federal Charter School Program, 105
Federal Housing Administration, 50
federal support of school choice movement, 90–115; accountability movement, 101–2; bipartisan nature of, 104; Bush and, 102–3; Clinton and, 104–6; DeVos and, 114–15; Johnson and, 90–91; magnet schools, 103–4; *A Nation at Risk* and, 98–101; Nixon and, 90–95; No Child Left Behind Act, 107–10; Obama and, 111–14; Reagan and, 95–99, 101; school vouchers, 110–11; Supreme Court and, 106–7
Ferguson, Herman, 81
Fine, Michelle, 171
Finn, Chester, 129, 143, 160

First to the Top law (Tennessee), 154
Florida: federal education funding
    for, 33; school performance in, 181
Floyd, George, 159
Ford, Gerald, 95
Forman, James, Jr., 146, 149
Forman, Stanley, 63
for-profit charter schools, 13, 130–31,
    179
Frankenberg, Erica, 121, 166–67, 181
Freedom and Capitalism (Friedman),
    43
freedom of association, 28, 30
freedom of choice in education,
    17–37; civil rights activism and,
    33–36; development of school
    choice, 19–30; ideology behind
    school choice, 30–33; introduction
    to, 17–19; northern cities, desegre-
    gation orders and, 37
Freedom of Choice in the United
    States (FOCUS) initiative, 35–6
freedom of choice plans, 28–30,
    33–35, 38, 46, 124
Freedom Riders and Freedom Rides,
    64, 139
Freedom Schools, 74
Freeman v. Pitts, 106
free market ideology, 44–45, 117, 123,
    125, 131–32, 175. *See also* Friedman,
    Milton
Free School movement, 118
Friedman, Milton: American Dream
    and, 39, 41–2; Chicago's historical
    racism, ignoring of, 60–61; Chica-
    go's segregated public schools and,
    59–61; Civil Rights Act, opposition
    to, 47, 61; education, views on,
    44–45; federal enactment of theo-
    ries of, 111; free market theories,
    40, 176; Goldwater and, 47–48; on
    integration, 45; legacy of, 164–65;
    libertarianism of, 46; mentioned,
    15, 37; New York liberals and, 48;
    Republican Party and, 41, 48; rise
    of, 38–49; school choice, devo-
    tion to, 164–65; on segregation

in Chicago, 59; structural racism
    in philosophy of, 39; on teachers'
    unions, 183; at University of Chi-
    cago, 49, 54; White privilege and,
    42
Friedman, Rose D., 41, 164
Fuller, Howard (Owusu Sadaukai):
    as activist, 139–42; community
    engagement, 145–46; on integra-
    tion, 148; on local school control,
    175; mentioned, 157; Milwaukee,
    school reform activities in, 149–54;
    New Orleans schools and, 161; on
    school choice, 162–63; on segrega-
    tion, 169; Williams and, 210

Gaither, Milton, 134
Galamison, Milton, 67, 79
Gallup poll on charter schools, 10
García, Lily Eskelsen, 207
Gardendale City, Alabama, racism
    in, 168
Garrity, Arthur, 74–75, 76
George, Gary, 152
Georgia: *Brown v. Board of Education*,
    response to, 23; Citizens' Councils
    in, 24; continued school segrega-
    tion in, 25; public funding of pri-
    vate education, 124
Goals 2000: Educate America Act
    (1994), 104, 105
Goldstein, Dana, 100
Goldwater, Barry, 47, 72
Goodman, Andrew, 96
Great Depression, 39–40
Great Migration, 49
Great Society programs, 41
*Green v. County School Board of Kent
    County*, 26, 35, 73
Greer, Elisabeth, 198
Gressette Committee (South Caro-
    lina), 30–31
*Griffin v. County School Board of Prince
    Edward County*, 24, 34
grit, 42
Gross, Robert, 125
Guggenheim, Davis, 133

Hannah-Jones, Nikole, 148, 167, 213
Hansberry, Carl, 51
Hansberry, Lorraine, 52
Hansberry v. Lee, 52
Harlan, John, 169
Harlem, New York City, public schools in, 143–44
Harlem Children's Zone, 12–13, 132
Hastings, Reed, 185
health, impact of desegregation on, 212
Hentoff, Nat, 66
HEW (Department of Health, Education, and Welfare), 33, 59, 69, 94
Hicks, Louise Day, 74
Hirsh, Arnold, 50, 56
Hollings, Fritz, 31
Holt, John, 66, 134
Home Owner's Loan Corporation, 50
homeschooling, 133–35
Home School Legal Defense Association, 135
housing: housing covenants, 42, 50; housing speculation in Chicago, 52; redlining, 39, 50
hunger strikes, 199, 202
Hyde Park, Chicago, Blacks in, 54–56
Hyde Park–Woodlawn Improvement Society, 51

Illinois Blighted Areas Redevelopment Act (1947), 53
Indianapolis, school segregation in, 167
individual actions, importance of, 211–12
Individuals with Disabilities Education Act (1990), 186
inner city problems, racism and school desegregation efforts, 83–88
Institute for Justice, 145
Institute on Race and Policy, 176
integration: de facto segregation defense against, 147; fair integration, 150; Friedman on, 45; impact of, 169. *See also* desegregation

Jackson, Mahalia, 51
Jansen, William, 70
Jefferson, Thomas, 7
Jefferson County, Alabama, racism in, 168
Jencks, Christopher, 124, 125
Jenkins, H. Harrison, 31
J4J (Journey for Justice), 198–99
Jim Crow laws, 22
John Philip Sousa Middle School (Washington, DC), 146
Johnson, Derrick, 157–58
Johnson, Lyndon B.: Daley and, 59; desegregation, support for, 90–91; Elementary and Secondary Education Act, signing of, 32, 90; fiscal policy under, 41; Marshall, appointment of, 35, 88; Watts insurrection and, 83
Johnson, Rucker C., 211
Journey for Justice (J4J), 198–99
judiciary, 94–95. *See also* Supreme Court

K12 Inc., 137
Kaminsky, Todd, 206
Keating, Kenneth, 71–72
Kennedy, Robert, 72
Kennedy, Ted, 74, 108, 144
Kenwood, Chicago, Blacks in, 54–55
Keyes v. School District No. 1, Denver, 87
Keynes, John Maynard, 40–41
Kilfoyle, Marla, 200–201, 206
Kimpton, Lawrence A., 54
King, Martin Luther, III, 13
King, Martin Luther, Jr., 27, 60, 64–65, 84, 140, 201
Klunder, Bruce, 139
Knowledge Is Power Program (KIPP), 131, 170, 187, 197
Kobrovsky, Larry, 122
Kojima, Aiko, 178
Kozol, Jonathan, 66, 118, 124, 143–44
Krasowski, Joseph, 68
Kryczka, Nicholas, 120

Laats, Adam, 14–15
Landsmark, Ted, 62–63, 88
Langley, Grant, 152–53
LaRaviere, Troy, 192–93, 195–97, 205, 212–13
Latinx communities: support for school choice, 12, 141
"law and order," 92, 102
Lee, Anna, 51
legal challenges to school choice, 208–10
Lewis, John, 17–19, 21, 27, 36, 63
Liberation Schools, 78, 79
libertarianism, 46
Lightfoot, Lori, 205
Little Rock, Arkansas: Little Rock Central High School, 20–21; public school closures in, 23–24
localism: community control movement, 78–83, 124; community empowerment, 176, 178–80; defensive localism, 55; local level, importance to school choice resistance movement, 190; local school board elections, dark money in, 183
Los Angeles: charter schools conflict in, 184–85; school choice in, 184–86; Watts insurrection, 83
Louisiana: *Brown v. Board of Education*, response to, 23; Citizens' Councils in, 24; voucher program, legal challenge to, 209. *See also* New Orleans
Love, Stephanie, 154, 159, 178–79, 198

MacLean, Nancy, 47
magnet schools, 97, 103–4, 119–23
Malcolm X Liberation University, 140, 149
"Manifesto for New Directions in the Education of Black Children" (Fuller and Smith), 152
Marshall, Thurgood, 35, 64, 88
Maryland, student activism in, 203
massive resistance to school desegregation, 19–21, 27, 31, 35, 43

McGrath, Christopher, 206
McRae, Elizabeth Gillespie, 74
Meier, Deborah, 118, 180
Memphis: charter schools in, 179; Memphis Lift, 158–59; resistance to school choice in, 197–98; school reform in, 154–59, 167–68
Michigan: charter schools in, 127; community control movement in, 80; school performance in, 181. *See also* Detroit
Mill, John Stuart, 3
Milliken v. Bradley, 87–88, 91, 95, 120, 121
Milton and Rose D. Friedman Foundation (EdChoice), 9, 114, 123, 164
Milwaukee: school choice in, 146, 210–11; school reform efforts in, 149–54; voucher system in, 125–26
Milwaukee Parental Choice Program, 103, 153
Minnesota: charter schools in, 103, 129–30; school segregation, legal challenges to, 208
Mississippi: *Brown v. Board of Education*, response to, 23; Citizens' Councils in, 24; continued school segregation in, 25; *Evers v. Jackson Municipal Separate School District*, 34; federal education funding for, 32; Freedom of Choice in the United States (FOCUS) initiative, 35–36; public funding of private education, 124; school privatization in, 26
Missouri v. Jenkins, 106
Moore, David, 197
Morgan v. Hennigan, 74
Morton, Felisha Reyes, 194
Moses, Bob, 79, 203
Murray, Patty, 138

NAACP: Boston, activities in, 74; *Brown v. Board of Education* and, 7; on charter schools, 13; Chicago branch, reports on school segregation, 57; in debate over school

choice, 157–58; Legal Defense Fund, actions by, 121–2; Milwaukee branch, 152; school choice debate and, 157–59; school desegregation, actions on, 22, 27
National Charter Collaborative, 156
National Civil Rights Museum, 12
National Commission on Excellence in Education, 97
National Education Goals Panel, 104
National Education Standards and Improvement Council, 105
National Governors Association, 100–101
National Teaching Academy (NTA, Chicago), 198
A Nation at Risk (National Commission on Excellence in Education), 10, 98–101
NCLB (No Child Left Behind) Act (2001), 107–10, 112, 113
Network for Public Education (NPE), 181, 200, 206
Nevada, *Schwartz v. Lopez*, 209
New America, Education Policy Program, 182
Newark, White flight from, 85
New Hampshire, voucher system, 124
New Jersey: charter schools in, 190, 209; Urban Hope Act, 190, 194
New Orleans: school choice in, 117, 160–61, 184; school performance in, 181
New Right, 47, 89
New Schools for Chicago, 112
NewSchools Venture Fund, 110, 113
Newsom, Gavin, 185, 208
New York City: charter schools in, 166; community control movement in, 79, 80–83; desegregation efforts, 66–69; liberals of, Friedman and, 48; teachers' unions in, 99
New Yorkers for a Balanced Albany, 206
New York State, shifts in state legislature, 206

Nixon, Richard, 72, 89, 90–95, 96
No Child Left Behind (NCLB) Act (2001), 107–10, 112, 113
no-excuses and school discipline, 187
nonprofit charter schools, 131–32
Norman, Keith, 158, 159
the North and northern states: racism in, 62–63; school desegregation in, impact on legislation and politics, 71–76; segregation in, 42; teachers' unions in, 99; views of desegregation, 64–66. See also *names of individual northern states*
North Carolina: desegregation efforts in, 106–7; resegregation in, 167; school segregation, legal challenges to, 208
North Division High School (Milwaukee), 149–50
northern cities, desegregation orders and, 37
NPE (Network for Public Education), 200, 206

Obama, Barack: educational reform strategy, 204; Emanuel AME Church killings and, 8; mentioned, 206; Promise Neighborhoods program, 132–33; school choice, actions on, 104, 111–14; school choice, support for, 14; school choice under, 154
Obama, Michelle, 194
Oberndorf, Bill, 185
Ocean Hill-Brownsville, New York City, community control movement in, 79–81
Ohio: charter school profits, 174; Cleveland, voucher system in, 125–26; teachers' unions in, 183
Oklahoma, Red for Ed movement in, 207
Oliver, John, 174
online education (virtual schooling, cyber schools), 135–38
Operation Transfer (Chicago), 57
Opportunity Zones, 160–61

Orfield, Gary, 95, 121, 166–67
Orrin, Cardell, 148–49, 157

Paine, Thomas, 3
*Parents Involved in Community Schools
v. Seattle School District*, 147
Parks, Rosa, 64
parochial schools, 106, 125–26
Payne, Charles, 203
Penn-Nabrit, Paula, 135
Pennsylvania, cyber charters in, 137
people of color: failing public schools,
reactions to (*see* civil rights claim
to school choice, racism and);
impact of poor public education
on, 145–46; northern Whites'
response to, 93; voice of, 210. *See
also* Black, Indigenous, and People
of Color (BIPOC) individuals; Latinx communities
Philadelphia, student strikes in, 191
philanthropy supporting education
reform, 110. *See also* Bill and
Melinda Gates Foundation; Eli and
Edythe Broad Foundation; Walton
Family Foundation
Philips, Kevin, 92
Phillips, Anna, 185
Plessy v. Ferguson, 22, 169
Podair, Jerald, 81
police in schools, 84–85
politics: of Black achievement, 78, 80;
teachers in, 206–7. See also *names
of individual states and cities*
Poor People's Campaign (1968), 201
Porter-Gaud School (Charleston,
South Carolina), 2
Powell, Lewis, 94
Prince, Edgar, 172
Prince Edward County, Virginia, pub-
lic school closures in, 24, 34, 46
private schools, 25–27, 29, 86
private segregation academies, 117
profit motive in education, 13, 171,
173–74
Promise Neighborhoods program,
132–33

P.S. 144 (Harlem), 144
public education (public schools):
challenges of choosing, 213;
charter schools as threat to, 133;
Chicago's segregated, 57–61; closures of, 23–24, 34; criticisms of,
143; deterioration of, 27, 143, 144
(*see also* failure of school choice,
deterioration of public education
and); disdain for, 89; disinvestment
in, 118, 173–76; homeschooling
versus, 134; impact of race on,
165; integration of, appearance of,
34–35; LaRaviere on, 196; *A Nation
at Risk* on, 10, 98–101; perceptions
of, as violent, 84; privatization of,
25, 26, 75–76, 106, 128, 199; public
opinion on, 96, 100; public school
enrollment, importance of, 213–14;
racial makeup of, 11–12; secession
of communities from public school
districts, 168–69; types of alternatives to, 4; vouchers as challenge
to, 127–28
Public Funds Public Schools (PFPS),
208–9

race and racism: in education system,
188; housing covenants, 42, 50;
impact on school choice failure,
165–70; racial divisions, perpetua-
tions of, 8–9; in school choice, 4–6,
10, 11; school choice as racially
neutral, 103, 104; social capital
and, 178; structural racism, 39.
See also civil rights claim to school
choice, racism and; desegregation;
integration; people of color; racism
and foundations of school choice
model; segregation
Race to the Top Program, 112–13,
154
Racial Imbalance Act (1965, Massachusetts), 74
racism and foundations of school
choice model, 62–89; Boston, busing in, 62–64; busing controversy,

media portrayals of, 76–78; Chicago, resistance to busing in, 69–70; community control movement, 78–83; desegregation, northern views of, 64–66, 70–71; desegregation, White resistance to, 88–89; inner city problems and, 83–86; New York City, school desegregation efforts in, 66–69; northern school desegregation, impact on legislation and politics, 71–76; suburbs and busing, 86–88

Rakes, Joseph, 62–63, 74, 88–89

rational choice theory, 42, 44–45

Ravitch, Diane, 110, 200

Reagan, Ronald, 48, 95–99, 101, 119

Red for Ed movement, 204–5, 206

redlining, 39, 50

Redmond Plan, 69, 120

Rehnquist, William H., 97, 126

Renaissance 2010 plan (Chicago), 112, 113, 196, 202

Republican Party, 41, 48, 89, 91–92, 172

resegregation, 147, 166–67

resisting school choice through counternarratives and coalitions, 189–214; achievement gap and, 211–12; in Charleston, South Carolina, 189, 197–98; civil rights perspective on, 210–11; coalition building, 198–203; counternarratives, 194–95; desegregation, impact on Whites, 212–13; Dickerson and, 190–92, 195; direct action and, 203–5; educators as political actors, 205–8; individual actions, 211–12; information sharing, 192–94; LaRaviere and, 192–93, 195–97; legal challenges, 208–10

Reynolds, John, 149

Rhee, Michelle, 183–84

Rickford, Russell, 78

right-to-work (anti-union) legislation, 47

Riley, Richard, 101, 104

Roberts, John, 147

Rockefeller, David, 56

Rodriquez, Refugio "Ref," 185–86, 208

Roof, Dylann, 8

Rooks, Noliwe, 137, 174–75, 179

Roosevelt, Franklin D., 40–41

Roth, Stephen J., 86, 120

Rothstein, Richard, 212

Rouhanifard, Paymon, 190–91, 193

Royal Swedish Academy of Sciences, 43

rural areas, online learning in, 136

Ryan, James, 88

Sadaukai, Owusu. *See* Fuller, Howard

Salters, David, 168

Sanders, Bernie, 162, 197

Sanders, Raynard, 162

Save Camden Public Schools, 195

Scholarships for Opportunity and Results (SOAR) Act (2003), 127

scholarship tax plans, 127

school buses, 63. *See also* busing

school choice: bipartisan support for, 104, 111, 159–60; Black support for, 145–46; Chicago, Friedman and school choice in, 38–61; choice districts, 9; choice schools, racial makeup of, 11–12; civil rights claim to school choice, racism and, 139–63; failure of, deterioration of public education and, 164–88; federal support of school choice movement, 90–115; freedom of choice in education, 17–37; ideology of, 117; introduction to, 1–15; racism and foundations of school choice model, 62–89; as resistance to desegregation, 27; resisting through counternarratives and coalitions, 189–214; school choices, multiplicity of, 116–38

school choice model. *See* racism and foundations of school choice model

school choices, multiplicity of, 116–38; alternative school movement, 118–19; charter schools, 128–33;

free school movement, 118; home-schooling, 133–35; introduction to, 116–17; magnet schools, 97, 103–4, 119–23; online education (virtual schooling), 135–38; vouchers, 123–28. *See also* charter schools; vouchers

schools: as not businesses, 176; parochial schools, 106, 125–26; private schools, 25–27, 29, 86; school reform, bottom-up approach to, 214; school-to-prison system, 14; small schools movement, 118, 124. *See also* charter schools; magnet schools; public education (public schools)

school vouchers. *See* vouchers

Schwartz v. Lopez, 209

Schwerner, Michael, 96

secession of communities from public school districts, 168–69

segregation: *Brown v. Board of Education*'s impact on, 17–21; in Chicago, 39, 42–43, 49–54; Civil Rights Act and, 32; de facto segregation, 57; de facto vs. de jure, 59–60, 71, 72, 87, 93; natural segregation, 54, 70, 71, 73; in New Orleans, 160; in Northeast, 146–47; northern, 59–60; perpetuation of, 147–48, 195; resegregation, 147, 166–67; school segregation, attempted solutions for, 78–83; school segregation in Chicago, 57–61; segregation academies, 26–27; vouchers and, 4

segrenomics, 174–75

Segrue, Thomas, 55

Sellers, Cleveland, 140

Sessions, John, 27

Shanker, Al, 82, 128–29, 131, 133, 211

Siegel-Hawley, Genevieve, 181

silent majority, 89

Sillers, Walter, 18

Sippel, Drew, 155

slums and slum clearance, 53, 55, 66

small schools movement, 118, 124

Smith, Adam, 3

Smith, Michael, 152

SNCC (Student Nonviolent Coordinating Committee), 27, 64

social and economic capital, 176–78

sorting mechanisms for school choice, 176, 177

the South and southern states: *Brown v. Board of Education*, response to, 19–21, 23–26; equalization plans, 22–23; federal funding for, school desegregation and, 32–33; school desegregation in, 91, 105. See also *names of individual southern states*

South Carolina: *Brown v. Board of Education*, response to, 23; Citizens' Councils in, 24; continued school segregation in, 25; freedom of choice plans in, 35; Gressette Committee, 30–31; post–Civil War education of African Americans in, 3; school privatization in, 26. *See also* Charleston, South Carolina

South East Chicago Commission, 56

"Southern Manifesto" (on resistance to desegregation), 19–20

Southern Poverty Law Center, 13

Southern Regional Council, 26

special needs/disabled students, 186–88

states: charter school legislation, 9; constitutional commitment to public education, litigation on, 209; interventionist, 44; states' rights, 96–97, 102. *See also* North and northern states; South and southern states; *names of individual states*

Stax Records, 155, 156

Stennis, John, 36

Stewart, Potter, 87

St. Louis, White flight from, 85

Stovall, David, 179, 194, 202

structural racism, 39

student activism, 203

Student Nonviolent Coordinating Committee (SNCC), 27, 64

suburbs, 65, 86–88, 92, 167–68
Supreme Court: education cases,
106–7; resegregation, facilitation
of, 147; on voucher programs, 109
Supreme Court (specific cases):
*Alexander v. Holmes County Board
of Education*, 26, 34, 35; *Board of
Education of Oklahoma City Public
Schools v. Dowell*, 106, 147; *Bob
Jones University v. United States*,
97, 117; *Brown v. Board of Education*, 7, 17–18, 44, 64, 67, 70, 143,
169; *Buchanan v. Warley*, 50; *Coit
v. Green*, 117; *Freeman v. Pitts*,
106; *Green v. County School Board
of Kent County*, 26, 35, 73; *Griffin
v. County School Board of Prince
Edward County*, 24, 34; *Hansberry
v. Lee*, 52; *Keyes v. School District
No. 1, Denver*, 87; *Milliken v.
Bradley*, 87–88, 91, 95, 120, 121;
Missouri v. Jenkins, 106; *Parents
Involved in Community Schools v.
Seattle School District*, 147; *Plessy
v. Ferguson*, 22, 169; *Swann v.
Charlotte-Mecklenburg Board of
Education*, 73, 107; *Zelman v.
Simmons-Harris*, 110, 126–27, 145
*Swann v. Charlotte-Mecklenburg Board
of Education*, 73, 107

tax credits, for private school costs,
97
teachers and teachers' unions: attacks
on, 183–85, 191, 204; charter
schools and, 128–29, 130; *A Nation
at Risk* and, 99–100; in politics,
206–7; right-to-work (anti-union)
legislation, 47; strikes by, 203–5;
United Federation of Teachers
(UFT), 81–83
Teach for America, 182, 184
Tennessee, school reform in, 154–57.
See also Memphis
testing mandates, 102, 107–8, 109,
111

Theoharis, Jeanne, 82
Thomas, Cal, 164
Thompson, Allen, 36
Thompson, Tommy, 103, 125, 140,
153–54
Thurmond, Strom, 7, 92, 93
Till, Emmett, 20
Timmerman, George Bell, 28
Todd-Breland, Elizabeth, 57, 78, 83
Trump, Donald: on African Amer-
ican children, education of, 12;
charter schools, proposed support
for, 219n12; DeVos, nomination
of, 114, 172; on school choice, 144,
163; school choice rhetoric, 159;
school privatization agenda, 162
tuition grants. *See* vouchers
Turner, Bobby, 131

United Federation of Teachers
(UFT), 81–83
United States constitution, lack of
mention of education in, 189–90
University of Chicago, 39, 43, 49,
54–57
Urban Hope Act (2012, New Jersey),
190
urban renewal, 53

Vallas, Paul, 202
venture philanthropists, 110, 113
Veterans Administration, 50
Villaraigosa, Antonio, 185
Virginia: *Brown v. Board of Education*,
response to, 24; continued school
segregation in, 25; Defenders of
State Sovereignty and Individual
Liberties, 28; freedom of choice
plans, 46; Prince Edward County,
public school closures in, 24, 34,
46; private schools in, 26–27;
States' Rights Party, 30
virtual schooling (online education,
cyber schools), 135–38
vouchers: DeVos's support for, 115;
discussion of, 123–28; historical

use of, 3–4; origins of, 25–26; philanthropic support for, 110–11; public funding for, 110; Reagan and, 97; Wisconsin voucher program, 153–54

Waldron, John, 207
Walker, Scott, 207
Walker, Wyatt Tee, 142–46, 179
Wallace, George, 92
Walsh, Camille, 68
Walton, Alice, 185
Walton Family Foundation, 110, 114, 170, 171, 186
Wang, Jia, 181
Waring, Thomas, 25
Warren, Elizabeth, 159, 162
Washington, DC: charter schools in, 166; John Philip Sousa Middle School, 146
wealth, impact on school choice, 170–71
Webb, Roblin, 157
Webb v. Board of Education, 57–58, 60
Weir, Margaret, 55
Weiss, Joanna, 113
White, Bobby, 156
White, Kevin H., 76
White, Terrenda, 179, 211
White Circle League, 50

Whites: *Brown v. Board of Education*, response to, 18–21; charter schools and, 2–3; desegregation's impact on, 212–13; northern, 64–66, 93; profit motives of, 175; race, lack of understanding of, 7; race-neutral rhetoric, use of, 169–70; school integration, responses to, 67–71; southern, states' rights and, 28; in suburbs, 65, 167–68; White flight, 4, 49, 52, 73, 85–86, 117–18, 120, 123; White fragility, 81; White privilege, Friedman and, 42; White resistance (*see* racism and foundations of school choice model); White rights, defense of, 28–29
Williams, John Bell, 35, 72
Williams, Polly, 146, 152, 153, 210
Willis, Benjamin C., 57, 58, 59
Winter, William, 101
Wisconsin: private school voucher plan, 140; teachers in politics in, 207–8; teachers' unions in, 183; voucher program, 153–54. *See also* Milwaukee

X, Malcolm, 89, 140

Zelman v. Simmons-Harris, 110, 126–27, 145